down to earth

Rhonda Hetzel is a retired journalist
and technical writer best known for her award-
winning blog, 'Down to Earth'. Rhonda lives
with her husband, Hanno, on the Sunshine
Coast, where they happily tend a food garden,
gather eggs and occasionally look after grandchildren. Rhonda is a keen volunteer worker
and is often found presenting simple-living
workshops in her community.

Rhonda Hetzel

down
to
earth

a guide to simple living

VIKING
an imprint of
PENGUIN BOOKS

For Hanno,
Shane and Kerry

A new beginning...

2020 was a year like no other. When uncertainty and fear became part of our daily lives, I saw many people start to think deeply about how they live and what 'home' means to them. After the first month of lockdown it was crystal clear that we all need our homes to be safe places.

There is no simple solution when you ask, 'How can I change my life to create a resilient and secure future?' But there are steps you can take to create a haven for you and your loved ones. My books, *Down to Earth* and *The Simple Home*, were originally written for those who wanted to slow down and simplify life. Now, they are also guides for creating a home that will provide safety and comfort during the uncertain years ahead.

Large-scale public health events and natural disasters such as fires, floods and weather events force change on all of us. Simplifying how you live allows you to deal with those changes while using your home to shelter, grow, cook, bake and store food. You'll live with fewer chemicals and less waste. Intelligent money management and budgeting will help you to conserve resources and live on less than you earn so you're able to support yourself if the hard times return.

There is a clear way forward when you use the information in this book, take control of what you do each day and work consistently to a plan. You'll be able to make simple and effective changes that will reward you with a home that is productive, nurturing and generous. I hope you find inspiration and encouragement here, too, because we all work to our potential when we're motivated and focused on a sustainable future. And I believe we need many more people to be working towards that goal.

Rhonda

Contents

LIVING SIMPLY

I was pulled into simple living before I knew what it was. It crept up on me using the smallest of steps and didn't reveal its true beauty and real power until I was totally hooked. I was searching for a way to live well while spending very little money. What I found was a way of life that also gave me independence, opportunity and freedom.

A change of heart

Had I known what profound and beautiful changes were awaiting me, I would have had a change of heart much sooner. About ten years ago I eased myself out of shopping, fashion, eating out and other non-essential spending. I felt like I was taking a giant leap into the unknown and everyone was asking me, 'Why!?' Now times have changed. There has been a worldwide financial crisis, a grey tsunami of retiring baby boomers is beginning to influence our lives as they leave the workforce and many move towards government pensions, and many more people are worried about the economy, the environment and the future. Clearly the time is right for a simple change. But it's not just for those who are facing difficulties. Even if recent years have treated you more kindly, simple living will have something to offer you. It's not just a refuge in a sea of environmental and economic calamity, it's a beautiful and significant life choice in itself.

I was pulled into simple living before I knew what it was. It crept up on me using the smallest of steps and didn't reveal its true beauty and real power until I was totally hooked. I was searching for a way to live well while spending very little money. What I found was a way of life that also gave me independence, opportunity and freedom.

I live with my husband, Hanno, in the hinterland of Queensland's Sunshine Coast. We've been married more than thirty years and have two sons, Shane and Kerry. They have both left home and settled down to build lives with their partners, Sarndra and Sunny. We've recently welcomed our first grandchildren. Life, as we move into our later years, looks pretty good.

I guess you would say we're 'retired' but we still work almost every day, making bread, jams, relish and soap, cooking from scratch, growing vegetables, recycling and mending what we use in our home. We aim to live productive lives, so while many of our contemporaries are travelling in caravans or planes we're pleased to be home-bodies, finding satisfaction in our simple home, and excitement and adventure in a backyard full of fruit, vegetables, chickens and wildlife. Rhythms, seasons and daylight rather than clocks, calendars and investment portfolios guide our days. We are in a fortunate position to be able to live this way and we both find it very satisfying to be active at this stage of life and to feel enriched by what we do.

Hatching a new life

After many years working as a journalist and technical writer I was burnt out. I'd just finished a major contract for a big company when I realised I didn't want to work for a living any more. I wanted to stay at home and rebuild my spirit. I wanted to look after my family, slow down, collect eggs and honey, and sit and dream in my garden. I also wanted to feel more alive.

What I had been doing was working in a job I didn't like so I had enough money to pay for a lifestyle I didn't want. I was shopping for clothes and shoes to make me look like everyone else. I was buying things for my home to make me feel comfortable in a place I didn't take the time to feel comfortable in. And I was buying food to comfort and nurture because I didn't feel at ease in my life and I didn't have the time or energy to cook the food I liked. This destructive behaviour seemed to be quite acceptable and, from what I could see, my family and friends were doing a similar thing. Continuous consumption was even encouraged by our government, who told us that shopping was good for the country and we were 'growing the economy'.

We live on a limited budget but
I am richer now than I've ever been in my life.

And the strangest thing is that when I was living in this way, I didn't think about the sadness I was feeling. I didn't realise I was unsatisfied and I didn't see the need for change. I believed I was the queen of my realm, that the more I had and the more dollars I spent, the more power, strength and independence I had. When I stopped spending I realised how pathetically wrong that was. I had actually been giving away my independence.

Now that I look back on it, I must have been a bit crazy to believe that I could just stop shopping without changing the way I lived too. I thought I would just stop the mindless spending while finding satisfaction within my own home, and that would be that. I didn't know then that the charm of living without shopping, and of making do with what I had, would open up a whole new world for me, where independence and opportunity would live side by side and lead to a kind of gentle liberation.

Luckily, at that point, I discovered that others had walked this road less travelled before me. I found a group of writers who had been explaining their philosophy to the world for many years, so I started reading. I found *Walden* by Henry David Thoreau online and devoured it within hours. I ordered books from America that were not yet available in Australia – *The Simple Living Guide* by Janet Luhrs, *Your Money or Your Life* by Joe Dominguez and Vicki Robin, the *Encyclopedia of Country Living* by Carla Emery, and *The Complete Tightwad Gazette* by Amy Dacyczyn.

I also discovered blogs. Here was a world I had never known about, where real people were writing about things that interested me. I could see into their lives, get to know their families, understand how they lived and be part of a community that supported one another. Once I found blogs, it didn't matter much that I didn't personally know anyone who was doing what I was doing; I felt comfortable in the company I kept online. In those early days I didn't find many people blogging about living my dream life, but I really enjoyed the blogs about family and frugal living. I also found blogs about global warming, lightening your footprint, going green and peak oil, but none that wrote about what I wanted to do – change how we live in the most fundamental and practical way.

I started my own blog and called it 'Down to Earth'. Instead of adding my voice to the fast-growing group of people who were writing about environmental disaster and post-peak survival, I decided I would write about our ordinary daily lives and how we were simplifying, and let that be my manifesto. I believed where radical change was needed was in the business of day-to-day living which, if done mindfully, could hopefully lead us to a good life. I hoped that writing the blog every day would make me accountable and give us a clear record of what we were doing.

I realised that many of the things I spent my money on I could do or make myself: I could make clothes, I could cook, I could do my own housework. But once I started doing those things I found that I'd lost many of those skills. I'd forgotten how to sew and knit because I'd been paying someone else to make my clothes. I'd forgotten how to cook from scratch because I'd been buying food that didn't require me to exercise my mind or spend my energy on making my favourite dishes. When it came to housework, all I knew was to get products from the cupboard and start wiping. I was a grown woman and I didn't know how to look after my family or myself properly. I'd forgotten the skills that had been passed on to me and I was almost completely dependent on others to help me live.

You don't have to be a genius to shop; all you need is money, or a credit card, and some time. Not shopping, on the other hand, requires a multifaceted strategy. You need to know how to create, cook, clean and sew; you need to make do with what you have, to reuse, recycle and repair. You need to barter, grow, store and preserve – and it helps if you like doing it. You have to discover for yourself the true beauty of being able to look after yourself, your family and your home with a minimum of outside help. The beauty is there if you look.

We live on a limited budget but I am richer now than I've ever been in my life. I know how to live. I have the skills to survive a crisis. I have the strength and knowledge to produce my own food and to store it. I can clothe myself and others. These are life-engaging and self-empowering skills. But the real skill here is to do it and love doing it day after day. Relearning those lost skills, and then using them, are acts of subversion because you're not doing what women and men in our times are supposed to be doing. Nurturing your family and yourself with cooking, gardening, repairing, dressmaking, knitting, creating, recycling and all the other things you learn to do in your post-consumerist life not only enriches your spirit, but also makes you an independent force. May the force be with you.

What is simple living?

So what is simple living? There are many answers to that question, but for me it's about living a life that's not complicated by wanting or having too much. It's being satisfied with enough, whatever that may be. It's a way of reigniting the excitement of everyday living because you throw away the rulebook and live according to your own ideals. It allows you to discover the significance of home life and how your home can nurture you. It's a lifestyle that allows you to live well on little money, thereby enabling you to build a family and a home that is based on authenticity and love, rather than on fashion or what is expected of you. It helps you regain power and independence by making you stronger and more self-reliant. It builds sustainability into your family life and home. For me, simple living has allowed my husband and me to live every day to its fullest and to grow and prosper at a time when we thought we would be doing the opposite.

This way of living is not about deprivation or being thrifty. It will help you get rid of many of the harsh chemicals you live

with by replacing them with simple household cleaners you make yourself. It will encourage you to cook from scratch, so you and your family can eat food that is not weighed down with preservatives or artificial colourings and flavours. It will show you that your home is your personal shelter and the one place you can rely on to nurture you and your family. If you let it, I believe your home and what you do there will shape the person you become. It did that for me; it can for you too.

'Simple' tends to describe the nature of the activities in this kind of life, not the amount of effort involved.

Overall, simple living is about finding peace, joy, beauty and satisfaction within ourselves and in that place we've been told it never is – our homes. It is about regaining the power to direct our own lives and become doers rather than buyers. It's about becoming independent and discovering that happiness is not bought; it is developed gradually in the day-to-day activities of life.

But what about the name: 'simple living'. Is it really simple? People tell me that I do more work than they do and that my life is therefore far from simple. It's true that it generally requires more effort to produce what we need than to buy it. But 'simple' tends to describe the nature of the activities in this kind of life, not the amount of effort involved. I know now that simple doesn't mean effortless or easy; it means plain and uncomplicated. Sometimes it just means simpler than the more common, commercial way of doing things. For instance, it is perhaps easier or more convenient for me to buy my bread from the supermarket, but if you consider the plastic bag the bread is packaged in, the preservatives that allow it to sit on the shelf for days, the artificial flavourings, and the oil and transport chains that have delivered it to the shop, then the bread I bake at home is simple. I buy my flour in bulk bags made of paper, and the yeast in large aluminium bags that last me six months. Is making a cotton tote bag to carry your grocery shopping simple? It might require more effort, but it's simpler than using plastic bags that kill marine life, clog up our oceans and contribute to landfill. Is staying at home to work simple? Compared with working to earn money so you can buy everything you need, yes it is. Yes, sometimes I curse and carry on about things I don't want to do, but most of the time this work is enriching and satisfying and, in our lives, significant.

> Home is where I want to be now. I want to spend my time living quietly, giving to my community when I feel I have something to offer, and working in my home so I can live in the fine style I have come to know. It may not suit everyone, and it may seem like a lot of hard work and sacrifice to some, but I love it, even if at times I don't understand why it resonates so deeply within me.

Moving towards simplicity

A simple life can manifest in many ways, but generally the lifestyle varies depending on the stage of life you're currently at. Hanno and I are older folk and we had the delightful opportunity to give up work completely, to grow food in our backyard and to produce a lot of what we need to live. If you're at retirement age, I believe there is no better discovery than this. If you're middle-aged and have some form of debt that you're working to pay off, living more simply will help you do that. If you're younger, the possibilities are endless. If you are debt-free you can move through your twenties and thirties creating a life that doesn't centre on excessive possessions and debt. However, if you regret some of the lifestyle decisions you've already made, it's not too late – you can now work towards sustainability and the elegant sufficiency of 'enough'.

The path is different for all of us. My way of living won't suit all of you; you have to define for yourself what you want your life to be, then slowly move towards that life.

No matter what your life becomes, it will probably involve some of these changes:

- thinking about what kind of life you want to live – this is a deliberate choice; you don't have to stay the same as you are now
- controlling your spending with the aim of being debt-free
- saving for important things you believe will make your life better

- reskilling and learning how to look after yourself and your family
- shopping in a different way
- eating healthy, local, and possibly organic food
- growing some of your own food
- disposing of disposables

- cleaning with green products
- managing your time and establishing routines
- cutting back and making do
- looking after what you own
- making home your centre
- connecting with your family and community
- changing your definition of success
- becoming independent.

Today, when you finish reading this chapter, I want you to think about how you want to live. Find a notebook and write down all your ideas. It doesn't matter if it doesn't make sense; you can edit it later. Just let the ideas flow. Your first task is to write two lists.

This is the first list I wrote all those years ago. I add it merely as a sample that you might find helpful when creating your own.

I want my life to provide me with:

- a reason to get up every morning
- interesting and productive work
- contentment that occasionally explodes into happiness
- a framework in which to live simply
- the opportunity and continued ability to learn skills that facilitate our lifestyle
- a strong and generous family circle that supports every member of our family – during the good times and especially when it's tougher
- opportunities to express generosity, kindness and empathy
- the strength to be a role model to the younger women in my family
- the enthusiasm and perseverance to take charge of my home and make it a place of comfort, welcome and warmth.

I hope that everyone wishing to change how they live will make their own list so that values and goals are clearly evident. Positive change doesn't always happen by itself; it sometimes needs a nudge. Lists give you a good starting point – not only will they confirm your intentions, they will also be a guide.

The next list you need to make is of all the things you need to change to make your first list a reality. This is the list that breaks down something like 'taking charge of my home' into specific actions like 'learn how to cook from scratch' and 'start a vegetable garden'. If you want to list the individual tasks you want to include in your daily life, do so. These two lists are your life plan and your action plan, they will be the starting point to your new, simpler life. I hope you're ready for this; it's going to be a wonderful and significant journey.

Doing it together

So far it sounds like the transition from our old lives to this new way of living was seamless and easy, but that's not quite true. One of the things I struggled with was Hanno's reaction. He didn't understand what I wanted to change and when I explained this half-baked idea I had, he wasn't happy. He had retired after forty years as a diesel fitter in the mining industry and had bought a little shop in Montville selling furniture, prints, lamps and gifts, and he didn't see a need to change.

While Hanno liked the idea of giving up paid work, he thought it was idealistic and unreasonable to think that two people on the verge of retirement could do so without suffering financial conse-quences. His response when I posed the question was a firm, 'No!' I respected his decision but I didn't agree with it. I went ahead with it anyway. I had already closed down my writing business, and when he went out to work every day I worked on my plan at home, learn-ing as much as I could. I didn't know how much we needed to live on and I had no idea of the work involved, but I intended to find out.

The only money I had to spend was the grocery money. It was my only tool, so I used it. I started to stockpile groceries, I increased the number and variety of vegetables we were growing and bought a few more chickens. I went from spending $300 a week on grocer-ies to spending much less by using those new (to me) methods. I put money into an emergency fund so we had a cushion in case some-thing went wrong. Over the next few months I built up our vegetable garden further, taught myself to bake good bread, bought a water-bath preserver and started preserving and freezing our excess food. I read everything I could get my hands on. I started remembering how my mother and grandmother had worked in their homes. The whole time I never mentioned to Hanno what I was doing.

By the time I brought up the subject of Hanno giving up work again, about nine months later, our two sons had left home and there were just the two of us to look after. When he saw the amount of money I had saved from our normal grocery money he was shocked. He understood then that we didn't need a large amount of money to live on. We'd paid off the mortgage and credit cards and I had drawn up a budget that showed we could live on $350 a week, including our rates, groceries, insurances, car and dog registrations – everything. (This later increased to our current $400 a week.) He was almost convinced we could do it.

Not long after that he closed our shop in Montville and we started the freefall into our new life. Hanno applied for the age pension, which helped cover some of our ongoing expenses, but he wasn't completely convinced we could do it until we'd lived the life for six months. After we'd done that, he agreed it was not only possible for us, it was right and it felt good. He dived right in.

I think when it comes to change, one partner tends to see the possibilities before the other. It can be frustrating for both parties because one is convinced it can be done and the other is convinced it can't be. I took the soft approach, and it worked. I thought the best way to show it could be done was to do it. Everyone who shops for groceries each week can do what I did. You can show your partner that cutting costs is not only possible, it's sustainable over a long period. And when you suddenly produce the money you've saved, it opens up all sorts of possibilities.

I am sure that many who read this book will be in a similar situation to ours. If your partner is hesitant about a life change, change yourself and work towards your dream alone first. There are many things you can do on your own. Show what is possible, then you'll have something more tangible to discuss when you raise the subject again.

Bloom where you are planted

Last year we had a tomato bush growing in the grass, next to the hard surface of our back verandah. It came up out of nowhere; it was not planned, or planted by either of us. It just arrived. We held up the bush with sticks and a couple of pieces of metal from an old card rack. It grew to be healthy and huge – much bigger than our planned and carefully planted tomatoes. We ate the tomatoes from that plant for a few months. They were delicious and every day they were like unexpected gifts. Life doesn't always go according to your plans so when you're not in your ideal situation, bloom where you are planted.

I cannot stress enough that simple living is not about a particular geographical location; it is not something that happens only in the countryside, nor is it confined to a certain city, or to the suburbs. You do not have to live on a farm or a homestead or in a cave. A simple life can flourish anywhere. Simple living is more about a powerful change in attitude and how you apply that change to the way you live. You could be living in a tent on the top of a mountain, an apartment block in New York City or a beach house in Australia. Your home could be the suburbs of London or Paris, the wild open spaces of Alaska or any crowded city in the world; a simple life is possible anywhere. It's not about where your home is, it's about where your head is.

> *It's not about where your home is,*
> *it's about where your head is.*

The vision of packing up and leaving the city to live a simple life in the country is a common one, but it is not a realistic vision for many people. It's often a romantic, idealised dream to live a life uncomplicated by traffic, pollution, crowds, violence and uncertainty. Sometimes people move to a location that looks perfect, but when they get there they can't find a job, the schools are too far away and the idyllic simple life they dream of is still out of reach. Their life is still complicated, just by different things.

One of my favourite aspects of simple living is that you make do with what you have, and that includes your location. It's an old-fashioned notion and the opposite of what's currently in favour: instant gratification and having what you want at any price. Simple living is not about buying a lifestyle, it's about building a life – using what you already have. And just like making a meal using basic ingredients, what you end up with is something suited exactly to you, not someone else's idea of what you should want. So no

matter where you're living, you can make it better by altering your attitude, making a few simple changes and making the best of what you have.

Your location is only a small part of your simple life. You can also concentrate on these other activities:

- building a strong family or network of friends
- earning a living and reducing debt
- simplifying your everyday activities
- reducing your spending
- reskilling yourself for the life you want to live
- contributing to your community
- getting to know your neighbours
- slowing down and living with a peaceful mindset
- cultivating generosity and kindness
- decluttering your home
- being aware of your environmental responsibilities
- reducing your use of water, power, fuel and gas
- reusing, reducing and recycling
- being grateful for what you have and making do.

If location is an issue for you, maybe you can start on these many other aspects of simple living, and in time, location might sort itself out. Make the best of what you have right now while you work towards your dream. Indeed, making the most of every day is as much a part of simple living as slowing down, growing vegetables, and all the rest. I can't tell you what will give you a life of happiness, enjoyment and satisfaction – that is for you to decide. What I hope is to give you the motivation and the information to help you start moving towards simplicity, and to tell you as clearly as I can that you can start living your simple life today.

Living deliberately

'I went to the woods because I wished to live deliberately, to front only the essential facts of life, and see if I could not learn what it had to teach, and not, when I came to die, discover that I had not lived. I did not wish to live what was not life, living is so dear; nor did I wish to practise resignation, unless it was quite necessary. I wanted to live deep and suck out all the marrow of life, to live so sturdily and Spartan-like as to put to rout all that was not life, to cut a broad swath and shave close, to drive life into a corner, and reduce it to its lowest terms, and, if it proved to be mean, why then to get the whole and genuine meanness of it, and publish its meanness to the world; or if it were sublime, to know it by experience…'

From *Walden* by Henry David Thoreau

Living simply is much more than a financial strategy; it's more than your location, more than how you manage your home or plant your vegetables. It's about you: how you think about your life and how you express your values every day. Anyone can learn to budget, make yoghurt, knit dishcloths and grow tomatoes; the real trick is for your actions to reflect your simple philosophy. What good is it to list the hundred things you've accomplished if you're not made happy by what you do, if you aren't renewed by it, and if you don't do it with grace, humility and generosity?

Living deliberately means thinking about what you want your life to be and making the decisions you need to make to take you there, rather than just reacting to what life throws at you. It requires a period of thought about you and your values, and how to live according to those values.

When you deliberately choose this way of life, you will be making life-changing decisions and taking steps to put those changes in place. You'll probably simplify your daily activities, reduce spending on non-essential items, start paying off debt, develop a more independent mindset. There will be many things you'll do differently, but if you do them well, if you really throw yourself into your life, if you *live deep and suck out all the marrow of life*, not only will you be living deliberately, you will be changed by it.

Independence, freedom and choice

How will you go about living the life I've described here? Stop living according to the expectations of others and focus on building a life that is unique to you. It's okay to say 'no' to others and 'yes' to yourself. Be mindful, make your own decisions, work out what will work for you and don't feel guilty or undecided if your family or friends aren't doing or don't understand what you do. Imagine your own life, and how you want it to be, then work to make that vision a reality. Don't be put off, don't listen to the naysayers; go with your heart and do what is right for you. I don't fit in the over-sixty pigeonhole, and I do not look to those around me for validation. That has helped me build this life I live. If I'd listened to all the unwanted advice I got when I started to change, I'd still be in debt and wondering, 'Is this all there is?'

The sum total of this life is much more than the individual parts because it adds up to give us independence, freedom, choice, security, joy and the comforting knowledge that we make our lives what they are. Like any good organic system, it creates a cycle that shows us that what we put into our lives gently returns to us in new and wonderful ways.

This book is in your hands because I wrote down what worked for us as we were changing how we lived. I realised it was becoming a guide that others could use too, and I was lucky that others saw that potential as well. In the following chapters I've written about how Hanno and I deal with our finances, how we shop and store food, how to make cleaners, laundry liquid, soap and bread, how to organise and declutter and how to plant a productive garden. There is information about family life, housekeeping and self-reliance, and a whole lot more. You don't have to live how your friends or neighbours live, and nor do you have to live how I live. Remember, this is a menu, not a prescription. Gather the information you want, then choose what will fit into your life. No one knows your life – or the life you want – better than you. So be guided by me and this book, by your family and friends, but in the end, make the life you want – even if it's different from everyone else's.

And if you want day-to-day contact with like-minded folk, or if you want to ask questions about your change, just visit my forum (downtoearthforums.com) and make contact. You'll be greeted by many people from all over the world who, like you, are striving to live more simply.

AGES & STAGES

As you grow older, you'll care less about what others think. If you're sure the way you're living is right for you, never be put off. There will be times when you question your choices; that's good! Don't forget to have fun along the way and look for the beauty that each day holds. Sometimes it's difficult to find when you're so busy, but it's always there. This way of life should be full of opportunities for relaxation, enjoyment and learning. Grab them every time they crop up.

Decade decisions

Almost everything in this book can be learnt at any stage of life, at any age. However, just for this chapter, I want to focus on a few adult stages of life, and see how simple living might fit into those stages. Because in each stage of life – and these can generally be defined by each adult decade – you grow and have different needs, and while you live each day to its fullest, you also prepare for what will follow.

The trick in every stage of life is to get through it with the people and things that make life worth living, without being saddled with debt. The one debt that will travel with you through a few stages is a mortgage; try not to have other debts with it that tie you down. Let me stress here that money should never be the most important thing in anyone's life, but it helps us live in the present and build for the future, so it will feature heavily at every stage. Money, or more accurately, debt, can make or break the plans you have for yourself.

As you go from one stage to the next, be mindful of what you've learnt in the previous decade and build on it. Always follow your

own path and define for yourself what you want to include in your life. This kind of life is flexible so if something that worked in the previous decade doesn't work for you now, don't be afraid to change it.

Remember, this is my version of simple living, so please model it to suit yourself. These are examples to give you ideas for what you might do.

DECLUTTERING EACH DECADE

You might find different things are important to you in each decade. While there are possessions that you will have with you all your life, some things you must have in your twenties are forgotten about when you're thirty, forty or fifty. At some point towards the end of each decade, it is wise to declutter and to get rid of those items you no longer need, and to open up your life for new life to flow in. There is information about decluttering in the Home chapter.

Simple living
in your twenties

When I look back on a life of well over sixty years, there is one recurring question that I wonder about and hear others asking as well: why didn't someone tell me this when I was twenty!

If you're lucky and smart, you'll never stop learning. What you learn at school and university are just the basics to set you up for life; you should continue to learn as you grow older.

Your money and your life

Unless you come from an incredibly wealthy family, work will be a part of your life. Expect to work for what you get and do your fair share. Despite what you may hear and read, work is a significant part of our lives and it will teach you more than you expect it to. When you reach your twenties, lazing on the beach or sleeping in are rewards for the hard work you do, not part of your everyday life.

Some people go through their teens knowing they'll leave school, study at university or TAFE then develop a career in a certain field.

But from my observations and personal experience, many people don't know what they want to do; they just know what they don't want. No matter which category you fall into, I want to encourage you to develop a positive attitude towards work. Whether it is paid work or work in the home, working gives a solid framework to our lives. It usually enables us to earn money to build a future and it places families on firm ground.

When you start working for the first time there can be a very strong urge to buy everything you couldn't have when you were younger. As soon as we start earning a bit of money, most of us want to create our own style – in what we wear, how we spend our time, where we live and which car we drive. It's one of the ways we separate ourselves from childhood. The ability to earn and spend money is a modern marker of adult life, and this is often exploited by advertisers urging us to buy more than we need.

Learn how to budget as soon as you start earning your own money, and live within your means. This way you'll be in control of your money instead of spending every cent you earn. At some stage in their late twenties or early thirties, most people settle down and think about buying a home. If you arrive at that point in control of your money, with little debt and maybe even the beginnings of a home deposit, you will have placed yourself in the best possible position.

Discovering shared values

If you meet the person you want to be with permanently, it's essential that you talk with them about their values. Without it sounding like an interrogation, find a way to discuss finances, children, ambitions and goals. Your values don't have to mirror the values of your partner exactly, but they'll need to be fairly close on the important things. If you're hoping to live a quiet, debt-free life, it's important to know if your partner aims for a yacht and a ten-car garage. If you hope to settle down with a couple of kids in your version of semi-rural paradise, it's best to know if your other half wants to be childless and travel six months of the year. Finding someone whose goals and ideas about the future are sufficiently aligned with yours will smooth your path towards the life you want and ensure that it is a shared journey rather than one filled with unbridgeable differences.

Becoming the authentic you

Now is the time when you'll start shaping your character and what kind of person you'll be later in life. Take control of your life; don't just react to what life throws at you. Take time out, think carefully about what kind of life you want for yourself, what your values are, what you value in other people and what your ideal life would be. Make plans to live that ideal life and then do it.

This decade is the launching pad for your life. If you can establish yourself on a firm foundation right now, learn the skills that you need, create a circle of supportive friends and maintain a good relationship with your family, you'll be setting yourself up in the best position to continue through to the next stage, and that one is a real spinner. If you thought your twenties were high-energy, just wait – you're in for the ride of your life in your thirties.

Quick tips for your twenties

- Start becoming more self-reliant so that you can look after yourself throughout your life without having to rely too heavily on others.
- Find a mentor or role model. It could be someone in your family, a colleague, or someone you meet along the way. Ask questions, watch how they conduct themselves and be aware of their values and how they apply them to their everyday life.
- Move on from friends who drain you or who are negative or toxic.
- Travel if you can – even if it's just to the next state.
- Get rid of possessions that are no longer useful.
- Discover more about yourself – this is the time when you work out what kind of person you are, what you hope your life will be and how to work towards those elusive goals.
- When you leave the family home, try to stay close to your family. They are important.
- Start saving for your retirement.

Simple living in your thirties

So, you've finally reached your thirties. It's not as bad as they said, right? Hopefully you've landed here with only a few debts and a passion for living simply. If you have, you're in the driver's seat. If you do have heavy debt, there is still a lot you can do to untangle yourself before it strangles you. If you can set yourself up properly here, if you budget and pay off debt instead of adding to it, you'll be fine.

Building your family

Statistics tell us that if people haven't become attached in their late twenties, now is the time they start settling down. There is something about our thirties that compels us to find a partner, settle down, take stock of our lives, mature and, for many of us, start having children. If you don't live with a partner, all the same things apply but there will only be one income and you will make all the decisions.

If you haven't already dived into marriage or parenthood, talk to your partner in depth about what you both want. Some people don't want children, others want many. Some assume there will be one parent at home raising the children. Others believe children can be looked after in childcare or by an accommodating grandparent while the parents work to pay off the home. Don't assume you know what your partner is thinking – this is an important part of your life and you need to talk about it. And it is better to work out your strategy early, rather than waiting until things aren't working out how you want them to. No matter what you choose to do – stay at home to raise your children, work from home, go out to work, or some combination of these options – this decade will be dotted with times you'll feel overwhelmed and tired. It goes with the territory, but it has the potential to make you stronger and more resilient. One thing I know to be true: working as a team, especially when times are tough, bonds you to your partner like nothing else. Hardship teaches valuable life lessons.

> *Working as a team, especially when times are tough, bonds you to your partner like nothing else.*

Starting a family can be a minefield of conflicting messages and influences. But if you have a close relationship with your partner and if you live true to your values, your thirties will be when your family shapes itself into a firm and supportive unit. Be a role model for your children. That is the most important thing you can give them – it's more valuable than any toy or fancy bit of electronics. Give of yourself to your children and you'll get the best back from them. Your children see you when the outside world doesn't; they see you behind closed doors, when you aren't on your best behaviour. Those are the times they learn how to behave because they'll do what you show them.

Developing financial security

What you do now could set you up for life. If you have the means to buy a house and it makes financial sense, do so. Whatever you do, choose wisely. Staying within certain frugal parameters can give you a home that you love without burdening you with debt that will take your entire life to repay. If you pay off your mortgage as fast as you can, living in your own home can give you a feeling of security right through to your older years. If you're not already in your own home but intend to be at some point, start making plans to save for a house deposit. It's better in the long run to save a hefty deposit rather than a meagre one, or – and I hope you don't do this – borrow the entire amount. Step up and save a large deposit. Even if it means waiting a few more years to buy, you will pay much less interest over the course of the loan.

There are so many things you can do now. If you're married or living with a partner, work out a savings plan. If you are both working, try to live on one wage and use the other one to save a house deposit or repay the mortgage. Living on one wage is a wonderful strategy to live by. If you can do it you'll be debt-free much faster. This is a time of sacrifice. You'll work hard, go without, regret decisions made, wish you'd done things sooner, or never, but in the long run, if you stick to your plan, you'll come out of this decade stronger, more self-assured and convinced that you can attain your goals.

Working towards your future

The thirties decade is all about consolidation. It's about bonding as a family, establishing priorities and boundaries, working towards common goals, becoming the person you want to be and, again, being very careful with debt. There is always a money trap waiting to spring, so be careful, know your limits and stay strong. Refusing the temptation of excessive spending is good for your soul as well as the bank balance. Although you might hear otherwise, being thrifty and saving your money is not being cheap or miserly. It's a mindset that will help you achieve your goal of living well and being content. If you hear criticism, remember your goals and stay focused. By staying true to your values you can become self-confident and feel a sense of enrichment that will carry you through those times when your friends can't quite work out where you're coming from.

As you grow older, you'll care less about what others think. If you're sure the way you're living is right for you, never be put off. There will be times when you question your choices; that's good! Don't forget to have fun along the way and look for the beauty that each day holds. Sometimes it's difficult to find when you're so busy, but it's always there. This way of life should be full of opportunities for relaxation, enjoyment and learning. Grab them every time they crop up.

Quick tips for your thirties

- Shop at thrift shops for clothes and children's needs.
- Stop using disposables unless you absolutely have to – especially nappies. Modern cloth nappies are comfortable for babies, can be reused for all your kids and don't add to landfill. And, according to statistics, you'll save about $3000 per baby using cloth nappies rather than disposables.
- Don't get into the habit of giving your children expensive gifts and clothes. Your children want to spend time with you and to feel loved – that is the most precious gift available, and it can be given every day.
- Declutter and give away or sell things you no longer use or love.
- Be a role model for your children.
- Learn how to knit, sew and mend.
- Do an audit of your own assets and liabilities – do you need your second phone, cable TV, a second car? Get rid of everything you don't need that is adding to your cost of living.

Simple living
in your forties

During your younger years I'm sure you heard all the negative silliness about ageing but now that you're in your forties, you'll realise you're in the prime of your life. You feel confident, ambitious and capable. You are at the height of your money-earning power, so you can pay off more debt now than at any other time and you might start to see the light at the end of the tunnel. Hopefully, with a bit of hard work and determination, you'll pay off your mortgage soon and keep putting something aside for your retirement. And don't add to your debt burden by trading up when you've paid off a sizable portion of your mortgage. If your family has grown a lot, a larger home makes sense; otherwise, stay where you are and be content with what you have – bloom where you are planted.

Funding your retirement

If you're working, you will be putting a set amount of money into your superannuation for your retirement. You can add more if you wish and receive tax benefits for doing so. It's a wise investment.

I want to make two important points about funding your retirement:

- If you are debt-free, you do not need as much as most investment brokers say you need. For example, Hanno and I live well on less than $30 000 a year.
- Keep all your superannuation funds in one account. Each time you change jobs throughout your working life, make sure you have the details of your chosen superannuation account to give to your new employer.

Growing into your life

As you age you'll realise that you don't have to please everyone around you. You mature, and part of that maturity is to be content with what you have and what you are. This is the time of life when your children have grown out of their highly dependent stage and with that you get more time to yourself. You get an inkling of how things will be when your children leave home and make their own lives. You'll have the time now to learn new skills and develop your hobbies – cooking, painting, sewing, gardening, hiking, camping, or a hundred other things – and get enjoyment from the things you choose to do.

If you don't have children, you probably have a group of friends you rely on. Make sure you put time into your friendships so they continue to nurture and support you as you grow older. You'll probably be more financially sound now and if you've been paying extra on your mortgage, now is the time you see the results of that. If your finances are in order you might decide to travel or take up new hobbies. Whatever you do now, stay on track while you do the things that make you happy and fulfilled.

If you choose to live like Hanno and me, it's the time to develop your home and land so it can support you in later life. If you haven't already done so, you might add chickens to the backyard, or bee hives, aquaponics, a couple of milking goats. Of course, you should learn all you can about whatever you add. Do you need more fences? You should do that now. Whatever requires strength and energy, do it now because later, you'll have less money, your strength will start to decline and you'll wish you had thought to do it earlier.

If you're hoping to retire with some degree of self-sufficiency, now is a good time to concentrate on learning all the relevant skills – if you haven't already. You'll need to know how to bake, make jams and preserves, mend clothes and shoes, and grow vegetables and fruit. If you're a couple, it's a good idea to divide the chores and learning between you, each taking the things you enjoy doing. I like doing the inside tasks like cooking and sewing and Hanno enjoys being outside, so he does the vegetable gardening and home and yard maintenance, and I am the homemaker. You and your partner might find that the opposite works for you.

Quick tips for your forties

- Check the state of your superannuation. Make sure it's all in one fund and if it isn't, move it to the one you believe to be the most successful and stable.
- Know your children's friends.
- Show your children how to make green cleaners, how to treat stains, and how to wash and iron their clothes. There are instructions for making cleaners in the Housework chapter.
- Do some volunteer work.
- If you want to be self-sufficient, or close to it, when you retire, start reading about the skills you'll need.
- Continue to educate yourself. Find books that will show you what you need to know, and blogs to see how ordinary people live from day to day.
- Declutter and get rid of everything you don't use or want in your life.

Simple living
in your fifties

What you're aiming for at the end of your fifties is to have your children out in the world, working and set up in their own homes. You'll want your mortgage to have been paid off and your home to be supportive and comfortable, and you'll want to have learned the skills you need to help you live the way you have chosen. If you can say you've successfully done that, then you are set because soon you'll reach the time when all your work pays off. You can retire, do whatever you want to do every day, and live life to its fullest measure.

Auditing your home

This is the final stage of your working life so you'll be paying off debt, checking that you have the assets you need to go into the later stages of life, and ensuring that your home and car are in good order.

Do an audit of your home while you're still earning money. You'll need to look at it in a different way now – you want it to support you in your older years, not be a burden. Now might be your last chance to change what you don't like and what doesn't work for you. Look at your furniture – is everything in good order? You might need to replace a few items. Thrift shops are full of old or antique furniture that may suit you – furniture that was made to last many years. Even if you have to have things recovered, revarnished or repainted, you're likely to end up with a sturdier and longer-lasting piece than you would buying cheaply made new furniture.

If you want to live in a smaller house when the children leave home, think carefully about the type of home you'll need. What facilities and services will be available over the next twenty years? Take your time with this decision and be mindful of how you want to live in retirement. Do you want a vegetable garden and chickens? Will you use your kitchen more or less? Do you want a sewing room or a shed? Do you want to be on one level or will you cope with stairs when you're older? You will have to keep all these decisions in mind when you look for your new home.

Decluttering again

You need much less in your home when the kids move out, so it is a great time to declutter again. You can give them some of your odds and ends as they leave home and start living their own lives. If you want to keep pieces of furniture or dinnerware in the family but no longer need these things in your home, maybe your children would be keen to be keepers of these treasures. Give away or sell everything else you don't need.

Teaching your children

Children need to be taught life skills all through their lives, and their teens and twenties are no exception. Now you're at the pointy end, you have to reinforce what you've been teaching them all their lives. Now it really counts. As in previous stages, make sure you are a good role model for them and always be the kind of person you want them to be. This is the time when you teach them about being a good and fair employee, talk to them about treating their friends and acquaintances with respect, and help them further develop self-respect and confidence.

There are also the practical skills like saving, driving, shopping for groceries, storing food, cooking and looking after their own clothes (how to wash and iron them, for example). Even if you've encouraged saving and focused on money management before, now is the time to reinforce it because there will be a lot of peer pressure to spend. This can be the most difficult time for a parent, but it's also the most rewarding. If you can send well-adjusted, confident children out into the world, fully equipped with the life skills they need, as well as the formal education of schooling, you will have given your children their very best chance of a happy and successful life.

Quick tips for your fifties

- Learn all you can about what you want to do in retirement. This might be the ideal time for art or sewing classes, or for asking your friends to teach you how to knit, crochet, replace a tap washer, change a tyre, or any other activity you might want to take up to support your life.
- Become a mentor or role model. Offer to help others learn the skills you've gained over the years.
- If you're making the transition from cooking for a family to cooking for two, or just for yourself, you might need to look through recipe books for new ideas.
- Declutter again and get rid of everything you don't use any more.
- Think about your financial future before you leave work. Do some research and work out the finer points of your post-work life and how you'll fund it. If you will be on a pension, go to Centrelink now to ask about it, and what discounts and rebates go with it.

Simple living
in retirement

When you think about it, the only time working and middle-class people get to do exactly what we want every day is on holiday and after retirement. I guess we have a fairly free and easy life in childhood and as teenagers, but even then there are people telling us what to do and when to do it. Retirement, whenever it happens, is all about freedom: the freedom to do exactly what you choose to do each day, the freedom of time. And even though the weekly wage stops, if you've gone through several simple decades and arrive at retirement's door with no debt, no mortgage, a roof over your head, money in the bank, some investments or a pension, you'll be fine. If you have chosen not to buy a house, or have never had the opportunity to do so, make sure that where you are living now allows you long-term tenancy and security. If it doesn't, or if you know you'll have to move in the future, do it now, before you get older. Strength will start to decline in this stage and it's best to get the physical work over with sooner rather than later.

Things are different when you retire. Many of your expenses drop, your priorities change and you'll have time to shop for bargains and to make a lot of the things you used to pay for. Depending on where you live and what benefits your government gives its seniors, you'll have to look at your budget now and make all the necessary changes. In Australia, when you're on an age pension, you get discounts on your property rates, ambulance subscription, public transport, telephone charges and pharmacy costs. Hanno and I decided to keep our private health insurance, even though it's expensive, as it gives us peace of mind to know that we can get medical help, choose our own doctors and go to hospital if we need to without having to go on a waiting list. You may decide differently – it's up to you.

Before you sit down to redo your budget, find out exactly what you're entitled to and claim it – it's one of the many reasons you've been paying tax all these long years. There are other benefits too: recently I parked my car in a senior's parking spot for the very first time. It was close to the front door of the place I was going to. I felt like a bit of a fraud, to tell you the truth, but the sign said 'senior parking' and I am a senior so I parked there. Nice. Check out the businesses in your area as well, because many give seniors' discounts.

Your daily work

In the months before you retire, start thinking about what you'll do every day when you stop working for a living. If you've always gone out to work you might find it difficult to adjust, but if you have something planned, whether it be home-based, volunteer-based or out in the community at a club or library, you won't be sitting there on the first day wondering what to do.

Hanno and I are as busy as we want to be. We decided to be

productive in our retirement, to grow as much food as we could and to find as much con-tentment and happiness doing that as we could. That involves all sorts of home-based tasks like house maintenance, gardening, cooking, baking, recycling and mending. Living like this gives our days variety and interest, and even though we've been working away here for several years now, it still feels fresh. We take breaks whenever we want them; we take days off and sometimes we go for a drive to a nearby country town. It's a peaceful and rewarding life full of the enrichment that comes from being active and self-reliant.

If you have the opportunity to do voluntary work in your community, grab it with both hands. In my experience, it has been rewarding and life-changing.

Your history

I believe it is my duty as an older woman to pass on what I know to those younger than I am. Older people are our connection to the past and if we don't tap into that, many traditional skills and memories will be lost. If you still have older relatives, ask them about your history. Even if you're not interested now, I guarantee there will come a day when you will be interested and if your loved ones are gone then, you will never know. Write down what they tell you so you can pass your family history on to your children.

And speaking of history, get rid of everything in your home that you don't need. Ask your family if they want that extra set of dinnerware. Donate old clothes to charity.

Your health

Stay active and look after your health because things can come back to bite you in your sixties and seventies. I have been lucky so far – I haven't had any health issues and am confident that I'll be out in the backyard in my eighties, yelling out: 'Hanno, the magpie geese are back!' Exercise your mind every day, keep learning new things, and stay con-nected with your family and friends. Aim to be a valuable member of your community by continuing, or starting, voluntary work at your local school or neighbourhood cen-tre. Continue to cook from scratch and eat wholesome food. Even if it's for you alone, it's important that you eat well and drink plenty of water every day.

Many people have an unrealistic idea of old age. They think we oldies are helpless and feeble and not capable of much. We may not be able to lift what we once did and we may be taking a nap after lunch, but we're still waking up every morning eager to get stuck into our tasks and get as much from the day as we can. I believe that if we stay active, in mind and body, we will live to a grand old age in our own home. I think the key to this is to have a good relationship with your family so you have their support if you are ill or have some heavy work you need help with. If you aren't in the best of health, you may want to move closer to your children or even move in with them.

Don't be scared of ageing. If you're in good health you'll have many years as a senior and they can be wonderful years. Older age has many rewards, and retirement – and the freedom that comes with it – is one of life's golden eggs.

Quick tips for retirement

- Remain active and involved. Do some classes if you have special interests.
- Volunteer in your community – this will open up a whole new world for you.
- Eat well and make sure you have one good meal every day. The rest of the time you can live very well on fruit, water and tea and toast.
- Have regular medical check-ups.
- Remember you're not perfect. That is a good thing.
- Don't cut yourself off from family and friends.
- Put your feet up and relax. Read, knit, do some research, enjoy the grandkids, travel, join a club, study or teach. Whatever you spend your time on now, enjoy it. You deserve it.

Simple living throughout your life

The rest of the book will focus on things you can do at any age, but here are some quick tips to get you going.

- Learn how to write a budget and stick to it.
- Shop wisely. You don't need everything you want.
- Learn how to cook from scratch. Over the years it will make you healthier and it's much cheaper than relying on convenience food and fast food.
- Learn to bake. It's a lot of fun and people will love you for it.
- Learn how to stockpile groceries and store food.
- Plan your menus.
- Plan your grocery shopping.
- Pack lunches for work and school. Buying lunch every day is an unnecessary expense.
- Learn how to sew, knit and mend.
- Try to cut back on your phone and internet bills.
- Take water with you when you go out.

- If you have some outdoor space, use it. Learn to grow food.
- Learn how to preserve or freeze your excess food.
- Read.
- Disregard advertising. It is there to create an insatiable want in you. Don't give it any power; march to the beat of your own drum.
- Reuse, repair and recycle.
- Get enough sleep.
- Learn how to make your own green cleaners.
- Learn how to read your electricity and water meters. That skill will help you save a significant amount of money and natural resources over the years.
- Look for entertainment that is free or close to it.
- Don't aim for perfection; expect to make mistakes and learn from them when they happen. All mistakes are learning opportunities.
- Always support your family and friends and be kind to yourself.
- Look on Freecycle (freecycle.org) or ask around when you need something. You may be able to swap or barter for what you need.
- Dry your laundry outside whenever possible. If you don't have a washing line, string one up.
- Keep learning new skills to support the life you want.
- Stay focused on the changes you want to make in your life.

R.K. ALLISTON

LONDON

THE IDEAL GARDEN TWINE

STRING IN A TIN

Soft, Pliable and Strong
Natural Green Shade Harmonises with Foliage

Waste
Proof

Will Not Tangle

Wet
Proof

USED FROM THE POCKET
BOTH HANDS FREE

DRAW TWINE FROM CENTRE OF SPOOL

SAVING & SPENDING

I used to live my life creating what I thought was happiness with new products bought at the shops every week. I was hoping to fill the void within me but when the excitement of the purchase wore off, the void was back, bigger than before. That emptiness has gone now. The space has been filled with optimism for the future, contentment with the present, and acceptance of the past.

Reclaim your life

Selling your life hours

If you're working for a living, or your partner is, then you are selling life hours for money. Each year has only 8760 hours in it, giving us – if we live to be eighty years of age – just over 700 000 hours in an entire lifetime. There are only 168 hours in a week, and you sleep for about fifty of them, so you have to be sure that the life hours you sell give you the best value. Wasting money or hours cheats you of your life.

'The cost of a thing is the amount of what I will call life which is required to be exchanged for it, immediately or in the long run.'

Henry David Thoreau

Think about your money in terms of the hours spent earning it. When you realise that what you buy costs the hours of your life that you spent earning that money, you will be ready go to the next level of creating a budget, spending less, and planning your financial future. If you have debt you might make a decision to not accumulate any more and to work out a plan to be debt-free as quickly as possible. If you can start saving and focus on paying off debt, wonderful rewards will come your way because making that last payment on your mortgage or credit cards will be one of the most memorable times of your life. On that day you will become genuinely independent and you'll live better and breathe easier because of it.

We must have money for food, shelter, clothing and the practicalities of life, but life isn't just about day-to-day living; it's also about joy.

When you're debt-free you're not beholden to anyone or any bank, and your life decisions are based on your needs and not the need to repay monies owed. You can cut down your working hours, if that is what you wish to do; you can continue working because you enjoy it or you can save for your retirement, education or travel – or whatever is really important to you and your family. The focus here is to identify your priorities. What do you love doing? What makes you feel really alive? What excites you and makes you jump out of bed in the morning? Whether it be cycling, reading, painting, going to the movies, travelling, learning, cooking, looking after pets, or anything else, those are the things you should save for. Simple living isn't about spending nothing at all and making yourself miserable because you're frugal; it's more about living within your means and not wasting your hard-earned money on things you don't want or need.

Don't let anyone convince you that you should never spend on the profound or pleasurable. We must have money for food, shelter, clothing and the practicalities of life, but life isn't just about day-to-day living; it's also about joy. If your particular joys cost money, include them in your budget and save for them with your other expenses.

A change in attitude

Back in my spending days, credit-card debt and a mortgage were big parts of my life. I didn't take much notice of it at the time because shopping gave me other priorities, but while I was working to pay off what I owed, I was building even more debt. I thought it was normal to have everything I wanted, that debt was a part of every life. We are encouraged to think that way. The average Western lifestyle always gives you new things to crave; it keeps encouraging you to spend beyond your means. That will never change. You have to change instead.

We cleared our debt by only buying essentials. We stopped using our credit cards and paid them off, then kept only one for emergencies. When the cards were paid off, we put all our spare money into our mortgage and paid it off in eight years, rather than the twenty years we had signed up for. Instead of making monthly payments, we paid fortnightly. That alone knocked several thousand dollars off our interest payments. It wasn't easy, but starting was the hardest part, and it got easier as we realised how much we were saving in interest.

Our other small steps were to stockpile groceries, grow vegetables, cook from scratch, stop buying convenience foods, and stop eating out except on special occasions. We cut our grocery bill in half, then in half again. We monitored our electricity and water meters, we checked bills and bank statements as they came in. (Yes, we found mistakes.

Always check.) We sold our second car, got rid of pay TV and stopped buying all those little things – like magazines, cups of coffee and bottles of water – that cost a lot of money over the course of a year. All those small steps allowed us to pay off our debts and reclaim our lives. You can do the same thing.

Being a spender is not sustainable unless you are incredibly wealthy – and even then it's pointless to spend just because you can. Simple living allows you to have what you need to live well, but within a frugal framework that encourages thrift, reusing, recycling, cutting back, and being aware of your impact on the environment. Within your new frugal framework it will be possible to build a rich life and find real happiness, but it will not come easily. Changing to this lifestyle requires a period of readjustment, in both attitude and behaviour. If you are like I used to be, and have been spending on whatever your heart desires, this period could be painful. You might fail a few times, and that's okay. You need to be strong. Just start again and don't let it beat you.

The key to money management

I have no doubt there are many effective ways to manage money but I am going to explain how we do it. Naturally it's a simple method; it requires a change of attitude from that of a consumer to that of a conserver, and it utilises and celebrates thriftiness. Money management is not my favourite topic but over the years I've come to realise that if we get the money right, everything else becomes much easier.

One thing stands out now just as much as it did when I first started taking my finances more seriously. The key to money management is simply this: spend less than you earn. If you can do that over a long period of time, no matter how much or how little you earn, you'll be in a good financial situation. The principle applies if you're earning hundreds of thousands of dollars a year or if you're on a pension.

Most of us know people who have gone broke despite earning a lot of money. Just think of all those celebrities who have declared bankruptcy despite earning millions of dollars. I know a couple whose household income was $200 000 a year for a number of years, while the rest of our circle made much less. That couple was always in debt – even though they earned a lot of money, they consistently spent it all, and then some. They ended up divorced and bankrupt.

The key to money management is simply this: spend less than you earn.

Hanno and I live by the 80/20 rule: we live on 80 per cent of our income and save 20 per cent. Our income is about $1700 a month, and we save around $350 a month. We live frugally, we have no debt, we buy second-hand and look for bargains when we need anything, but we live well; we're not mean-spirited or stressed by money and we feel satisfied and enriched by our life choices. Remember, it doesn't matter what amount of money you earn; the key to being financially secure is to spend less than you earn, and to do it consistently over the years.

Next I'll describe the five steps you can take towards debt-free living. The steps are quite simple but contain several elements and will need some thought about how to include them in your life. Managing your money well is one of the key components of a simple life and it will take time and effort, but if you can do it – if you can consistently spend less than you earn – you will notice a real difference.

Step 1: Track your spending

The first step in the process of cutting back and working towards a simple life is to track your spending. I doubt there is anyone who hasn't wondered at some point where his or her money went. Most of us know how much we earn in a week but few of us have a realistic and accurate idea of how much we spend, or what we spend it on. Often we're so tied up with work, the children, or things that are happening in our lives that we spend without knowing it. We may also be spending small amounts frequently without thinking how those small amounts add up over a longer period. Tracking your money will help you discover what your priorities are and what your current spending patterns are. You can then use that information to change habits and focus on positive spending, like debt reduction.

How to track your spending

Take a small notebook and pen with you wherever you go and every time you buy something, write it down in your notebook. When you

and your partner are both tracking your spending, both of you need to record everything you spend. You must be honest and consistent, and record everything – even the smallest amounts. Bills, coffees, movie tickets . . . everything. This is very important because what you are doing is making a record, for yourself, of what you do with your money. If you 'forget', or try to hide your spending, you might as well stop doing this right now and think about your purpose. If your purpose is to change the way you live and move towards a more sustainable life, then even though this process may be painful, it needs to be done.

At the end of each day, add up how much you've spent and how much of that could be called non-essential, and note those figures down. Knowing what you spend your money on and where you could save will help you when you come to the next two steps.

Your money-tracking list for a few days might look something like this:

MONDAY 15 APRIL	TUESDAY 16 APRIL	WEDNESDAY 17 APRIL
Groceries $39	Fruit and veg $36.90	Dress $120
Coffee $3	Coffee $3	Shoes $125
Fuel $25	Mints $1	Coffee $3
Lunch $7	Newspaper $2.50	Gift for friend $30
Phone bill $89.50	Postage stamp $1	Bottle of water $2
Credit card bill $70	Dinner with friend $30	Apple $0.50
Spent: $233.90	Spent: $74	Spent: $280.50
Non-essentials: $10	Non-essentials: $36.50	Non-essentials: $280.50

You'll have a fairly good idea of your spending habits at the end of a week, but keep tracking for a month to get a more accurate picture. You'll find that many of your bills will be monthly and it is only in the context of accounting for everything you pay during that time that you'll reveal the true nature of your expenses and spending.

Most of us know how much we earn in a week but few of us have a realistic and accurate idea of how much we spend, or what we spend it on.

At the end of each month, sit down with your partner and report on your expenses, or if you're single, set aside some time to go over your month's spending. Take the time to enter your figures in a spreadsheet or handwritten register so you can build up a long-term record of your spending. If you're in a partnership, the end of each month is a good time to have a discussion, when you have your monthly figure in front of you, about upcoming expenses and how much money can be put aside for debt reduction or saving that month. Please remember this is not a time for arguing about money or making your partner feel guilty. Be kind to each other and expect a few stumbles in the first couple of months.

Step 2: Reduce your spending

Whether you like it or not, to live simply you must reduce your spending. It's part of the territory. You will get away with not growing your own food; you don't have to keep chickens or goats, make soap, bake bread, sew or knit. You can live in the city or the country, you can work or not, you can be young or older. But the one thing everyone should do is reduce their spending.

While some of us don't have a problem with over-spending or debt, many of us do. If you have problems dealing with your money in a sensible way and continue to over-spend, this step might be difficult for you. Personal responsibility plays a huge role in getting yourself on track with your money. I cannot help you with that, except to say that it is up to you to make a decision to take control of your life and start to break that cycle of debt. You are the only one who can make that decision. You can read as much as you like about reducing debt but there comes a time when you have to stop reading and thinking about it and start doing it.

Think about the difference between needs and wants, then try to spend only on needs. When you have a budget you can relax more, but for now you need to cut your spending in order to change old habits and start building your new life. I'm not advising you to give up all your small pleasures, but choose your pleasures wisely and know, really know, what they are costing you. When you know the full cost of something – not just the monetary cost, but also what you have to give up and how long you have to work to pay for it – you might find you don't want it any more.

Things you can do to cut spending

There is more information about many of these suggestions in the following chapters.

- **Give up an expensive habit.** That might be alcohol, cigarettes, gambling, pay TV or recreational shopping. Be kind to yourself while you do it and when you succeed, reward yourself with a non-related activity that you love. If it is too difficult at first, cut down instead of giving up. After a period of time, try again. If you can't do it the first time, or the second, keep going. It is only a failure if you stop trying.

- **Monitor your insurance and electricity, gas, water and phone usage.** Make sure you're not wasting a cent on any of these essentials. Check your usage and costs every year and try to get a better deal by doing research and calling your suppliers and their competitors to discuss better value for the money you're spending.

- **Stop eating out and buying takeaway or convenience food.** When you buy pre-prepared food you pay for the time and expertise of the person who is making your food. You will have cheaper – and healthier – food if you buy the ingredients and make it yourself. With a bit of organisation, you'll be able to make your own food and, even on the busiest day, you'll be able to eat at home.

- **Start packing lunches and drinks** for the workers and students in your family. Take water in a bottle and a flask of good coffee or your favourite tea to work.
- **Cook from scratch.** It's much cheaper, tastier and healthier.
- **Don't waste food.** It is estimated that about 30 per cent of food bought for family homes is wasted. That's like taking your weekly grocery money and throwing a third of it in the rubbish bin. Eat your leftovers for lunch the following day or turn them into a new dish the next night.
- **Plan your menus.** Menu planning is another way of saving money. It's simply taking time to plan what you will eat during the next week or month, and having the ingredients already in your pantry and fridge. When you do that you will buy according to your plan, look for specials, waste less food and save money.
- **Spend less time in the shops.** The more you're in the shops, the more you'll spend. If you tend to wander through shops looking for things to buy, stop. If you shop weekly for groceries, go fortnightly instead. If you spend your lunch break browsing in clothes stores, go for a stroll around the block instead.
- **Start a stockpile.** Put aside $15–$20 a week to buy things on special that you know will store well and be used. Use that money when you do your regular shopping and see storable bargains. When you've built your stockpile to a reasonable size, you can do your grocery shopping much less frequently, thereby spending less time in the shops.
- **Rethink the way you give gifts.** Cut your gift list down to your immediate family and perhaps a few close friends. If you must buy gifts for a lot of people, organise it well ahead of time so you can fit it into your budget. Give homemade gifts or buy at thrift shops. Most people will appreciate a card with a thoughtful message or something that you've spent time making more than an expensive item.
- **Make your own cleaning products.** Instead of buying the numerous expensive

commercial products in the cleaning aisle, buy white vinegar, bicarb, laundry soap, borax and washing soda, and learn more about green cleaning.

- **Entertain yourself more cheaply.** Borrow DVDs, books and magazines at the library instead of buying them. Take a small, portable knitting or sewing project to fill in spare time when you're away from home. Instead of going shopping with a girlfriend, invite her over to your home, where you can make hot scones and coffee and use the time to talk. Invite friends over for a soap-making session, or to sew together.

- **Mend your things** rather than throwing them out. It might be sewing a button on a shirt, replacing a zipper, cutting a split from a hose and connecting the hose up again, or cleaning and sharpening you garden tools rather than replacing them. When I was a spender, I threw away good clothing simply because it was ripped or needed a button sewn on. I would rather have worked a few hours more to pay for a new dress or new shoes than repair them. Now I value my time, and myself, a lot more.

Cut down on small things

One of the easiest ways to decrease your spending is to cut down on small things. My downfalls were cups of coffee, magazines and newspapers, bottles of water, and lunch.

There were so many temptations that whispered, 'It's okay, it doesn't cost much.' Those whispers lied; those small things don't cost a lot as a single unit but if you keep buying them every time you go out, they add up to a shocking and disappointing surprise.

Let's take some time here to work out the cost of those little extras that give only fleeting satisfaction or quench a thirst. Buying a cup of coffee will cost around $4 – or more, depending on where you are. If you buy that coffee five days a week, forty-eight weeks a year (just looking at the working year), you'll pay $960 a year for your cup of coffee. You could make a substantial extra payment on your mortgage with that kind of money. One or two extra payments every year will slice an incredible amount of time and dollars off your mortgage.

If you buy one magazine or a daily newspaper, that will set you back about $8 a week or $1 a day – around $400 a year. A bottle of water might cost about $3. One every day while you're at work is $15 a week, or $720 over the space of a working year. And lunch – well, that could cost anything from $4 to $12, but let's agree on $8. Eight dollars a day, five days a week, will cost you $1920 a year.

Let's look at it this way:

- Coffee: $4 a day × 5 days a week × 48 weeks a year = $960
- Bottled water: $3 a day × 5 days a week × 48 weeks a year = $720
- Newspapers/magazines: $8 a week × 48 weeks a year = $384
- Lunch: $8 a day × 5 days a week × 48 weeks a year = $1920
- **Coffee + water + newspapers/magazines + lunch = $3984**

Nearly $4000! All for little comforts and conveniences that, with a bit of organisation, you could replace with coffee, water and lunch from home, and a book or magazine from the library. You will still have your comforts at work but they'll cost you a fraction of the price you'll pay picking them up at a café or shop each day, and with less throw-away waste. You don't have to be Einstein to work out that if you're earning an average wage of $1659 a week, before tax, almost $80 each week ($4000 across the year) is far too much to pay for the convenience of not having to do those things for yourself.

Become more energy efficient

Reducing your energy and water usage will help cut down your bills as well as your impact on the environment. Here are some energy-saving tips for the home.

- **Turn off appliances and chargers at the wall, and don't leave them on standby.** Reorganise your plugs to make this as easy as possible. For example, plug your TV, DVD player and stereo into one power board, which you can easily turn off when you go to bed. Try to do the same in the kitchen. (You can use a wall clock instead of relying on your microwave or oven clock.) Turn the monitor off when you leave the computer, turn lights off when you leave a room, and turn the TV off when you're not watching.

- **Minimise electricity-powered activities.** Sweep the floor instead of vacuuming, wash up by hand instead of using the dishwasher, and do less ironing.

- **Make your house more efficient.** Change to solar hot water, install skylights in dark rooms, replace old light bulbs with new, efficient ones. If you're in a cold climate, install double-glazed windows and insulated blinds.

- **Use less heating and cooling.** Set the thermostat lower/higher (depending on the season) during the day, and turn the heating or cooling off at night. Dress more warmly in winter and keep quilts and rugs on the couch to encourage the family to use them instead of the heater. Heat or cool the main living area instead of the whole house, and close the door when you're heating or cooling a room.

- **Wash your clothes in cold water and take shorter showers.** This will save both energy and water.

Step 3: Take control

After you've tracked your spending for a month to get a better idea of where your money goes, and have started to reduce your spending, you are in a great position to take control of your finances. This involves writing a budget, working out how much you can save, and organising your money.

Write a budget

A budget is an estimate of your income and expenses. When you write it all down, not only will you have a plan to work from, but you'll also have an accurate and honest account of your financial situation.

I know some people hate the idea of writing a budget. They see it as a restriction. I did too, until I did my own budget and realised it was a plan to help us wisely spend whatever money we had. Instead of being the restriction I had been fighting all those years, my budget turned out to be the most liberating of all the changes we made.

There are many ways to write a budget and if you've already

got one that's workable, stick with it. If you've never worked with a budget before, I'll explain how we do it below. There are only a couple of rules: you have to be honest, and, when you've written up your plan, you have to stick with it.

Write your monthly household income down on a piece of paper, or use a program like Excel and enter it into a spreadsheet. Check the resources at the back of the book for other electronic options. Below that, list everything you spend during a month. This will include your debt repayments (all mortgage, loan and credit-card repayments), utility, phone and internet bills, groceries, childcare, entertainment, gifts, clothes and so on. Use the money tracking you did in step 1 to help you.

Many bills are not paid monthly, so to work out an accurate monthly amount, collect your bills from the last year and add them up to get a yearly figure. If you don't have your old bills, estimate how much you spent last year based on your current bills. When you have an annual amount, divide it by twelve to give you a monthly amount. Remember to include once-a-year expenses like car registration, broken into monthly amounts, and irregular purchases, also in monthly amounts. In the sample budget overleaf I've included $100 for clothes and shoes, $80 for vitamins and $60 for optical as an example of putting aside money for items that are not regular purchases.

You might want to include an amount for pocket money. It's wise to give yourself a small allowance so you have money in your purse or pocket and don't feel isolated or deprived. Hanno and I have $50 a month each. Moving to a simpler way of living isn't about giving up everything you hold dear. It's more a modification of your behaviour that results in a better life.

Our budget looks something like this:

Total monthly income	$4000
Monthly expenses	
Insurance (house/contents, car, health)	$437
Phones (landline, mobiles)	$166
Internet	$99
Electricity	$25
Car rego and maintenance	$100
Vitamins	$80
Clothes, shoes, cosmetics, haircuts etc.	$100
Optical	$60
Groceries	$280
Chook and dog food	$50
Bulk food/flour	$100
Health and pharmacy	$100
Petrol	$180
Garden supplies	$50
House maintenance	$75
Pocket money	$100
Postage	$20
Total monthly expenses	$2022

Once you've calculated how much income you have in your budget, as well as how much you spend each month, you need to make sure you have enough income to pay all your expenses. As you can see in the sample budget, the income is $4000 and the expenses are $2022. The difference between these two is $1978, of which we save $1000 and the remaining $978 can go anywhere, such as a debt repayment.

If you find that your expenses are higher than your income, go to your money tracking and see what you can cut out or cut down on to give you that money you need to balance your budget. This is where you'll have to make some sacrifices. Even if you can cover your expenses with your income, you may still want to reduce spending in some areas so you can save more, or pay larger amounts off your debts.

Work out your savings

If you're in the fortunate position of having money left over, work out how much you want to save and organise to transfer that money to a savings account every month. If you are part of a couple, make sure you do this together so there is a shared responsibility and a shared commitment towards your future.

It's a good idea to give yourself a little leeway when calculating how much to save. In our case, our income is $2500 and our expenses are $1382. The difference between these two amounts is $1118, so we've calculated that we can save $700 per month. The remaining $418 could go anywhere. If we had debt it could be a debt repayment. At the moment, we are using this spare money to buy our solar panels. While it's good to be ambitious with your savings plan, don't cut it too fine, otherwise you might be tempted to dip into your savings to cover unexpected expenses.

Organise your money

Organising your bank accounts and knowing which money you'll use to pay for which expense are essential parts of taking control of your finances. We have two bank accounts: a working account and a savings account. The working account receives Hanno's pension and any money I earn, and we make sure we have enough

money in this account to cover our bills and withdraw cash. Our monthly savings amount, along with whatever extra money we did not spend the previous month, is transferred to our savings account.

We pay our bills by direct debit straight from the working account, and withdraw cash from the same account to pay everything else. I have found this system to be very simple and effective. We know exactly how much we have for spending and we know we have money in the bank to pay the bills.

This is not the only way you can effectively work with your money. Some people prefer using a debit card to using cash. They like the convenience of plastic and the record of transactions the bank provides. If that is how you operate with your money, and it's working for you, don't stop.

If you decide to use the system we use, you'll have to work out how much you need to leave in your bank account each month to pay your bills by direct debit, and how much you'll spend each month in cash. Go back to your budget and sort your expenses into two groups: the regular bills that you will pay directly from your working account, and all the other expenses, which you will pay with cash.

The amount of money you need to pay your regular bills stays in the bank until your bills come in, then you pay them by direct debit, BPAY, or whatever your chosen method is. Make sure any quarterly or annual bills that are due in the current month can be covered with what you have in your working account.

PAY YOUR BILLS ON TIME

Make sure you know when your bills are due and pay them on time. Late fees are a waste of money. A good way of reminding yourself about payments is to mark them on your calendar or diary, or enter them in your computer so you'll be reminded a couple of days before each payment is due.

For your other expenses, the cash ones like food, groceries and fuel, you'll need to withdraw money from the bank each month. We divide the cash we withdraw into categories – groceries, bulk food, fuel, and so on – and place it in labelled zip-lock bags. That way, we know how much we have left to spend on each category at any given time. Jars, a divided drawer, or sections in your wallet would work just as well for this purpose.

When you shop for groceries, you take the cash from the grocery money stash. If you have to pick up garden supplies or fill up your car with fuel, take money from those containers. Only take out what is needed and return what you don't spend.

When you near the end of the month you may find a container is almost empty. If you need more money for that category, take it from another bag that you know will not be used that month. If you have money left over at the end of the month, put it towards your debt, emergency fund (see the next section) or savings account.

Watch what you spend in the first couple of months and adjust your amounts as you need to.

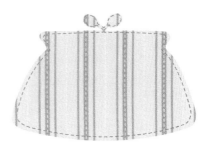

Step 4: Start an emergency fund

Whether you are forced to live on a small amount of money each month, or you do so by choice, it is a good idea to have some money set aside for emergencies. I am aware that this will be a stretch for some, and may even be impossible. If that is your situation, and you have absolutely no money left over at the end of the month, you can still work towards being debt-free, but you'll have to do it without this safety net.

The unexpected does happen and most of us will have times when the dog needs to go to the vet, the car blows a tyre or the refrigerator breaks down and you have to either pay to have it repaired or buy a new one. Enter the emergency fund. You'll have the cash to pay for your needs and you won't have to use a credit card. The amount will depend on your circumstances and the number of people in your family. For two generally healthy people $1000 should be enough, but for a larger family, or if there is chronic illness in the family, you'll need more. When times are tough you might also need more: when you start hearing the words 'economic downturn' or 'recession', start adding more money to your emergency fund.

If you have money left over at the end of the month, or however long your budgeting period is, use it wisely. We often have between $25 and $100 left over in our zip-lock bags at the end of the month and that always goes either in the emergency fund or, if we have enough in there already, into our savings account. When you've built up your emergency fund, if you're actively paying off debt you can use the money left over at the end of the month to make an extra payment.

Start a change jar

Create opportunities for saving spare change by having a change jar. Find a container and put it on your desk, dressing table or hall table – anywhere you will see it when you get home – and start putting your change in it. If you have any spare small notes, put them in too. It will be easier for you to save coins if you have somewhere to put them when they come out of your pockets or purse at the end of the day. Slowly but surely that change will build up and you'll have another source of money with which to boost your emergency fund. If your emergency fund is large enough you could put this money in your savings account, or pay off debt. You could also use your change jar funds for something special, such as:

- buying special birthday or Christmas gifts
- investing in eco and organic yarns if you're a knitter
- buying craft materials
- saving for a longed-for appliance such as a good kitchen mixer or breadmaker.

Don't raid the jar! It's not for thoughtless spending; it's part of your savings so whether you pay off debt with it or buy something you need or want, it's money you saved for that purpose. Well done.

Step 5: Pay off debt

So far we've focused on tracking, budgeting, cutting back on spending, and saving. Now, how do we use some of those savings? When you have saved your emergency fund, it's time to pay off your debts. If you can get rid of your debts it will liberate you and you can get back to the business of living your life.

Unless you come into a lot of money and use it to pay off your debt, there probably won't be one big thing that will help you with debt reduction. However, living a more simple life will give you plenty of small opportunities to cut back and pay off debt while still living well.

I have no doubt some readers, particularly younger ones, will not yet have acquired major debt. Often people start thinking seriously about future debt when they get married or make a lifelong commitment to a partner, as there are so many possibilities ahead. So what do you do if you're in that situation? It's a good idea to talk about your hopes for the future and choose ways to work sensibly towards what you both want. The common hopes of buying a home, travelling and having children all cost a lot of money. But you're in an ideal position.

If you're both working, commit to living on one income. The other income can go straight into the bank to finance your future plans. And just to give you a quick estimate of what that might mean, if you can save $500 a week, you'll save $26 000 in a year. What a lovely nest egg that would be! At the same time, you'll be getting into great habits that will help you if and when you do take on a mortgage. So as you read through this book, even if you currently have no debt the suggestions and strategies all still apply to you. But instead of paying down debt, you'll be building up assets.

Deal with your credit cards

Credit cards are bad news. They epitomise the idea of spending beyond your means. Many people say they use a credit card only to pay for goods online, and then pay the bill in total when it is due. Statistics don't bear that out. Most people pay interest on their cards every month, even though the interest is usually very high. The cards are so convenient, using credit to buy things is like a slippery slide of happy shopping – until you hit rock bottom with a bang. Even if you think you're on a good thing with credit-card rewards, the amount of money you have to spend to get even a small reward is not worth it.

The first step in reducing your credit-card debt is to stop using them. This can be a big step for those who are used to paying with credit. Take the cards out of your wallet and put them in a drawer at home so you won't be able to use them when you're out. If you can't resist the temptation of buying whatever you see, cut those cards up.

The first step in reducing your credit-card debt is to stop using them.

I grew up at a time when there were no credit cards and people used to save for what they wanted before they bought it. And when you brought home something you'd saved for, you would look after it and make sure it lasted. Of course, those were the days before we all bought cheap products that regularly need to be replaced. People aren't prepared to wait any more; they want what they want *now*, and credit cards facilitate that attitude.

Now the emphasis is on quantity, not quality, and we often look for cheapness instead of value. The common feeling is that if you don't like what you have, or if it breaks, just buy another one. It's cheap and easy, yes, but it creates more debt, more greenhouse gases, more landfill. It's not cheap and easy, or sustainable, in the long term. If you want to get off that never-ending carousel of buying, convince yourself that less is more, look for quality in what you buy, stop using your credit cards and pay them off.

I have no doubt that while you're paying off your debt you will get a letter from the bank telling you that as you're such a good customer, they're kindly raising your credit limit. Always remember this: it is not in the bank's interest for you to pay off your debt quickly or completely. When you do that, they stop getting your money. They will tempt you. *You* will tempt you. You'll say you've been so good, you deserve a reward. And yes, you do deserve a reward: to be debt-free. Never stray from that thought.

When you get rid of your debt burden you will look at spending in a different light. You will know how difficult it is to pay back and you won't want to go back there. So, when you get that letter from the bank extending your credit, write back and tell them to *decrease* your limit. If you used to have a $5000 limit, lower it to $2000. When you pay off more, lower it again. It will reduce your temptation in this period of debt reduction. If you decide to keep just one credit card for emergencies in future years, the bank will be happy to increase the limit again, and your habits will have changed so you won't be tempted any more.

Snowballing debt payments

I think American finance expert Dave Ramsey's system of snowballing debt payments is a very good way to go. Instead of paying off the debt with the highest interest rate first, pay off those smaller debts first. This will get rid of a few debts fast. List all your debts, from smallest to largest, along with their minimum repayments.

Your debts list might looks like this:

Debt	Minimum repayment
Dad – $300	$50/week
Credit card 1 – $870	$26/month
Credit card 2 – $2000	$60/month
Car – $9790	$310/month
Mortgage – $187 355	$1350/month

This is the order you pay them off. With your emergency fund in place, look for all those dollars you've saved by taking lunch to work, not buying magazines, reducing your phone and internet plans and not buying new clothes and shoes. If you have any cash left over at the end of your budgeting period, it should go towards paying off that first, smallest debt. If you don't have leftover cash, go back to your tracking notebook and see what you can stop buying or cut down on to give you that spare money.

So, to pay off that first, smallest debt, instead of paying the minimum amount, you pay more:

Debt	Minimum repayment	Actual repayment
Dad – $300	$50/week	**$150**
Credit card 1 – $870	$26/month	$26
Credit card 2 – $2000	$60/month	$60
Car – $9790	$310/month	$310
Mortgage – $187 355	$1350/month	$1350

Instead of taking six weeks to repay Dad, you'll take two weeks, and wipe one debt off your list. When that first debt is paid off, put the money you were using to repay it towards the second debt. So, in addition to the minimum repayment you were making on the second debt, you add the money you had been paying on the first debt, as well as any extra cash you have left over that month.

Debt	Minimum repayment	Actual repayment
Credit card 1 – $870	$26/month	$26 + $150 = **$176**
Credit card 2 – $2000	$60/month	$60
Car – $9790	$310/month	$310
Mortgage – $187 355	$1350/month	$1350

When credit card 1 is paid off, start working on credit card 2.

Debt	Minimum repayment	Actual repayment
Credit card 2 – $2000	$60/month	$60 + $176 = **$236**
Car – $9790	$310/month	$310
Mortgage – $187 355	$1350/month	$1350

When credit card 2 is paid off, start working on the car.

Debt	Minimum repayment	Actual repayment
Car – $9790	$310/month	$310 + $236 = **$546**
Mortgage – $187 355	$1350/month	$1350

Once the car is paid off, you have only one debt – the biggest – left to pay.

Debt	Minimum repayment	Actual repayment
Mortgage – $187 355	$1350/month	$1350 + $546 = **$1896**

In effect, the payments increase, like a snowball: the more you pay off your debts, the sooner the debts will be gone from your life. This will keep you motivated to continue your debt reduction plan because you see results fast.

Mortgage calculations

It's a very interesting and convincing exercise to put your figures into an online mortgage calculator. There is a good calculator in the resources section at the end of the book. Play around with it, adjusting the amount of money you pay monthly or fortnightly and reducing the number of years. Keep an eye on the interest you will pay over the term of your loan. If you have a loan for $300 000, for example, over twenty-five years you will pay back the $300 000 plus more than $200 249 in interest (at the Australian standard interest rate at the time of writing). If you can manage to pay back that same loan in ten years, you'll pay back your $300 000, plus only $73 098 in interest. You will save yourself $127 151! If you can't manage ten years but pay it off in fifteen years instead, you'll pay back your $300 000 plus $113 096 in interest, saving you around $87 153. They're incredible savings and well worth the sacrifices you'll make to do it.

Family finances

Roles and responsibilities

It makes sense to have one person managing the money, and that person should be the one who does it best. Obviously, if you're single, there is no decision here – you'll look after your own money. If you are the one who is managing everything, you should be prepared to give a summary of your combined finances to your partner every month. This will not only keep you on track, it will also help your partner understand where the money is going and how much is being saved or paid off your debts.

Your budget can be written either by the designated money manager or by both of you. You can also both find grocery bargains, write up the shopping list and meal plans and, before babies come along, shop together. You both need to have a realistic idea of grocery prices. If you have young children and you're both working, take turns at the shopping – always with a shopping list – so that you both understand grocery prices and have a chance to save with your prudent and careful shopping. It is better to shop without young children if possible, as you need to be focused.

If your partner is working and you are a full-time homemaker raising children, then it is your partner's job to earn money and your job to save money. This is one of the most rewarding and important jobs. You will manage the money, actively look for ways to save, think carefully about your grocery shopping and look for bargains and ways to cut back. Try to work out a system where your partner looks after the children while you shop. Your weekly grocery money is important: it's a lot of money to spend each week and you need to do it carefully. You'll also need to work out a system to manage your food so it is eaten as fresh as possible and stored in such a way that none is wasted.

Work decisions

There is a common perception now that it's best for both people in a couple to work. While that is true for couples without children, I don't believe it's necessarily true for couples with young children. There is no doubt that working together to pay off the mortgage is a good thing to do, but you may find there is more *value* in having one parent at home to guide them through childhood.

You also need to work out if the second wage is really as beneficial as you think it is. When you add up the actual cost of having both parents in the workforce, you may discover it is financially sound to have one parent at home.

WHO SHOULD GO TO WORK?

The partner who can earn the most money, for the least expense and the shortest time away from home – or the one who most enjoys outside work – should be the one who goes out to work. If you are very lucky it might be possible to organise a part-time job for both parents, but this is rare.

Before you make the decision to have both parents working, calculate what it will cost you. Some things to consider are:

- loss of certain government benefits
- childcare or babysitting costs
- public transport, fuel costs, or running a second car
- equipment or tools of the trade
- new clothes and dry-cleaning
- haircuts and cosmetics
- lunches, coffees and bottles of water.

Include everything you know you'll spend money on. Be accurate and realistic because you'll use this to decide if work outside the home will actually contribute to your family.

As an example, if your new job pays $800 a week, you might lose $115 of that in taxes, making your take-home pay $685. You have to get to work, so you spend $35 a week on public transport or running the car. Your $685 is now $650. Childcare might cost around $250 a week, so now your income is $400. Take off the amount you need to spend on clothes and grooming, and your coffees and lunches and it might reveal that both parents working is sometimes not as financially beneficial as you think it's going to be.

You should consider related matters too – those factors that will lessen the impact of one parent not working. When one parent is at home with the children, they can shop for grocery bargains to make the most of the food budget, food can be cooked from scratch and they can bake bread – this is the healthiest way to cook and it's also the cheapest. Sometimes there is the opportunity and the space to grow vegetables and have chickens for eggs. If there is surplus in the garden it can be preserved by canning, freezing or drying, for eating later in the year – again saving money. Clothes can be sewn and knitted, and in general, there will be time to look after the things you already own.

If you choose to stay at home with the children, you can read to them, teach them how to write their name, how to count and identify colours. You could show them how to plant seeds, tie a knot or collect eggs, explain the role of chickens in the vegetable garden and show them, by example, what a joy simple living can be. You can be there when they come home from school, or you could homeschool them, and as they grow older, you'll be there to guide them. Value comes from many things, not only those with a dollar sign attached.

I think the ideal, which is not always possible, is that you both work hard to save for the deposit on a home and then pay off as much as you can on your mortgage while you still have the double income. When your babies come along, you can start on this next stage of your life – raising your children in a strong and loving family where both parents have a good balance between family and work.

> *Value comes from many things,*
> *not only those with a dollar sign attached.*

I have no doubt there are many couples who don't have a choice about staying at home; both must work to make ends meet. There will also young parents who decide to return to work, either full- or part-time, because they need a break from raising children, or they choose to develop their career, or they want to continue to make a financial contribution to their family.

This is not an easy decision but don't just go along with what everyone else is doing. Think about it and talk to your partner – preferably before you have children – and make the decision that is right for you. No matter which way you go, do everything you can to make it work for your family as a whole. The way you work at

home, and outside home, is your decision and no one else's business. There is no room for guilt here, or for people who try to make you feel guilty. Support each other and share the work at home if you're both working, and be confident in your decisions. If you're sure that your choice is the best for your family, work towards your goals together with no guilt and no regrets.

Saving for retirement

The baby-boomer generation, of which I am part, is about to make another huge impact on the world. We have started retiring and in just twenty years' time there will be more old people in Australia than young people. A few years ago the retirement age for Australian women went up to sixty-five. By 2023 the retirement age for men and women will be sixty-seven. It is possible that the pension age will keep increasing and might eventually cease to be paid. For many baby boomers, the superannuation scheme came in too late for us to take full advantage of it. But if that's not the case for you, I encourage you to budget for retirement and make sure you're part of a good scheme.

As I wrote earlier, keep all your superannuation funds in one account and make sure you give the details to your new employer each time you change jobs. If you let them put your contributions into the account they usually use, you'll end up fragmenting your investment. If you have money in several accounts right now, I encourage you to take some time in the next few weeks to contact those companies and instruct them to transfer your funds over to your preferred account. Find out if there is a fee for doing that, but in the long run you'll get a better return if consolidate your funds. You'll avoid transfer fees in the future if you give your information to each new employer.

No matter where you live or how old you are, look into the future. How much money should you have when you stop working? What will you need to support you through the rest of your life? How can you prepare now for a world you have no idea about? It's worth doing your best to answer these questions, but I believe the most practical way to approach retirement is to pay off debt and live simply.

Saving your money and your life

It can be quite difficult to change patterns of behaviour, but change is happening right now – all around the world. Many more people are using their cars less, and giving up the extras they used to take for granted. More parents are staying at home with the children, more couples are working part-time and some are setting up home businesses instead of returning to work. I think these changes have come about because despite being worried about the rising cost of living, people want to spend more time with their families. They have discovered that saving money at home can give them a good life.

There is always something you can do; it is never an option to ignore hard decisions. Making a plan and working according to your plan is always better than doing nothing. So start by tracking your money, then budget according to what you discover as well as how you want, or need, to live. As with most changes leading to a simple life, these suggestions are all small steps. But all those small things add up – even a saving of $10 a week will add up to $500 a year. That money could help with the mortgage or credit-card payments or be used to take the family away for a weekend.

When you think about your money and the amount of debt you have, or will have in the future when you buy a home, I hope you realise that money and debt, while important, should not make you miserable. Money can make or break any of us, and it certainly has the ability to break up relationships or put a strain on them at the very least. But money used wisely can bring pleasure and stability to a family. Being frugal and using that great simple-living tool – a budget – will help you organise your finances so that most of the time you have what you need, and sometimes you have what you want, and you will be in control.

Money used wisely can bring pleasure and stability to a family.

Overall, the less money you spend, the greener and more simple your life will be. But I'm sure there are many who, while living more simply, still want to travel, give to charities – either by donations or volunteering their time – as well as buy odds and ends that others might think of as frivolous in a simple life. Don't listen to anyone who wants you to go against your own wishes. If you'd like to buy a piano and think your life will be enriched by the music you play, save for a piano. If you will be enriched by travel or working in your community, do it – with a plan. Establish your priorities, budget for them and plan for them.

Decide what you want your life to be. If you're like most of us, you'll want to work enough to buy what you need to live, and pay off a house and maybe a car. You are reading this book so I presume you have lifestyle changes in mind. Some of us were spendthrifts in the past. We believed what advertising told us; we bought everything that appealed to us, kept up with fashion and made sure our homes were always up to date. It was only later on we realised that if we continued to do that, we would be working to pay for our shopping sprees for the rest of our lives.

We are all different and have different needs but we should all conserve our life hours for real living. Examine your life and think about what you want. If you have a partner, make a plan together and see it through together. I hope that plan turns into a guide that helps you along the way and leads you to the kind of life you long for.

HOME

Your home should be the one place where you and your family know with absolute certainty they are loved, where they can relax and be their true selves, where everyone can recuperate from being at school or at work, and have fun, help, be productive and creative and learn how to live. Your home is where children should develop their values and where parents should strive to live by theirs. Home is far more than just furniture, bricks and mortar.

Finding home

There was a time when I would have been bored waking up in the morning knowing everything that would happen to me during the day. Now, that is what I hope for. I love knowing every nook and cranny of my home. I love doing the same thing at the same time; I relish the familiarity of it all. I don't have to think too much about what will crop up, there is no anxiety about not knowing, and the day rolls along with one thing following the other and minute by minute the hours become another day.

The strangest part of this kind of familiarity is that it feels fresh every single day. I rise, shower, write, eat breakfast, bake bread, work in the garden, sew or knit, care for the animals and do my general chores every day, and each time it feels new, like this day is one of a kind. It never gets boring; it gets better.

We have turned our very ordinary brick house on a one-acre block into a home we thrive in. We have organic vegetables growing in the backyard. Rainwater is harvested from the roof and on that same roof, the sun is heating our water, skylights send light to the kitchen, laundry and bathroom, and whirlybirds spin and extract hot air from under the roof. Fruit is growing to juicy maturity; plump heritage-breed chickens lay eggs every day and scratch around eating insects and weeds. Thousands of compost worms devour our kitchen waste and they, in turn, sometimes become food for the chickens. A creek flows by, providing water for a rainforest that gives us protection from the wind, and within the confines of that rainforest embrace, regeneration and life goes on.

Inside our home, bread is baked, sauces made, jams processed and stored. Gifts are made for family and friends, the house is cleaned, soap is hardened, books are read, ginger beer is brewed and afternoon naps are sometimes taken on the verandah. Dinner is made from backyard produce and provisions stored in the freezer, stockpile cupboard and pantry. Life is slow and peaceful here.

A simple home is not necessarily the biggest and best house in the street. It is not identified by how it looks. The worth of this home is gauged by the way people live, how they share their lives, what they give importance to, the way they raise their children, the boundaries they set, the work they do to provide that nurturing space and possibly by a hundred other things that are more difficult to define – but responsibility, respect, self-reliance, warmth, generosity, kindness and care are all in the mix.

I am sure that when many people start out in adult life, they think the hardest part will be working to pay for, equip and furnish their home. But the challenging part of adult life,

with a partner or alone, is setting up a home that feels like a home. Your home should be the one place where you and your family know with absolute certainty they are loved, where they can relax and be their true selves, where everyone can recuperate from being at school or at work, and have fun, help, be productive and creative and learn how to live. Your home is where children should develop their values and where parents should strive to live by theirs. Home is far more than just furniture, bricks and mortar.

*The prize is not having an outstanding house;
it's having an outstanding life.*

It doesn't matter what stage of life you're at; keep your eye on the prize. The prize is not having an outstanding house; it's having an outstanding life. It's tough juggling life, family, home, work, money, friends, hopes and wishes. Sometimes you fail. But in those times when it comes together – when you look and see what you hope to see, when you hear a quiet 'I love you' and know it is meant in its truest sense, when you want to announce to the world what a wonderful family you have but instead keep it inside you to nourish and grow, when you think you've failed but realise you haven't, when you put the family to bed at night and sit, content – those are the times that will make up for the uncertainty and toughness of it all. As I look back on my long life of family and home-building I know for sure that it was not just the good times that made Hanno and me what we are today, it was the hard times too.

We don't get a lot of encouragement to build stable and happy families. The encouragement seems to be focused on success, creating wealth, spending to help the nation, and acquisition, and while those elements have some importance, they are secondary. Our real mission is to build productive and healthy families, which will create productive and healthy communities, which, combined, build the nation. I want to gently remind you that what you do at home is significant and meaningful, and that creating a warm and productive home provides the ideal environment for your family to thrive in.

Setting up house

Whether you're single and living in your first apartment, a young couple buying your first home, a married couple with a few children, a single parent, a single solo adult, or baby boomers moving towards retirement, you can create a simple home that won't burden you financially or emotionally. When you build a comfortable and nurturing home, you'll feel like you've sailed into a safe harbour, that you're where you can be your best. Don't confuse the shell of the home – the bricks and mortar – with the essence of what a home is. You can create a beautiful home in the plainest shell. Don't fall for real estate advertising that tells you lifestyle is attached to a building. Let me be very clear about this: buying a simple home that is within your budget and can be modified to suit you and your family is the best investment. It doesn't have to be new or in the best suburb; it needs to be able to sustain what you want to do, to provide a feeling of relaxation and security to all who live there and be within the budget you've set yourself. That is relevant at every stage of life as you move from house to house. Don't be tempted by flashy, extravagant houses. What good is it if you have to spend most of your income paying off a mortgage and you have no money or energy left to enjoy life?

If I were setting up a home today with the same sensibilities and knowledge I have now, I'd buy a well-loved, solid old cottage, a home with character. I'd reject new, cheaply made furniture and go for either second-hand, handmade or good-quality family hand-me-downs that would last many years and could be repaired and repainted when needed. I wish I could say I did that the first time around, or even the second, but I was caught up in the conspicuous-wealth syndrome back then and I bought things that were fashionable. I should have known better.

Don't confuse the shell of the home – the bricks and mortar – with the essence of what a home is. You can create a beautiful home in the plainest shell.

By the time we arrived at our current home fourteen years ago, I'd had a change of mindset and knew that large houses only benefit large families and real estate agents. We were quite happy to settle in our very simple brick slab house. It was within our budget and an easy distance to most of the facilities we needed. For the first couple of years, the house didn't feel right but then I suddenly realised that if I wanted to feel comfortable at home, if I wanted a safe and pleasant place to live where I could nurture my family and myself, I had to make that space myself; it wouldn't just happen. So we set about making a home using things we already had, we changed cupboards to maximise efficiency and carefully placed furniture where it would aid productivity and relaxation. We changed the house to reflect a much more productive life; we decluttered and kept only what we needed or would pass on.

A comfortable, safe and peaceful home will not only support people who, like us, are at retirement age, or younger couples raising children. This type of home is essential for those who go out to work. If you're in paid employment, you need a place where you can relax and unwind. If you allow it to, your home will prepare you for work and help you be at your best when you're out earning a living.

SWEDISH STYLE

One of my grandmothers was Swedish, so buried deep within me is a love of the Swedish style of furnishing a home. It relies on plain and simple wooden furniture that is painted in beautiful tones of white, milky blue or sage green, with bright splashes of red. Items suitable for renovating can be picked up at roadside throw-outs or bought at garage sales or in op shops, then sanded back, scrubbed and repainted.

You don't create a home by creating the perfect showpiece – that's just a furnished house. A home is created first in the heart and then it is pieced together, with all members of the family playing their part, to make it the kind of home you can all thrive in.

When you start to furnish and decorate your home, don't rely on what you'll find in a retail chain store. When it comes to appliances, it's a good idea to buy new or near-new energy-rated, good-quality items that are built to last and can be repaired. But everything else can be recycled, made, repaired and reinvented. Look around and see what you already have, ask around to see if anyone in your family has furniture they no longer need, walk around your neighbourhood the next time there is a kerbside pick-up and see what you can find. Chairs and couches can be covered with homemade cotton covers sewn to fit the shape. Curtains and soft furnishings can be homemade, and bit by bit you'll build your new home into something unique, rather than a carbon copy of a thousand other houses nearby. It is also a very frugal and environmentally sound way of furnishing a home. Be innovative and bold, invent your own style, and create a home you really love without breaking the bank.

Building strong families

Let me say this clearly. Homemakers – the women and men who build stable families and communities – are an essential and significant part of who we are as a society. Whether that is acknowledged by our political leaders or not, they are the glue that holds us all together. Yes, we need commercial enterprise and entrepreneurs to keep our nation moving and commercially viable. We need big business to provide some of the products we use. We need to maintain our civic responsibilities and support our law enforcement and armed services organisations; we need to elect honest politicians. But unless we form stable families on which to build those civic institutions, we won't amount to much. Families are the foundation of our nation.

Make your mark, stand tall and know that your contribution is important. Providing comfortable and secure homes places our children and working people on solid ground. We are the ones sending them out capable of making the most of their work and school lives; we are the ones setting the tone for what our children will become.

I am not silly enough to believe that our children grow up to be our mirror image, but we can have a significant input into the type of people they grow to be. Model the behaviour you want to see in them. Teaching kindness, generosity, tenderness and humility helps build character and forms a stable foundation on which to build a life. Show your children that you enjoy life and that your family makes you happy. That will be one of the greatest gifts you will give them. Be proud of your work and show it. Show children how they can contribute to the family – they will grow up with a realistic view of life and feel valued because they help the family function. This should start when children are two or three years old. They can pick up their toys and help set the table, then progress to more complicated jobs as they grow.

> *Show your children that you enjoy life and that your family makes you happy. That will be one of the greatest gifts you will give them.*

Older children need that kind of guidance too. Traditionally, mothers would pass on their knowledge to their daughters. Times have changed. Now it's sons and daughters who need this information, as well as the confidence to apply it to their own lives. This is not a gender issue, it's about basic life skills and learning how to look after yourself. It is quite common now for young women and men to not know how to iron a shirt, or how to cook. It is time to rekindle interest in basic domestic skills and for all of us to encourage women or men of all ages who want to stay at home and raise children to see that as a viable, worthwhile life choice.

I hope there will be many things of which you will be proud when you're my age. If you can say you launched your children into the world as decent people; if you can say that most of the time you did your best; if you know that you supported and encouraged other men and women in their tasks; if you know that you helped build a strong and supportive community, you will have done a fine job, not only for yourself and your family, but for your country as well.

Keep your family close

I think children learn a lot when they gather with the family around the dinner table. This is the one part of the day when everyone can sit and relax, talk about what happened that day, and listen to what everyone else did. This is the time when we show, rather than tell, what our family values are. If you don't take the time to reconnect every day, children drift off in their own world. We need that time to let them know they're an important part of the family, that you support them and if they need help, you're there. It needs to start early, from the time they're eating from a tiny bowl, and continue right through until they leave home. Each stage has its own unique lessons; each stage prepares for the next. There will be requests to sit in front of the TV and to eat in their rooms, but the answer to that should always be no. They won't understand the significance of the family gathering until they're older. No phones or iPods at the table. No disruptions; all else can wait. This family time comes first, no exceptions. That thirty minutes can make or break a family.

As I get older I understand how crucial the family unit is. Children who have been nurtured by a loving family and have seen active parents working towards a greener and simpler future undeniably have a better chance of doing that themselves. There are many things a child can do without, and you don't have to fret if you can't, or don't want to, supply iPods, mobile phones, fashions and computers, but never be ungenerous with the love. Children want their parents' love and attention more than anything else. Acceptance, kindness and love delivered in full measure, consistently over the years, builds character and confidence in a way no product ever can. The trick is to start early and never stop.

Growing up

I have often thought that modern society has divided into two camps: adults and children. Governments, corporations, media and the advertising industry are the adults and the rest of us are children. They speak; we listen. We are expected to be dependent and compliant; we are told constantly that we will be made happy with 'stuff', that part of modern life is to carry a large amount of debt and if we work hard, we'll be able to pay off our life as we live it and retire at sixty-five or seventy to enjoy what we have.

Advertising is ubiquitous. Wherever you look, there will be an advertisement telling you what to buy, where to get it and how wonderful you'll feel when you buy it. When we wake in the morning and turn on the TV news, advertising is there to greet you. Read the paper – more ads. Go to work or to the park and you'll probably pass billboards and advertising signs along the way. You come home to relax and if you turn on the TV, every few minutes ads will be telling you what you can't do without and how to get it.

We have messages coming at us every day about what's right for us and how we should live. Advertising makes us look outside our homes to find what satisfies us. It teaches us that when we see what we like, we should have it. It never teaches prudence or patience; quite the contrary, it encourages us to go into debt to buy whatever our hearts desire. We are encouraged to work our entire lives so that big business remains healthy, the country prospers and we skill ourselves in how to earn a living rather than how to live a life.

You can't buy the experience of living well, the sense of being happy and safe or the inclination towards satisfaction. These are all handmade treasures.

I love living in a prosperous, multicultural country, with all the advantages that offers. I'm grateful that our country has a sound financial base, a thriving business community and a compassionate welfare system. I don't want that to change. I want us to. I want us to stop believing the message that one size fits all, and to see for ourselves the value of stepping outside what is considered normal. I want us to grow up.

We should stop listening to outside advice about what makes us happy and fulfilled and find out for ourselves. Take your life by the throat and give it a good shaking. Step away from what you are expected to do and instead do what you wish to do. My heart's desire is to live well, to be happy and safe and to feel satisfied by what I do each day. For me, happiness is realised every day by being at home and working to give my family and myself a quieter, safer, healthier life. I grew up the day I discovered that work at home is satisfying and significant. I felt stronger and smarter when I started learning how to look after myself and realised I did not need to shop to have what I need. I feel like I'm really living now and that what I do is important and has purpose. And that has made all the difference. If you know what you're doing is meaningful and helps you live as you wish, it gives you the courage, strength and every reason to keep going.

Since I started living as I do, I have achieved all my desires. I have never seen any of them advertised on TV or in the slickest magazine. It's obvious you can't buy the

experience of living well, the sense of being happy and safe or the inclination towards satisfaction. These, my friends, are all handmade treasures; you have to make them all yourself. And you do it at home.

Starting small

I want you to find happiness too. I can't say what will make you happy – only you know that. I can tell you that happiness isn't one thing. It's a whole lot of tiny fragments you find every day that add up to a deep feeling of contentment.

I encourage you to develop your skill base. Learn as much as you can about doing the things you want to do. Start small, with one thing at a time, and you'll probably find it will lead you on to other things. You could start by making your own laundry powder (there is a recipe for it in the next chapter) or baking bread (check the Recipes chapter for instructions). Maybe you could start stockpiling so you don't have to shop as frequently as you do now. Cook

a meal from scratch or start cleaning with non-chemical cleaners. It could be anything. Your start might be to make your bed each morning so you can look forward to a lovely warm and cosy bed when you go to sleep each night. Maybe you could start by making up a roster of chores for the children so everyone helps at home and you start teaching them how to look after themselves. You might start walking

to work or making sure you take twenty minutes out of an otherwise busy day to make a cup of tea and sit quietly to relax. You might turn off the TV or the lights more often, or start monitoring your usage of electricity or water. Maybe you'll mend a ripped shirt instead of throwing it away, or cut up old towels for rags. Or maybe you'll just read this book and let it all percolate for a while, before getting started. There are so many small ways to start, but once you have, it's easy to add another small thing, then another.

You will find that as you do this, your focus will be on your home. Do your tasks slowly and that will help slow your mind too. See the work you do at home with respect. It's not an annoyance; it will make your home, and your experience of living there, better. You're building a new way of life. As you work towards what you want for yourself, you will see that each thing you learn makes you stronger and less reliant on what you find in the shops. And once you discover the joy of doing for yourself, when you're capable of providing for many of your own needs, nothing else will be good enough for you.

Be the friend you want to find

It is tough, no one is denying that. We are battling hard economic times and trying to stick to our budgets while food and fuel prices are increasing. Some homemakers, also in the paid workforce, wonder if they are missing important milestones in their children's lives but the need for an income keeps them working. Stay-at-home mums are raising children and running their homes – some are doing it easily and gracefully, others feel guilty that they aren't contributing to the family's income, or are suffering the criticism of 'friends' who say they should get a job. It's tough and confusing, whether you stay at home or go to work.

But we can make it better by supporting other homemakers. Be proactive. Invite a new neighbour in for coffee and celebrate ordinary domestic life together. Take a magazine and flowers to your sick neighbour. Encourage others in their work. Share recipes and tactics. Take the washing off your neighbour's line if it starts raining while they're out. Show younger homemakers that while this job is difficult, never-ending and unpaid, it is also incredibly satisfying, enriching and wonderful. Lead by example, guide others with your strengths and accept assistance when you need it. Be the friend you want to find.

Modern living with an eye to the past

I was born in a time when, like all our friends and neighbours, we did most things in a similar way to how they'd always been done. We grew vegetables in the backyard, made most of what we ate from scratch, made our own clothes and knitted woollies to keep us warm in winter. We soaked our grains before eating them, drank non-homogenised milk and homemade ginger beer, spread our bread with butter and ate what today is seen by some as an unhealthy diet. In those days most food was unprocessed and there was no such thing as 'low-fat' foods. It was also commonplace for people not to have cars, home telephones, TVs or a lot of clothes.

In the fifties and sixties, men worked and brought home their wages and most women worked in the home, looking after the children, cooking, budgeting, gardening and sewing. I don't want to go back to those days – I found that era particularly repressive and I think many people who romanticise the fifties housewife were probably not there to experience what it was like. I love living in an age when we have an enlightened view, the internet and democracy. However, now it seems that many modern lives are geared around a large mortgage and two incomes, and having less time at home means we pay someone else to make most of what we need. We have been deskilled and dumbed down because we don't use the life skills that used to be common.

When new products came onto the market in the 1950s, there was a genuine belief that many of them would make life easier. Of course, there was the ever-present profit motive too but now a new element had been added to the equation: dependence. Producers want us to be dependent on their products and they use fear to achieve this. I doubt scaring us was originally their strategy, but it is now. When I see advertising for cleaners that promise to kill bacteria that harm our families; when I hear that people throw out perfectly good food because it happened to be out of the fridge for a few hours; when homemakers doubt their capabilities and don't think they can handle soap-making, well, I just shake my head and wonder why.

> *We've set ourselves apart from the natural world and we've traded our independence for convenience. I think we've lost out on that trade.*

All that convenience has robbed us of our knowledge and skills. We don't know how to cook for ourselves. We don't see the need to garden when we can buy what looks like fresh fruit and vegetables at the shops. We don't know our cuts of meat because we prefer to buy them pre-sliced and unrecognisable on a plastic tray, so we forget that for every bite of tender beef, lamb, pork or chicken, an animal has died. We don't preserve our excess food because we're scared of that word, 'botulism' – and because we never learnt how. We clean everything in our homes with chemicals that give us an environment so clean, our babies are failing to develop resistance to everyday bugs. In a nutshell, my friends, we've set ourselves apart from the natural world and we've traded our independence for convenience. I think we've lost out on that trade.

Short of time?

Retired people, parents who stay at home to raise their children and those who establish a home business might find they have plenty of time to do things for themselves instead of utilising all of life's modern conveniences, but what of the many more people who work for a living outside the home? How do they fit in here?

I am convinced these same skills would be as effective for people who work for wages and don't have the amount of time Hanno and I have. Once-a-month cooking, where you take some weekend time to cook up batches of several dishes that will freeze well, is one way of being able to put nutritious home-cooked food on the table every night when you come home from work. Another way is to develop a series of recipes for the slow cooker and load it in the morning so you come home to a fully cooked meal just waiting to be dished up. Planning your menus in advance also helps save time.

Making soap takes about thirty minutes and one batch will last, depending on the size of your family, for one to three months. A batch of laundry liquid takes about thirty minutes to make and will last many months. Laundry powder is even quicker: two minutes and it's finished. A large stockpot of dog food will take about fifteen minutes to prepare and will cook, with no input from you, for an hour. Then you just place it in containers for freezing and you have dog food for at least a week.

You can buy the supplies for your stockpile when you do your weekly grocery shopping, and when you've built the stockpile to a reasonable size you can cut back on the grocery shopping, going once a month or bi-monthly, saving you lots of time. Sewing and mending can be taken up any night after dinner or on the weekend. Knitting will pass the time well if you take public transport to work, or during lunchtime when you're

socialising with colleagues. You and your partner can discuss and set up a budget on a weekend morning, then work at cutting back, saving and recording your spending as you both go about your normal week.

If you're short of time, it always helps to make things easy for yourself. Many house chores are gentle tasks but they can seem like hard work, especially at the beginning. Set your home up to help you work in this new way. For example, if you want to make compost, have a covered bin in the kitchen to hold all the kitchen waste you'll use in the compost. If you want to make your own laundry liquid, buy washing soda, borax and soap the next time you shop so that when you have time, the ingredients will be there, waiting. If you want to cook from scratch, buy a good cookbook you can rely on. I recommend *The Thrifty Kitchen* to you. An Australian book, written by Suzanne Gibbs and Kate Gibbs, it's a most delightful and encouraging introduction to good cooking in the home kitchen that fits well within our simple framework.

Learning
traditional skills

There are very few commercial enterprises that offer to teach traditional skills like sewing, knitting, crochet, leather or metal work, jam making, preserving, food storage or wine making. A large proportion of businesses have little interest in raw materials or ingredients; they're more interested in providing products that are ready for us to use. We've been more interested in that in the past fifty years too. But now it's time to get back to our roots, learn traditional crafts, and help these crafts, and ourselves, live on in this modern world. Don't think of this as being old-fashioned or lowering your standards by going backwards. If anything, you'll be better off.

There is no doubt that the best way to learn most things is to have someone beside you showing you how to do it and how to fix mistakes. I am sure you'll be surprised at how generous and friendly older people are when asked about a skill. But because most of us have never been taught traditional skills, finding someone with the skills to pass on may be difficult. If you have no one close by to ask, you can do your research about various products and ways of tending to your housework online. YouTube (youtube.com) has thousands of videos that show you how to start knitting and crocheting, how to sew a seam, how to cook and make soap and butter, as well as many other old skills. Books and blogs are also an excellent way of learning various skills.

And don't forget to think! You can work things out, even if you've learnt that you shouldn't – that you should rely on others to do the thinking. Gathering the skills of life will teach you that being self-reliant is a fine way to live. We're not talking about rocket science here – this is the everyday work of women and men that has been part of our lives forever. Don't let it slip away from you and your children. Learning, and then teaching, will open up a rich life that will allow you to live well.

It's time to get back to our roots, learn traditional crafts, and help these crafts, and ourselves, live on in this modern world.

You don't have to learn every skill, but try to learn a lot about the skills you do take on. If the only part of a simple life you have the time or inclination for is cooking, then learn every aspect of it, so that in addition to being able to do it, you understand it, can modify what you do and pass that skill on. For instance, baking bread isn't just about the ingredients and method, it's also about understanding the chemical processes of baking so that you can improve the bread you make and fix problems that occur.

Sewing

Making aprons, shopping totes, napkins, tablecloths and tea towels is really easy if you have a good pair of scissors and a sewing machine. Even without a sewing machine, you could make all of these simple household items with a bit of hand stitching.

If you need a few ideas and some encouragement, and you have access to the internet, there is a very good site called Polka Dot Chair (polkadotchair.com) which features general home sewing, projects using scrap material, how to make face masks, sewing with vintage fabric, bags, pillows, quilts and general craft sewing.

Start off by making the things you need in your own home: table-cloths, quilts, table napkins, or any number of items you could use. If you have small children, making or modifying clothes will be on your agenda. After you become more confident, you might then move on to making your own clothes.

Nightgowns and pyjamas are quite easy to make and perfect for a beginner, as they don't have to fit the figure well. If you manage to get it right, that's great, but if you don't, no one will know and you'll be improving your sewing skills with each garment you make.

Mending

I feel real shame when I think of all the clothes I threw away because they needed minor repairs. Now I love mending. It's very rewarding to be able to mend something so it continues to be of service to us. I commonly patch bed sheets, repair hems, sew on buttons and clips, darn holes and generally keep things going as long as I can.

Collect items that need mending in one place until you have enough to make a mending session. If you've never mended any-thing before, you'll need a guide, and you'll find a good one in the resources at the back of the book. You'll also need a sewing kit with needles, cotton, scissors and a thimble and, if you're sewing on buttons or clips, you'll need the originals or replacements. Then it's just a matter of finding a comfortable chair to sit on and about thirty minutes.

Knitting

I have been a knitter for a few years now and it's one of the needlecrafts I really enjoy. I love the idea of making something in such tiny increments – one stitch at a time – and out of it comes something beautiful and useful.

One of my favourite knitting projects is the ordinary kitchen dishcloth. Made with either light- or medium-weight pure cotton, they're efficient for washing dishes, can be added to clothes in a regular wash cycle and will last for years. I haven't bought wipes or dishcloths for years and happily use these homemade dishcloths and recycled rags. If you want to learn how to knit, making a dishcloth is an easy first project that will produce something functional.

DEB'S WAFFLE WEAVE DISHCLOTH

This is a lovely pattern for a dishcloth from Deb at the Homespun Living blog (homespunliving.blogspot.com). You'll find many other patterns on the websites listed in the resources at the back of the book.

Materials

- 1 ball 8-ply cotton yarn; additional yarn for coloured stripe (if desired)
- Needles size 6 (US) or 8 (UK)

Abbreviations

K: knit, P: purl

Directions

1 Cast on 38 stitches
2 K 3 rows for border
3 Row 1 (right side): K

4   Row 2: K 3, P to last 3 stitches, K 3

5   Row 3: K 3, (P 2, K 1) 10 times, P 2, K 3

6   Row 4: K 3, (K 2, P 1) 10 times, K 5. Repeat these 4 rows, 6 times

7   If a coloured centre stripe is desired, change yarn now and work rows 1–4 in desired colour 2 times. Change back to main colour and work the 4-row pattern, 6 times

8   Rows 61–75: K

9   Bind off and weave ends in

ASCOT SCARF PATTERN

This is a nice little scarf pattern of plain, purl, knit two together and yarn over. It is one of my favourites – quite simple and a good practice exercise. It makes an excellent gift.

Materials

- 1½ balls 8-ply pure wool
- Needles size 10 (US) or 4 (UK)

Abbreviations

K: knit, P: purl, YO: yarn over, K2tog: knit two together

Directions

1   Cast on 34 stitches

2   Rows 1–8: K

3   Row 9: K 1, YO, K2tog and repeat these 3 stitches until the last stitch, ending with a K

4   Row 10: P

5   Repeat rows 1–10 until the scarf is the length you want

6   Finish with K 8 rows, cast off and weave ends in

You'll need to find some way of fixing the scarf on the neck. I chose two press studs that are hidden under some crocheted flowers. I set the press-studs at an angle to allow the scarf to fit in around the neck but open up a little towards the shoulders.

Creating your own gifts

A lovely ongoing project is the creation of gifts for friends and family. If you do this throughout the year, you won't be rushed or pressured to spend a lot of money at Christmas or when birthdays come around. One of the best things about crafty gifts is that they're usually small, so they're the ideal project to take with you when you have to go out and wait somewhere – like on the train, at school sports or at the doctor's office.

Most people love to receive handmade aprons, shopping bags, scarves (like the Ascot scarf), fabric handbags, embroidered cloths or tea cosies. You could make up a lovely gift by putting together some handmade dishcloths or a loofah with some soaps, or a basket of homemade cleaning products. Homemade food is also always appreciated. You could make a good sourdough loaf and include the sourdough starter in a preserving jar for the recipient to use in their own breadmaking. Another popular food idea is to make up a small selection of your homemade preserves. A little tray or box of jams, relish, pickled onions, preserved lemons, lemon butter or pasta sauce would make a unique gift. If you prefer to give drinks you could make some lemon cordial and ginger beer, or a few small jars of homemade tea leaves such as dried rosella, chamomile, peppermint or lemon balm.

You can also make charming cards at home. One year I made cards that had a little square of knitting that I had knitted with toothpicks. I rolled up the end of the wool into a tiny ball and left the toothpicks in, like miniature knitting needles. People always love receiving something original that you've spent time on, and taking time with the presentation of a gift will make it even more beautiful and special.

An open invitation

Tasks such as mending, sewing, knitting, preserving, cooking from scratch and simple cleaning may have seemed irrelevant to you in the past, but now might make good sense. All these skills are a perfect match for modern life; most of them will save you money and all of them will support an eco-friendly lifestyle. Using the skills I grew up with helps me run my modern, thrifty home efficiently. I know how to make do and mend; if I need to, I can make half a kilo of minced steak feed ten people and I can turn an old wool jumper into a pair of baby pants. Hanno can fix a washing machine, lawn mower and many of the other appliances we use. Developing and relearning these homemaking, gardening, cooking and home maintenance skills allows us to remain productive as we grow older.

And you can do it too. You can learn how to make pasta sauce instead of buying it in a jar, and you can make your own pasta – you don't need a pasta machine. There are many delicious summer drinks to make instead of relying on a bottle of fizzy soft drink. Homemade bread, cakes, biscuits, yoghurt, custard and ice-cream are all more nutritious and delicious than their store-bought cousins, and if you can teach yourself how to make sauces, jams, relish, gravy and dressings, not only will you be better off financially, but you'll also be eating far fewer preservatives, flavour enhancers and colourings. Soap and laundry powder made with your own hands is better on your skin than anything you can buy. You will be wearing unique clothing if you learn dressmaking,

crocheting and knitting. If you mend, re-use, produce and maintain, you'll reduce your contributions to your local landfill dump. You'll make great steps towards sustainability and self-reliance if you stop buying disposables and learn how to make replacements for those frequently bought items like dishcloths, napkins, paper towels, tampons and nappies. Learning how to grow some of your own food and how to preserve and store that food will develop your resilience during hard times or emergencies.

All these skills are a perfect match for modern life; most of them will save you money and all of them will support an eco-friendly lifestyle.

These are easy skills to learn. And learning these things and doing them daily, or as often as you can, has the potential to change you in wonderful and significant ways: it will help make you capable, productive and independent. Regaining independence is not difficult. It is there for the taking but it is not purchased, or available to the faint-hearted. Be bold, step up and take back what is yours. You'll be better for it, and self-confidence and autonomy will be your fine reward.

HOUSEWORK

When I came to live this gentler life I discovered that doing the work needed in my home slowed me down and made me think about my daily activities in a different way. It would be a significant and valuable gift if I could make my home a place of comfort for everyone who lived there, and for those who visited, rather than a chaotic jumble of disconnected and generally unfinished chores that didn't encourage anyone to relax.

Housework
never ends

I used to be one of those people who looked down on housework as something to be avoided at best, and demeaning at worst. You could work all day doing what needs to be done in your home, or you could work to a schedule and have your chores organised according to the days of the week, but even if you stuck rigidly to your schedule, you'd still have to do it all again tomorrow or next week. Because housework never ends.

I used to struggle with this. When I first starting living simply, this was the one thing that didn't just fall into place for me. I didn't have a problem with most of the chores themselves, but I had real trouble coming to terms with the endless nature of it. I wanted to get joy from the simple things that made up my day, but how could I want to do any chore, and get joy from it, when it would never end? No matter how well I did what I had to do, there would always be more housework to do tomorrow – and some chores, like washing the dishes, would have to be repeated a few times every day. I knew

I had to find a different way to look at my chores.

One of the things that impressed me about my husband early in our relationship was his attitude of, 'It has to be done, so I'll just do it.' So I started with that, and I just did what had to be done. I made sure I sprinkled all the things I enjoyed – like cooking, gardening and mending – throughout the week so every day there were chores I liked doing. I did the same with things I didn't like so much – such as cleaning toilets, ironing and vacuuming. That worked! But no matter how many times I packed the dishwasher or cleaned the shower, or how well I did it, it still had to be done the next day or the next week.

Then it hit me like a tonne of bricks. If housework never ends, then I should get rid of that feeling that if I clean the fridge out or mop the floor, then it's done. Over with. Finished. Completed. If housework never ends, then I never have to finish it. Eureka!

When I stopped thinking, 'I'll work through my chores and get everything finished but then everything will get messed up again so I'll have to start over,' and replaced it with, 'I'll do the ironing, mopping, bed-making, washing up and baking today and I'll do the mopping, sewing and baking tomorrow,' it made a real difference. Instead of a new start and finish each day, it was a continuous stream that I could break away from whenever I needed to. I continued mixing chores I liked with those I didn't like so much, and that worked well for me. I also changed things to better suit the way I liked to work. I prefer sweeping to vacuuming, so now I vacuum once a week and sweep the rest of the time, and this still keeps the floors clean. I stopped using the dishwasher and started washing up by hand, and found I liked it. I stopped ironing everything we wore and now just iron our going-out clothes and the tablecloths and pillowcases that

I like ironed. I stopped washing everything that had been used once and now only wash what is dirty or smelly – this has helped reduce my washing to two loads a week. All these things have made a big difference to the amount of housework I do and it's also cut back on our power and water usage – a big plus.

If you're not royalty, very ill or impaired, or incredibly wealthy, and you want to live in a clean home, then housework is a part of your life. If it's inevitable, you should try to make the most of it. You might end up liking it. Rethink how you work. Just because you've always done something one way, it doesn't mean it has to be like that forever. If you can modify something to better suit how you work, do it. Include the family in the housework. Teaching children how to look after themselves from a young age is a gift, not a burden. Expect your partner to help; work as a team and then relax together.

Housework never ends, so don't try to finish it.

Streamline your tasks and don't aim for perfection. Take breaks. Do everything you do well, understand the reason for the work and look for the pleasure in it. Be proud of what you achieve every day because you are providing a good home for your loved ones, you are making the most of the resources you have and looking after what you own. Stop thinking that you'll never get through it all. Housework never ends, so don't try to finish it. Just do as much as you can do or feel like doing today, and continue with it tomorrow.

Time and inclination

I know, having had years of experience dealing with readers on my blog, that there will be a wide range of people reading this book. You might be older and moving towards retirement, middle-aged with teenagers at home, single or married, have children or pets; you might want to dive into self-sufficiency or just dip your toe into simple-living waters. You may be a student, just married, a stay-at-home mum with ten children, a twenty-year-old eager to learn how to live simply or a thirty-something who is looking for a meaningful life change. No matter what your age or situation, I encourage you to decide for yourself what level of housework you're comfortable with.

Hanno and I are retired and spend a lot of time at home. Housework and home maintenance are a welcomed part of our lives and a natural part of our days. We have the time and the inclination to keep on top of our work and we are happy to do it. If you're working, ill or have a lot of children or other commitments, you may have neither the time nor the inclination to do anything but basic and necessary cleaning. That is fine.

Think about what you're capable of, work out a cleaning schedule that will work for you, then live happily with that decision. Do not feel guilt about not doing every-thing that is suggested in this chapter – this is a guide for a wide range of readers. Some will want complete guides and routines, others will be interested in the process but not feel compelled to do it all, and some will be happy to do the basics. Whatever you decide to do, that is your decision.

The mother of reinvention

In former times, homemakers took pride in presenting their homes as warm and nurturing places in which they carried out their tasks, cooked, baked, and offered hos-pitality to visitors. But traditions, short cuts, family recipes, household journals and thoughts about organisation and routines have not been passed down from those times. There was a break in that tradition because, since about the 1970s, the popular view of housework has been that you either do it as fast as you can, or ignore it until something becomes unavoidable.

When I came to live this gentler life, I discovered that doing the work needed in my home slowed me down and made me think about my daily activities in a different way. Instead of getting through the housework as fast as I could, I slowed myself to do each job well. I realised I liked doing a lot of my daily tasks when they were carried out in a mindful manner. The slowness allowed me to think about the work as I was doing it, about how that task connected to the others that followed. It showed me that all the work connected and helped make our home the place in which I wanted to live.

That change showed me that being at home had the potential to nourish my soul. It would be a significant and valuable gift if I could make my home a place of comfort for everyone who lived there, and for those who visited, rather than a chaotic jumble of disconnected and generally unfinished chores that didn't encourage anyone to relax and enjoy being there. It was not easy – in fact, there is more work to be done when you live this way – but each new day brought challenges and joys and, by taking one small step at a time, I got to where I am now. The journey is never over. Simple living is not a destination or a reward that you move towards; the journey itself is the prize.

CRAFTS ARE A PART OF YOUR HOUSEWORK

Sewing, knitting, crochet, potting, organising family memories in the form of scrapbooking and photo albums, home brewing, wine making, wood, metal and leather work aren't separate activities you should feel guilty about taking the time to do. They are part of the mosaic of housework that makes simple life holistic and sustaining. If craftspeople live with you, you'll have a far more productive home than if they don't. Be thankful for those skills, build on them and teach others what you know.

A clean sweep

We all know it makes good sense to keep a clean house, to raise children to wash their hands before they eat and clean their teeth before bed and, in general, to maintain good levels of hygiene in the home. But you can be too clean.

Since television advertising started telling us about the benefits of 'whiter than white' and how to rid our homes of germs, we've been brainwashed into believing that every germ is harmful and must be killed and if we don't do that, we're not good housekeepers. That's hogwash. There are many medical studies around now showing us that exposing children to pets and normal household dirt is good for them. It builds up the immune system and allows the body to naturally develop antibodies that fight the harmful germs. When I was growing up, and even when my boys were young in the 1980s, it was common for children to play outside. Out there, among the dirt, bugs and grass, not only were they having fun swinging on ropes, riding bikes and whispering secrets, but they were also building bone strength, muscle tissue, good lungs and healthy immune systems. Nowadays children tend to play inside on computers and PlayStations, and inside is becoming increasingly clean. We have gone from the common family home with a dirt floor in the 1800s to stainless steel and a war against germs.

Take the pressure off yourself to kill germs; your aim should be to have a clean home, not a sterile one.

We are surrounded by millions of bacteria and viruses but only a small number actually cause us any harm; the rest we live with and have evolved with, and being exposed to them has probably helped build tolerance. When we do our daily chores, it is neither possible nor healthy to kill every germ. I'm not advocating that we leave our sinks dirty and not sweep the floor. Of course we continue to do those things. We also need to wipe handles, cupboard doors, remote controls, light switches and so on, but we shouldn't be using antibacterial wipes. Take the pressure off yourself to kill germs; your aim should be to have a clean home, not a sterile one. Soap and water, vinegar or bicarb will do the trick. Using bleach, peroxide or disinfectant every day is overkill.

Disposing of disposables

Disposable products have become so entrenched in the way we live our lives that we see them as normal. I looked up the meaning of the word 'dispose': cast aside, discard, fling, throw out, throw away, toss out. The trouble with the disposables we buy is that when we cast them aside or throw them away, most of the time they sit in a landfill rubbish dump somewhere, taking years to decompose. In the case of disposable nappies, it is believed they will take about 200 years to decompose. (Of course, no one really knows how long it will take, as disposable nappies have only been around for fifty years or so. Maybe they don't decompose at all; maybe a future earth will be full of slowly rotting, ever-present, dirty nappies.)

Landfill is not the only problem worsened by disposables. Products like tissues, paper towels and plates, toilet paper and napkins tend to decompose fairly rapidly, if they aren't coated with plastic, but valuable forests are cut down to create them, and their manufacture and transportation creates unnecessary carbon emissions. Marine life is killed by eating and being tangled in plastic ropes, bags and sheets.

So we try to do without disposable products as much as possible. We take drinks with us when we go out so we don't have to buy plastic bottles of drink or tea in a polystyrene cup. We've given up buying disposable dishcloths as we have our wonderful hand-knitted ones. Our grandchildren have cotton prefolds, wraps and fitted nappies. Their beautiful bottoms will, hopefully, not see the inside of a disposable nappy.

I've given up plastic shopping bags and have my own shopping totes, including little net bags that I've made for small items. We've given up paper towels, instead using old terry cloths and newspaper, and I always try to buy products with the least amount of packaging. A few years ago we replaced paper napkins with simply sewn squares of cotton. I have about a dozen, and we throw them in the washing machine when they're dirty and fold them straight from the line. They're not ironed.

I think you increase your potential for success if you have all these things ready to be used. Don't expect to make up rags when you spill something; you'll just go back to the paper towels. These activities make a powerful statement – for the environment, for your purse and for the life you intend to live.

Knitted dishcloths

My cotton knitted dishcloths last for years, and withstand a rigorous cleaning routine and frequent washing. Every day or two, depending on how dirty they are, I replace my dirty dishcloths with fresh ones. I put my dirty tea towels in the wash and get fresh ones from the drawer at the same time. In between times, I thoroughly rinse the cloth, wring it out and hang it over the tap or sink to dry. Few bacteria can survive dry conditions; they need moisture to propagate and thrive. Hang your dirty dishcloths and cleaning rags over the side of the laundry basket so if they're wet they can dry out rather than sitting wet in the pile of dirty laundry waiting to be washed.

Cleaning with rags

My definition of a rag is a piece of fabric that has been recycled to be used for cleaning or other household duties. I use rags for all my general house cleaning – moist for wiping up spills and dry for polishing.

Cleaning with rags is the ultimate in fabric recycling. I only recycle 100 per cent cotton or linen fabric, because it's so soft and absorbent, and the older it gets the better it is. Polyester fabric and poly/cotton blends won't wipe spills as well, and will never get to that soft fluffy stage that cotton and linen reach after many washes.

My cleaning rags are washed in the washing machine, dried on the line and stored in a ragbag that hangs in the laundry. If something really dirty or unhygenic needs attention, I use a rag to wipe it up and throw that rag out. That's the beauty of having a lot of rags: you can afford to throw out the odd one, and still have plenty for cleaning.

I don't add cleaning cloths for the bathroom and toilet to the ragbag; they are stored under the sink in the bathroom. I colour code my cleaning rags so I know not to use a bathroom cloth in the kitchen.

I believe the best kind of cleaning cloth is an old terry towel. When a towel has finished service as a towel, I cut it up into 25-centimetre squares to use as rags. We've become used to neat edges and perfection in our store-bought cleaning cloths. I usually don't worry about the edges of the terry cloths, as they don't fray a lot when I cut them out with pinking shears. To me, a rag is a rag and should look like one. But if you're worried about fraying, or if you want to use the rags as dusting cloths, you could run a zigzag stitch around the border to keep the edges contained. Linen and cotton do fray, so you'll need to run the zigzag stitch around all those cloths – you don't want to be picking up little pieces of cotton from your cloths as you dust. Generally, the zigzag stitch is fine on the edges, but if you like everything to be neat and tidy, feel free to hem or edge your rags. There are no rules here; do what suits you.

Homemade green cleaners

The advertising industry would have you believe that you need a specific product for each cleaning job in your home. That's not true. It's possible to make all the cleaners you need yourself, at home, and it doesn't take a lot of time. All the ingredients of homemade cleaners will cost you only a fraction of what you pay for supermarket cleaners, and you'll have enough for your various cleaning jobs for many weeks.

Many of the cleaners we make use old-fashioned ingredients like vinegar, bicarb, borax, washing soda and soap: all inexpensive and all available at most supermarkets. Making laundry powder or liquid and other various cleaners at home will not only save you money, but it is also a safer and healthier option – for you and for the environment. Before we proceed, though, I want you to understand that every chemical you use – including the safer ones – can cause environmental damage if used in high concentrations. When you start green cleaning, don't expect vinegar and baking soda to be as fast and effective as your commercial cleaners. They are gentle cleaners, and they're much safer in our waterways than any spray-and-wipe concoction you can buy. But even so, they need to be used sparingly.

You'll need bottles or jars to hold them, so recycle your own suitable bottles and jars or get them from a hardware store, two-dollar shop or your local thrift shop. Mark all your bottles to clearly show what they contain. If you re-use a bottle that previously contained another cleaner, make sure the bottle is completely clean and marked before you fill it with your homemade cleaner.

Home cleaning kits

I have found that having small kits suitable for different areas has been helpful, so I'm not rushing about trying to find bits and pieces I need for certain areas. I suggest you make up three small kits – one for the kitchen, one for the bathroom and one for general cleaning – and keep each kit close to its area.

Your home cleaning kits will include a small bucket or old ice-cream container, rubber or latex gloves (if you use them), scrubbing brushes, terry or cotton cloths or old pantyhose for cleaning or polishing, and whichever of the homemade cleaners you choose for that area, such as vinegar, bicarb and creamy scrubber. Recycled toothbrushes are a great help in small areas. When you finish with a toothbrush, soak it for an hour in a cup of water to which a spoonful of bleach has been added and then add it to your cleaning kit.

Remember the principles of good hygiene. After cleaning the toilet with your bathroom kit you do not want to clean the kitchen with the same cloths and brushes. You should not use the bathroom kit in the kitchen or the living room. You may like to colour code them or mark them in some way, perhaps by knitting cleaning cloths of a specific colour for each area. That can be a good ongoing project for when you sit and relax after dinner at night. There is a pattern for homemade dishcloths in the Home chapter.

My bathroom cleaning kit is a 4-litre bucket, baking soda in a flour shaker, white vinegar, liquid soap, at least four terry or cotton cloths, a bristle brush, a broom and dustpan, and a mop and bucket.

The basic cleaning tools

Although all of the ingredients recommended here are safe, some of them can be harmful if ingested. Please keep all your cleaning aids out of the reach of children, wash your hands after preparing your cleaning products and wear gloves if you have sensitive skin.

Ingredients for homemade cleaners

- bicarb (baking soda)
- washing soda (a naturally occurring mineral)
- borax (a naturally occurring mineral)
- soap – either homemade soap or yellow laundry soap (such as Sunlight or a generic brand), or soap flakes (such as Lux)
- white vinegar – the cheap variety in a 2-litre bottle
- powdered oxygen bleach (such as Napisan or a generic brand)
- lemon myrtle, tea-tree oil or eucalyptus oil – used sparingly
- liquid chlorine bleach – used sparingly and carefully

Basic home-cleaning equipment

- broom and vacuum cleaner
- cotton mop or squeegee
- 10-litre bucket
- small buckets or recycled 4-litre ice-cream containers for holding your cleaning kits
- spray bottles for vinegar
- shaker for bicarb – either a large salt shaker or a recycled jar with holes punched in the lid
- rags
- scrubbing brushes of various sizes

Experiment with your cleaners – you might need to add more of one thing and less of another. You may want to add essential oils like lemon myrtle, tea-tree, eucalyptus, lavender or rose to give your cleaners a pleasant smell. They are not necessary to the recipe but adding them does not detract from the cleaners' effectiveness.

Homemade laundry cleaners

LAUNDRY LIQUID

Makes 10 litres

Ingredients

- 1½ litres water
- 1 cup grated yellow laundry soap or homemade soap, or soap flakes
- ½ cup washing soda – NOT baking soda
- ½ cup borax

Method

Into a medium-sized saucepan add the water and the soap. Over a medium heat, stir until the soap is completely dissolved.

Add the washing soda and borax. If you use the grey water from your laundry on your garden, leave out the borax because it can build up in the soil and affect your plants. It is safe to use if you have a septic tank. Stir until thickened, and remove from heat.

Pour this mixture into a bucket, then fill the bucket with water from the tap. Stir to combine all the ingredients. The laundry liquid will thicken up as it cools and often separates. The more you stir it while it is cooling the smoother the liquid will be.

Pour the liquid into containers that you fill almost to the top; leave room in the container so that you can shake it before use. To make it easier to store on my laundry shelves, I use recycled 2-litre milk or juice bottles for this.

Use ¼ to ½ cup of mixture per load or monitor to see what works well in your washing machine. If you have stained clothes, rub some washing liquid on the stain and leave it for 5 minutes before you add the item to the general wash. That should be enough to remove stains like oil, chocolate, pencil or dirt.

This laundry liquid and the laundry powders on the next page will not make suds in the washing machine because they do not contain the chemicals that are added to commercial detergents to make them bubble. You do not need bubbles to wash your clothes or for the laundry liquid and powders to be effective. The agitation of the washing machine does most of the washing.

All these washing aids are suitable for top loaders and front loaders. I have been using them in my front loader machines for many years with no ill effects. I usually use the laundry liquid for stain removal and general cleaning as well.

Cost comparisons

Cost of bulk ingredients:

- 700 g soap flakes (9.3 cups): $7.49
- 1 kg washing soda (3.9 cups): $3.99
- 500 g borax (2.6 cups): $4.10

Cost of ingredients used in 10-litre batch:

- 1 cup soap flakes (75 g): $0.80
- ½ cup washing soda (255 g): $0.51
- ½ cup borax (190 g): $0.78

Cost in total for 10 litres: $2.09

At the supermarket, a 900ml bottle of Dynamo costs around $12. So, 10 litres of Dynamo would cost around $133. Not only does making your own save you more than $130, but you'll also have enough ingredients to make it several more times.

LAUNDRY POWDER

This is a powder version of the laundry liquid but it is not as economical. I sometimes use the powder because it's easier to mix up when I'm busy and in a hurry.

Ingredients

- 4 cups grated laundry or homemade soap, or soap flakes
- 2 cups borax
- 2 cups washing soda

Method

Mix all the ingredients thoroughly and store in a container with a lid.
Use 2 tablespoons per wash.

HEAVY-DUTY LAUNDRY POWDER

For use on greasy or dirty workers' overalls, football and sports uniforms or heavily stained fabric.

Ingredients

- 1 cup powdered oxygen bleach
- 2 cups grated laundry or homemade soap, or soap flakes
- 1 cup borax
- 1 cup washing soda

Method

Mix all the ingredients thoroughly and store in a container with a lid.

Use 2 tablespoons per wash. For very heavily stained clothes, if you have a top loader turn the machine off when the powder is completely dissolved and allow the clothes to soak for an hour, or overnight. Soaking will help remove stains. In a front loader, operate the machine to dissolve the powder and then stop the machine to soak the clothes. Leave to soak for an hour, or overnight, then turn the machine on and continue washing as normal.

STAIN REMOVERS

Organic stains caused by blood, coffee, tea and so on should be soaked in a bucket of clean, cold water as soon as possible. After soaking for at least an hour, rub the stains with a bar of laundry soap or ¼ cup of laundry liquid. If the stains don't come out, add 2 tablespoons of powdered oxygen bleach to a bucket of water and leave the item to soak overnight. After soaking, wash as usual in the washing machine.

Food stains can usually be removed by placing the fabric on a flat surface and applying a tablespoon of homemade laundry liquid. Rub the liquid into the stain with your fingers for about a minute, then add the clothes to the normal wash.

OTHER LAUNDRY CLEANERS

To **remove stains from white clothes**, mix together ¼ cup of hydrogen peroxide and ¼ cup of water and dab onto the stain. Leave for 2 hours and repeat if necessary.

For a **fabric softener**, just add ½ cup of white vinegar to the final rinse of your washing machine.

Assorted home cleaners

ALL-PURPOSE CLEANER

Can be used as a floor cleaner – tiles, laminate or vinyl – or for general cleaning of walls, counter tops or sinks.

Ingredients

- ½ cup washing soda
- 2 litres warm water

Method

Mix together and store in a sealed plastic container.

CREAMY SCRUBBER

Simply pour about ½ cup of baking soda into a bowl, and add enough liquid soap or laundry liquid to make a texture like very thick cream. Scoop the mixture onto a sponge, and start scrubbing. This is the perfect recipe for cleaning the bath and shower because it rinses easily and doesn't leave grit.

Note: If you plan to store the mixture, add 1 teaspoon of vegetable glycerin and store in a sealed glass jar; it will keep for about 1 month. Otherwise, make as much as you need at a time.

WOODEN FURNITURE POLISH

Ingredients

- ½ teaspoon olive oil
- ¼ cup vinegar or fresh lemon juice

Method

Mix the ingredients in a glass jar.

Dab a soft rag into the solution and wipe onto wooden surfaces. Seal in the glass jar and store indefinitely.

WOODEN FLOOR CLEANER

Ingredients

- 2 tablespoons grated laundry or homemade soap
- ½ cup vinegar
- 500 ml strong black tea with no tea leaves
- bucket of warm water

Method

Combine all the ingredients in the bucket and apply with a cotton mop.

WINDOW CLEANER

Pour a little vinegar onto a sheet of newspaper and wipe windows. Remove all the grime and polish the window with a clean sheet of newspaper.

HEAVY-DUTY WINDOW CLEANER

For use on very dirty windows. The soap in this recipe cuts through the wax residue from the commercial brands you might have used in the past.

Ingredients

- ½ teaspoon liquid or grated soap
- 3 tablespoons vinegar
- 2 cups water

Method

Put all the ingredients into a spray bottle, shake it up a bit, and use as you would a commercial brand.

STAINLESS STEEL CLEANER

This is very good for appliances with a buffed-steel appearance, like dishwashers, fridges and rangehoods.

Ingredients

- 1 cup vinegar
- ½ bucket warm water
- few drops eucalyptus oil

Method

Add the vinegar to the bucket of warm water. Using a clean rag, wipe the appliance over with the mixture and wipe dry.

Add the eucalyptus oil to a clean cloth and wipe the appliance, making sure all streaks are polished off.

SILVER CLEANER

This method works by a chemical reaction of the aluminium, salt and baking soda.

Ingredients

- sheet of aluminium foil
- boiling water
- 1 teaspoon baking soda
- 1 teaspoon salt

Method

Put the plug in the kitchen sink. Lay the foil on the base of the sink and add your silverware. Pour in enough boiling water to cover the silver.

Add the baking soda and salt to the water, and let it sit for about 10 minutes. The tarnish will disappear without you touching it.

FLOOR CLEANER

This is good for tiles, vinyl or laminate. To clean all but the worst floors, ½ cup of white vinegar plus 2 litres of hot water in a bucket and a clean mop will do. If you have a really dirty floor to deal with, add a squirt of homemade laundry liquid to this mix.

Other cleaning tips

Choosing a dishwashing liquid

Making your own dishwashing liquid is quite complicated, unlike the simple cleaners in this book. So read the label and make sure you buy one that is plant-based (not petroleum-based) and phosphate-free.

Tea-tree oil

Tea-tree oil can be used effectively against bacteria and fungus. If you have a very dirty bathroom, sink or floors, ½ teaspoon of tea-tree oil in a bucket of hot water will help disinfect those problem areas.

Cleaning your mop

A clean mop is a necessity when cleaning floors. If you start with a dirty mop you'll just loosen the dirt on the mop by making it wet again and then spread that on the floor. When you finish mopping, follow these steps to get your mop ready for the next session:

1 Rinse the mop out to get rid of the loose dirt.
2 Add a tablespoon of oxygen bleach to a bucket half-filled with hot water, and let the mop soak for 30 minutes.
3 Rinse the bleach out and squeeze out as much water as you can.
4 Dry the mop in the sun.
5 Store your mop on a hook off the floor, with the mop head facing down.

Cleaning crayons from painted surfaces

Make a thick paste with a few drops of water and baking soda. Wipe over the crayon marks and scrub off with a terry cloth.

Removing glue or stickers

Cover with eucalyptus oil and leave for 30 minutes. This will loosen the glue so you can scrape it off.

Safe and simple cleaning

There are three main cleaning areas in the home: the kitchen, the bathroom/toilet and the laundry. In the following pages I describe how to deep-clean these areas. When you have everything clean, keep it that way by doing a little touch-up each day. It only takes a few minutes to wipe down the fridge or clean up spills on the stove, but it will make a big difference to your overall workload because you'll only have to do a big clean like this every couple of months. However, if you are time-poor or ill, or just plain tired and need a rest, don't fret if your cleaning is left undone until you feel better and have the time to do it.

Simple green cleaning requires more effort than spray-and-wipe chemical cleaning, but your home will be safer using these methods. I expect you to use this as a guide, to modify it to suit your method of cleaning and your house. I hope you see that the emphasis is on elbow grease rather than chemicals. The products recommended here will clean thoroughly – if you start out with a dirty kitchen or bathroom, they might need two or three applications, but they will work. Whatever you do, make sure you use less and not more of everything. We are conservers, not consumers; let's try to keep everything to a minimum.

Green cleaning the kitchen

It will probably take a few hours to deep clean your kitchen, so put aside a morning or an afternoon to get it done. As well as the build-up of dust and dirt, there is usually grease in the kitchen, so that adds another element to your cleaning. The best way to deal with a kitchen is to work on getting it clean, and then do a little maintenance each day to keep it that way. Even so, you'll need to deep clean and reorganise every few months.

So, put on your apron and gloves and let's go through this step by step. You'll need your kitchen cleaning kit.

ACTION PLAN: *Kitchen cleaning*

The oven

* If the oven is really dirty, place an ovenproof dish containing a cup of hot water and a cup of vinegar in the oven. Turn the oven on until the mix starts to boil, then turn it off and leave for an hour.

* It is easier to clean a warm oven than a cold one, so if you haven't already given it the vinegar steam treatment (above), turn on your oven for a short time.

* Fill the sink with hot water. Remove the oven racks and wash them in the sink.

* Empty the contents of your kitchen cleaning kit out onto the kitchen bench. Fill the bucket with hot water and get your bicarb, vinegar and a rag. Wet the walls of the oven using a wet rag and sprinkle bicarb over every surface. Take a second rag and pour vinegar on it and wipe the bicarbed walls and floor of the oven. If you need a second round, apply the bicarb again and scrub.

* To clean the top of the oven, pour the vinegar onto a rag, then add bicarb on top of the vinegar, and rub that onto the surface. Repeat if necessary. When all traces of grease and grime are gone, wipe the oven with a clean, moist rag, then dry with a clean dry rag.

* Replace the racks and wipe the front of the oven with vinegar and dry with a rag.

The fridge

* Now check your fridge. If it needs cleaning, empty it completely, including the shelving and drawers. Check all the food and dispose of anything past its prime, preferably giving it to the chooks or worms or adding it to the compost.

* Working quickly (you don't want the food to warm up), take a small bucket of hot soapy water and a rag and clean the interior of the fridge. Dry with a clean cloth. When the fridge is completely dry, spray the interior of the fridge with white vinegar and wipe it dry again.

* Replace the shelving, drawers and food. Check the temperature – it should be no more than 4°C.

* Don't forget the seals on the door. Clean them with a toothbrush dipped in all-purpose cleaner.

* Check that the fridge seal is actually sealing. Put a piece of paper over the seal and close the fridge door. Try to pull the paper out. If it comes out easily, you need to replace the seal. Clean the outer fridge with a creamy scrubber and wipe dry with a clean cloth.

The dishwasher

* If you use your dishwasher daily, every month or so remove the filter and wash it in the sink with a brush and soap.

* Clean the seals on the inside of the machine with a moist soapy cloth. Check the spinning arm and make sure the holes are not blocked. If you see any part of the interior clogged or dirty, pay particular attention to it, cleaning it with your soapy cloth and wiping away any debris.

* Replace the filter and spray the inside of the dishwasher with vinegar. Run the machine on a short cycle.

Appliances

* Your homemade creamy scrubber is perfect for cleaning appliances and cupboard surfaces because it rinses off easily. Simply apply the creamy scrubber to the area and clean with a moist rag. When the appliance is clean, wipe over with a dry rag.

✳ To clean your toaster, turn it off and empty the crumb tray. Wipe the outside of the toaster with vinegar on a rag and dry with a clean rag.

The pantry

✳ Remove everything from the pantry and wipe the shelves with warm soapy water or white vinegar, then dry them. If you notice pantry moths or any sort of larvae, clean the pantry with the vacuum cleaner and use the small nozzle to get into all the joins.

✳ Check your storage jars. Whatever is in the pantry should be stored in sealed containers or in unopened packs. If anything needs to be topped up, do it. If something looks as if it's past its prime, throw it out – preferably in the compost, or as food for the chickens or worms.

✳ When you re-pack your shelves, keep similar things together and make sure everything is clearly marked. All your flours should be labelled and in one place, for instance; all your vinegars and sauces go together, various rices, dried fruits and spices are all labelled and stored together.

The stove

✳ So, the oven and fridge are clean and the cupboards are organised the way you want them; now clean the stove. Remove the bits you can, including the knobs, and wash them in hot soapy water in the sink, then dry. You can use either the creamy scrubber or the all-purpose cleaner for the surfaces of the stove. Either spray on the all-purpose cleaner or, using a moist rag, apply the creamy scrubber. Wipe it clean, then wipe over with a wet, clean rag. When it's clean, dry with a terry cloth and replace the parts you cleaned in the sink.

The benches

✳ Clear your benches and thoroughly wipe them with either the all-purpose spray or the creamy scrubber. Using a moist rag, wipe the benches, cupboard doors and handles and the splashback or whatever you have behind your benches and sink.

✳ Wipe dry with a terry cloth and replace everything.

The sink

* Now that most things have been cleaned, you can clean the sink. To clean a dirty sink, or to make one shine, wet the sink, combine equal parts of baking soda and coarse salt and sprinkle it on.

* Scrub the sink with a hard brush to remove dirt and grease. Make sure you get in all the areas around the taps and drain.

* About once a month, finish off with a litre of water in the sink, add a tablespoon of liquid bleach and remove the plug. You'll sanitise and clean the pipes at the same time. This will stop any debris building up and will eliminate smelly pipes. WARNING: Don't use bleach in your sink if you have a septic system. The bleach will kill the beneficial bacteria in the tank.

* Wipe with a dry terry cloth.

The floor

* You're almost finished. The only thing left now is the floor. Sweep the floor and scoop up the dust and crumbs and dispose of them in the compost or bin. Now you can wash the floor. Choose your floor cleaner depending on the type of floor you have. Combine all the ingredients in a bucket and wipe over the floor with a clean mop.

* Now clean your kit so it's ready for your next cleaning session, then wash your hands, stand back and admire your work.

Green cleaning the bathroom

This is the way I clean my bathroom. I do it once a week, and I wipe the vanity and taps during the week whenever I feel like doing it. I don't stress over it, I just do it as it suits my mood. This routine should take about fifteen minutes for an average bathroom. If it's dirtier or much larger, add another fifteen minutes.

ACTION PLAN: *Bathroom cleaning*

Prepare the area

✳ If possible, open doors and windows to allow a free flow of air through the room. Put on your apron and gloves. If you have a toilet in your bathroom, close the toilet lid after using it and pay particular attention to drying your surfaces. Bacteria generally need moisture to grow, so drying the surfaces after cleaning is a good habit to get into.

✳ Remove all the items you have stored in the shower, around your sink and bath. Put all towels and floor mats in the laundry ready for washing.

✳ Check the mould on the grout. If there is mould growing, make a paste of some bicarb, tea-tree oil and water and apply it to the grout with a toothbrush. Leave it while you get on with the rest of the cleaning. If the mould has been growing for a while, it might have eaten into the grout. You'll only be able to remove it if it's on the surface. Re-grouting the tiles is the only thing you can do for deeply embedded mould.

✳ Pour a cup of bicarb into the toilet, add a cup of white vinegar and leave it for a few minutes. It will fizz – that's okay.

The mirror

✳ Wipe the mirror over with a clean cloth and a splash of white vinegar. Rub with the same rag until it's dry.

The shower

✳ If there's a build-up of soap scum, wet the walls and sprinkle with bicarb, then scrub with a rag soaked in vinegar. If it's hard to get off, reapply and scrub with a stiff brush. If the shower is not very dirty, just sprinkle bicarb onto your damp (not wet) terry cloth and wipe all the surfaces.

✳ When you're satisfied it's clean, add about 1 litre of cold water to your bucket, dip a clean cloth into the bucket and wipe all traces of bicarb off. If you have a removable shower head, use it as a hose to clean off the bicarb.

* When you've finished cleaning, wipe all surfaces with a dry terry cloth. Pay particular attention to the glass and stainless steel surfaces as they will show water spots if you allow the water to dry on them.

* You have now used three of your cloths – one for bicarb and water, one for vinegar and one as a dry wiper. Keep these cloths as they are; you'll use them again soon. Depending on the state and size of your bathroom, you might need more dry wipers.

The bath

* Wet the bath with clean water and wipe it over with your bicarb-and-water rag. When it's clean, wipe with a dry cloth.

The sink

* If you have a toothbrush holder, clean it first with your clean rags using the creamy scrubber to remove all traces of toothpaste. Then wipe with a clean, moist rag, and dry.

* Now clean the sink with bicarb and water, or bicarb and vinegar if it's really dirty. Make sure you clean the taps, around the taps and the areas where the taps join the sink – this is where bacteria can build up so scrub those areas well with a brush. When it's all clean, wipe over with your dry cloth.

The toilet

* You've already poured the vinegar and bicarb into the toilet; now it will need to be scrubbed with the toilet brush. Make sure you get into every area. If there are stains in the toilet, you might have to repeat this treatment – scrub it and leave it for a couple of hours. Then come back and scrub it with the toilet brush and flush. Wipe the cistern, seat and lid with a clean rag dipped in warm, soapy water to which 4 drops of tea-tree oil have been added.

The floor

* Sweep the floor to get rid of all the strands of hair, dust and talcum powder.

* Half-fill a bucket with hot water and add a teaspoon of liquid soap or ¼ cup of laundry liquid. I have found that a broom cleans a bathroom floor better than a mop because it gets into the spaces between the tiles and around the toilet more effectively. Wet a clean broom in the bucket and drain it a little, then scrub the floor. Clean the floor of the shower recess using this method too. Make sure you get into the corners.

* When you're satisfied the floor is clean, empty your bucket and fill with clean cold water. Wipe the floor over with a mop and the clean water, making sure you remove all the soap and lather. Wring the mop out well and wipe the floor one more time, so you leave the floor moist, not wet.

* Let the floor dry. Take off your gloves and wash and dry your hands. Lay down your fresh floor mats and put out fresh towels. Now you can put your toiletries, creams and make-up back.

Clean your kit

* Now clean up your bathroom kit so it's ready for the next job. You want everything to dry out between uses, otherwise bacteria will build up in your equipment and it'll start to smell. Rinse the mop and broom in clean, cold water and wring out as much as possible. Stand them in the sun or somewhere they can dry completely.

* Wipe out your bucket, put it in your cleaning kit with fresh cloths and return it to the bathroom, under the sink if possible. Put all your cleaning cloths in the laundry to be washed.

Green cleaning in the laundry

Cleaning your laundry usually means wiping surfaces with a warm soapy rag and drying them off again. Every so often, run a cycle in your washing machine with a cup of vinegar and nothing else – just a short cycle will do. It will clean it out and remove any built-up soap scum. If you use a dryer, remove the lint every week or so. This is important because lint in a faulty dryer can be a fire hazard. Give the sink a good clean with the bicarb and vinegar treatment, then dry it.

Handwashing

Some clothing lasts longer and looks better if it is handwashed. Be guided by the garment label and your common sense. I have handwashed garments recommended for dry cleaning only; they survived the process and looked clean and smart when they dried.

To handwash effectively, half-fill your sink with warm water and add a small amount of liquid soap or dissolved Lux flakes. Put the garment into the water and thoroughly soak it. If it's a blouse, dress or shirt, take particular notice of the collar and underarms – you may need to wash these areas with a bar of soap.

For woollens or natural fibres like alpaca, be careful not to lift the garment by the shoulders. Support the weight of knitted items and don't let them hang loose – they will stretch. Move the item through the water and rub the underarms gently. When it is clean, squeeze it out but don't wring it. Twisting will stretch and weaken the fibres. Place in clean water and rinse until every bit of soap is removed. You may need to replace the water a couple of times.

Have some towels ready. Squeeze as much water from the item as you can, then place the garment flat on the towel. Roll the towel up tightly and press down to remove more water. Do this a couple of times, then take the garment outside and place it on a dry, clean towel in the shade to dry.

Drying your washing in the sun

There are a few daily chores that have not changed much in a hundred years. One of those things is hanging washing out to dry. Drying clothes outside is a task that connects you to your great-grandmothers. We might have plastic pegs and clotheslines now, but most of the other elements are basically unchanged.

Tumble dryers are among the most energy-intensive household appliances, and using them to dry your clothes will add to your electricity bills and to the carbon emissions coming from your home. Line drying your laundry, on the other hand, is remarkably efficient. All you need is the time and a bit of effort – sun and breeze are supplied free to everyone with the will to use them. If there is no wind, you could even do without pegs and just place the clothes neatly over the clothesline – or a fence or large bush. Back in the old days many women used lavender bushes to dry their clothes.

When the washing machine finishes the cycle, take the clothes out immediately and head to the line. If you leave the washing in the machine or in your washing basket you'll have more creases than necessary. The thing that makes the most difference when hanging washing is a shake and snap: shake the item and give it a sharp, hard whip-snap before you peg it up. You'll remove some of the wrinkles in cotton and linen, and help fluff up the towels.

If you're hanging brightly coloured or black clothing, turn them inside out to help prevent fading. Your whites will benefit from drying in the sun because it has a slightly bleaching effect. Woollens or any natural fibres like alpaca will shrink if dried in the sun. They should be laid out flat on a large towel and dried in the shade. Make sure you support wet woollen and alpaca clothing with both hands when you move them from the sink to the drying area.

> Generally we have good weather where we live, ideal for drying, and a line of clothes set out early in the morning will be ready to bring in after lunch. Hanno has built an all-weather line too, so in addition to our Hills hoist, that umbrella-shaped Australian icon, I can line-dry clothes on our back verandah, even when it's raining.

When you peg the item to the line, smooth it out with your hand and make sure the edges are straight. Straighten and smooth collars, sleeves, pockets and hems before going on to the next item. If you can hang your items straight, without creases, there's a better chance you won't have to iron them. This includes most jeans and some shirts.

On a rotary line, socks and underwear were traditionally hung in the middle, hidden by the larger items that were hung on the outer lines. I have to confess I still do this. If you have a long line, hang the lighter items in the middle and the heavier things on the ends of the line, where there is more support.

Peg towels, tea towels, pillowcases and napkins by two top corners, shirts and blouses upside down on the side seam, jeans (with the zip undone) and skirts by the waist, and dresses on the shoulder seam. Hang sheets, tablecloths and doona covers by the two top corners, then make a U shape with it and peg the bottom corners to the line behind it. This will create better drying conditions for these large items and, sometimes, the wind takes up the fabric like a sail. If you're using a circular line the wind will spin the line around. If you have enough room and sturdy coat hangers, you could hang dresses, shirts and anything permanent press on a coat hanger and peg it to stop it slipping along the line. Permanent press clothes are chemically treated so they don't wrinkle. They're generally trousers and business shirts and if you wash and dry them correctly they don't need to be ironed.

I like wooden pegs but here in our climate, they go mouldy and often end up marking the clothes. Plastic pegs will serve you better in humid or moist climates. And don't do what we do here and keep the pegs on the line. It's best to store plastic pegs out of sunlight; they'll last much longer if you take care of them.

If you intend to immediately iron anything you have hanging on the line, remove it when it's still slightly damp to make ironing easier. When the clothes are dry and full of the smell of sunshine, unpeg them, and place them in your basket. When you remove towels from the line, shake them again to fluff up the pile. Take the washing inside and fold it straight away. I do this on the kitchen table as it gives me enough room to work and stack everything. It's also a central place from where I can easily put away tea towels, napkins, dishcloths, towels and sheets as soon as they're folded and stacked. Don't put off your folding because if you do, you'll have creased clothes that will have to be ironed. I have been able to cut my ironing by 50 per cent by shaking wet clothes at the line, careful hanging, and folding as soon as the clothes are off the line.

Line drying is one of those things we can do that doesn't rely on electricity – it's just you and the pegs.

Hanging laundry is a wonderful thing to do. You might think of it as yet another chore but it allows you to take advantage of the outdoors, the fresh air and the sunshine. You are using the natural elements of your environment to help keep your clothes clean. It's one of those things we can do that doesn't rely on electricity – it's just you and the pegs.

If you haven't tried line drying yet, give it a go. Your clothes and household linens will last longer as they aren't subjected to the heat and constant tumbling action of a dryer. Yes, it does take more effort on your part to do it, but these gentle exercises are good for all of us. Hanging laundry is one of those little things that gives you the chance slow down and to be mindful of the many simple things you can do at home. If you can't line dry your clothes, choose an energy-efficient tumble dryer and look for every opportunity to dry clothes in the bathroom or on your balcony.

The rest of the house

I have explained how to clean the kitchen, bathroom and laundry, but what about the rest of the house?

All of us need to clean the floors, but how often you do that depends on the time you have and whether you have children or pets. Common sense will probably tap you on the shoulder if you don't have a regular cleaning routine; the trick is to work out a strategy that suits you and is easy and effective. I find that doing a deep clean with the vacuum cleaner once a week and sweeping the rest of the time works well for us. We have a dog but no children. If you're a working couple, you may be fine with the vacuum cleaning once a month; if you're a stay-at-home mum with small children, you may want to vacuum every day.

Here are some cleaning tips and suggestions for people with the time and inclination:

- About once a month, clean the skirting boards while you're vacuuming, and dust when you feel like it. If you're on a main highway, you'll need to do it more frequently.
- Another once-a-month task is to clean around light switches and door handles with your all-purpose spray and a clean rag. You can also wipe television and computer screens once a month with a splash of vinegar on a clean dry rag.
- Every three months, vacuum the lounge suite thoroughly. Remove the cushions and vacuum the crevices underneath.

Spring cleaning

Spring cleaning is traditionally done when the weather starts to warm up again after winter, but it can be done at any time of the year. Depending on how much time you have, you can do all the inside chores in one day, do one room at a time or put aside thirty minutes a day to work through what you need to do.

Plan and make a list of what you intend to do. Everyone's list will be different but most of us will have to clean windows, doors, screens and shutters. Some of us will need to wash curtains. Other common tasks will include:

- changing seasonal clothes; washing and storing what you won't be wearing for the next few months, including warm jumpers, gloves, hats and scarves
- changing bedding; washing and storing warm quilts, doonas and blankets
- turning the mattresses over and around
- washing pillows, pillowcases and cushion covers, and hanging them in the sun to dry
- vacuuming the house thoroughly, moving the furniture and white goods
- taking the rugs and mats outside for a thorough shaking, and letting them sit over a fence for a while in the sun (facedown to minimise fading)
- cleaning and organising the fridge, pantry and stockpile
- removing everything from the kitchen benches and cleaning thoroughly
- going through anything you accumulate throughout the year, like magazines, and getting rid of the old ones
- cleaning and organising your bathroom cupboard, safely disposing of old medications (the local pharmacy will probably take them back)
- washing the shower curtain
- soaking hair brushes and combs in a weak solution of chloride bleach or peroxide
- cleaning out any cupboard that needs it
- cleaning ceiling fans, air conditioners and fireplaces
- getting up on the roof and cleaning out the gutters, skylights and solar panels, and checking for cracks or damage
- checking and maintaining the lawnmower and other garden tools.

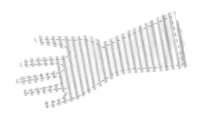

Cleaning you

You can get by with very little when it comes to showering and staying clean. A good homemade vegetable oil soap and some bicarb for shampoo and deodorant will be fine. Loofahs and a thick terry face cloth are excellent simple aids in the shower. However, many people like to use more than the basics so here are some recipes to try.

Cold-processed soap

I'm sure many of you are wondering, 'Why make soap when I can buy it cheaply at the supermarket?' Commercial soap is often made with tallow (animal fat), contains synthetic fragrance and dye and retains almost no glycerin. (Glycerin is a natural emollient that helps with the lather and moisturises the skin. The makers of commercial soap extract the glycerin and sell it as a separate product, as it's more valuable than the soap. Then they add chemicals to make the soap lather. Crazy.) My cold-processed soap is made with vegetable oils and when it is made and cured, it contains no harsh chemicals or dyes.

Making your own soap allows you to add whatever you want to add. If you want a plain and pure soap, as I do, you can have that, or you can start with the plain soap and add colour, herbs and fragrance. The choice is yours.

I have to start with a warning. If you are new to soap making, it should not be attempted when children or animals are around. The caustic soda burns, and if you spill it on skin you need to wash it off immediately under running water or vinegar. If you drop it on the floor or bench top, wipe it up straight away as it will burn the surface. When you mix caustic soda with water, even though it's not on the stove it will heat up considerably and will burn if you drop any on yourself or splash it in your eyes. This process will also create fumes. Make sure you mix caustic soda in a well-ventilated room. Many soap makers wear latex gloves, goggles and a mask. Please use these safeguards while you're learning to make soap. When you're experienced, you might be able to dispense with them.

Are you still with me after that warning? Soap making is a simple process that is made more difficult by using caustic soda. A form of caustic soda was originally taken from wood ash, but now caustic soda is made commercially by running an electric current through a salt solution. There is absolutely no way to make soap from scratch without using caustic soda. Even the 'natural soap' sold in shops is made using caustic soda. But the process of soap making – saponification – neutralises the caustic soda and by the time the soap is cured, no caustic soda remains in the soap.

If you make sure you're alone when making soap, if you have all your ingredients measured out and have a clean and clear work area, you shouldn't have any problems. The entire process should take about thirty minutes.

The recipe may change every time you make soap but the method of making it remains the same. If you do use a new recipe, check it with an online soap calculator first to make sure you have the correct ratio of caustic soda to water and oils.

PURE SOAP RECIPE

Makes 12 big blocks

This is a beautiful soap that is easy to make. I wash my hair with this soap and it feels like I've used the best shampoo. See the soap-making tutorial on my blog for photos of each stage of the process. Most soap ingredients must be measured by weight, not volume. The best way to mix your soap is to use a stick blender. It will get the job done quickly and, as the mixing happens under the surface, there is no splashing. Electric hand beaters will splash too much.

Ingredients

- 1000 g olive oil
- 250 g copha or coconut oil
- 450 ml rainwater, or tap water that has stood in a container for 24 hours to allow the chlorine to evaporate off
- 172 g caustic soda

Equipment

- newspaper to cover your work area
- soap moulds, a resin cake form, clean milk cartons or some other non-aluminium receptacle that will shape the soap
- scales

- stainless steel or cast-iron saucepan (not aluminium – the caustic soda will ruin aluminium)
- measuring jug – for measuring water (it's okay to measure the water by volume)
- small bowl (not aluminium)
- milk or candy thermometer
- stick blender

Method

1 Open windows and doors to allow good ventilation, and lay out the newspaper over your work area.
2 Grease your moulds (I use cooking spray) and put on your safety gear.
3 Weigh all your oils and place them in the saucepan. Measure out the water and leave it in your measuring jug. Measure out the caustic soda into a small bowl.
4 Clip the thermometer onto the side of the saucepan and place on low heat on the stove. Slowly heat the oils to 50°C.
5 Carefully pour the caustic soda into the measuring jug with the water, and stir gently until fully dissolved. Stand back a bit as there will be fumes coming from this mix as it heats up.
6 You need to have the oil at 45–50°C and the caustic soda at 45–50°C. When they're the same temperature, pour the caustic soda water into the oils, being careful to avoid splashing it. Mix for about 5–10 minutes with your stick blender, making sure the blender doesn't overheat. The surface of the mixture should be smooth.
7 When slight ripples form on the surface and remain there, stop mixing. This is the sign you look for that the soap has become stable and is ready to be poured into a mould. The mix should be thick, but pourable. This is called 'trace', and the caustic soda is almost gone by this point.
8 If you're going to add fragrance, add it when you reach trace and give it a good mix. If you want to colour your soap you need to buy soap dye or use natural

powders like turmeric, cinnamon or cocoa. Food colouring is not suitable because it's unstable.

9   Pour the mixture into the greased mould. I use a resin cake form that I bought at a two-dollar shop. Once the soap is in the mould, place a cutting board on the top and wrap it in a towel so it cools down slowly.

10 The next morning, or about 15 hours later, release the soap from the mould and cut it into whatever shape you desire. I don't fiddle with the shape; I just cut them into blocks with a sharp knife. I like my soap to look handmade, but many soap makers fashion their soaps to look very professional. You do what you want to do. I do stamp my soaps with a plain old rubber or potato stamp when the soap starts to harden – about 4–6 hours after pouring. This time period will vary depending on the temperature in your house.

11 Place the cakes of soap on a drying rack somewhere they can stay for a couple of weeks. Turn the soap over every second day to allow it to dry out evenly. I cure my soaps for about 6 weeks before using them. The drier they are when you use them, the longer they last. If you use your soap after a week or so, it will go soft when it gets wet and won't last long.

You can also pour your soap (while it's still in liquid form) into loofahs that have been cut into disks. Just wrap the bottom of the loofah in a small piece of plastic wrap so the hot soap doesn't run through. The next morning, or when it's set, just tidy up the top with a sharp knife and allow the loofah soaps to cure for a few weeks.

Skincare

While it's lovely to be given organic and natural skincare products as gifts, I tend to make what I need from what I have here at home. You don't need expensive potions; rely on Mother Nature to supply what you need in the form of oils, herbs and petals that will serve you just as well as anything you'll buy over the counter – without the chemicals.

FACE AND BODY MOISTURISER

Dry skin is best treated after you've had a shower or bath, when the pores are open. If you have dry skin, a simple rich oil, such as almond, sesame, vitamin E or olive oil, is all you need. Normal to oily skin will need a lighter oil, such as jojoba or avocado oil.

You can apply all these oils in two ways. Either apply the oil straight on to your skin and rub gently in a circular motion, or wet your hands with warm water, add a drop or two of oil to your warm, wet hands and then rub on to your skin.

QUICK ROSEWATER

Place a cup of firmly packed rose petals (that have not been sprayed with insecticide) in a saucepan. Pour in 2 cups of water and bring to the boil. Stir with a wooden spoon, bruising the petals as you stir. Let it simmer for 3 minutes and take it off the stove. Cover with a cotton cloth and let it sit until cool. Strain, making sure you get all the liquid out of the petals, and store in a sterilised, sealed jar or bottle for up to a month.

Splash rosewater on your face after cleansing, use as a fragrant hair rinse or as a spray-on fragrance for your ironing.

ROSE MOISTURISER

To make an excellent moisturiser, use 2 parts rosewater mixed with 1 part glycerin. Shake well to combine and use on the face or as a body lotion.

Glycerin is a natural product usually purchased from the chemist. It is extracted from commercial soap during processing.

SIMPLE FACIAL CLEANSERS

For dry to normal skin, rub skin gently with cotton wool dipped in milk. Leave for 30 seconds, rinse off and dry.

For oily skin, apply plain, natural yoghurt to the skin with fingertips. Leave for 30 seconds, rinse off and dry. Natural yoghurt and the lactic acid it contains exfoliates the skin. It is also a good moisturiser.

HERB WATER

Herb water may be used as simple skin tonics or for hydrating and cleansing the skin. Elder flowers and lime flowers are soothing on dry skin, comfrey and marigold are good for normal skin and chamomile and rosemary are excellent for oily skin.

To make herb water, simply take ¼ cup of fresh herb leaves or flower petals and place in a bowl. Pour a cup of boiling water over the leaves and petals. Cover the infusion with a cloth and leave for 3 hours to steep and develop. Strain through muslin and store in a glass bottle.

Herb water will keep for up to 4 days in the refrigerator but it is best to use it fresh.

> When using water for any of the herb and rosewater recipes, use either rainwater, spring water or tap water that's been allowed to sit in a bowl for 24 hours. That will allow the chlorine to evaporate.

LIP BALM

Melt 6 tablespoons of beeswax in a saucepan on a low heat on the stove. When it's melted remove from the stove and mix with 6 tablespoons of sesame oil and 2 tablespoons of honey. Stir until the mixture thickens. Store in a small jar for up to 2 months.

Selective filtering —
download & scan whether
you need it or not.

Micro _____

- micro_____ fees for global _____
- leas_____ rather than own_____
- Lon_____ rail tracks
- _____ on water

_____ Hardware
_____ that is possible
_____ final
_____ craftsman

_____ wallpaper

Designed to Death

ORGANISING
YOUR LIFE

Sometimes, when I have a deadline to meet, housework to do, and voluntary work, gardening, cooking and my family to tend to, I feel a slight panic – how will I ever get it done? At those times I've taught myself to step back, think about my work and be mindful of the kind of life I am living. This way, I get a clearer picture of how I can carry out my work efficiently and plan the day ahead. Above all else, I tell myself that my work has to be broken up into chunks, it doesn't have to be perfect and it doesn't all have to be done. That saves me every time.

Finding your rhythm

There is a simple key to almost everything you do at home – organisation. If you start out by decluttering, then get into the habit of organising your food shopping, cupboards, clothes, cleaning, washing, dishes, craft supplies and garden, you will almost always be able to do your housework efficiently. It will help a lot if you set everything up well at the beginning but don't be afraid to change what isn't working for you as you go along. What you are aiming for here is to get rid of all the things you don't need, manage your time well by developing a routine that will help you get through your chores, then work to your own rhythm every day.

Time management

Time management will help you do the work you need to do so you have time for the things you want to do. Time is managed most effectively if you're organised and work to a regular routine. You can work out for yourself what system best suits you and the amount of time you have, by first sitting down and thinking about your life and the many elements in it. Have a pen and notebook handy because you'll need to list your priorities and then go on to map out a plan of what will work for you.

It doesn't matter if you're a full-time homemaker, if you're working full-time outside the home or anything in between; you will benefit from shaping a way of doing your housework that is efficient, effective and productive. When we do certain things each day, we train our brain to expect that action. They say it takes about three weeks to modify behaviour and establish a habit, so don't expect it all to fall into place overnight.

Sometimes, when I have a deadline to meet, housework to do, and voluntary work, gardening, cooking and my family to tend to, I feel a slight panic – how will I ever get it done? At those times I've taught myself to step back, think about my work and be mindful of the kind of life I am living. When I do that, when I take a step back rather than racing headlong into it, I get a clearer picture of how I can carry out my work efficiently and plan the day ahead. Above all else, I have to tell myself that my work has to be broken up into chunks, it doesn't have to be perfect and it doesn't all have to be done. That saves me every time.

Slowing down

I grew up in a much slower time, a time when bread was delivered by horse and cart and a ginger beer merchant sold his product, from a cart, door to door. Believe it or not, that was the start of the commercialisation of food. Previously, mothers and grandmas had made bread and ginger beer at home. A few years later we started taking our saucepan to the local Chinese shop (very infrequently, I must add) for a treat of takeaway Chinese food – well before any thoughts of plastic or polystyrene containers. These were slow times with lazy Sunday roast lunches, talking to the neighbours over the back fence and train travel, when you'd take a Thermos flask of tea and sandwiches to eat en route. It was a time when you'd often hear, 'We'll do it tomorrow,' 'It has to cook for three hours,' and 'Let it sit and ferment for a few days.' Nothing was rushed.

When I was a young mum, I spent time with my family, worked full-time, studied for a degree, was on school committees, had to drive three hours each way to reach the shops, spent time with friends and generally had a good time. I was certainly busy, but I always took time to sit and talk to my sons and my friends, and if anyone asked me to do something I could usually fit it in. I don't remember feeling rushed, or stressed. And I'm sure other people were the same. Now I hear so many people say they're busy and you see and hear this message all the time in the media too: 'Everyone is busy.'

Slow down, think about what you're doing, experience it fully, and get something out of it.

Now, it's quite possible I'm wrong, but family life seems to be pretty similar to how we experienced it all those years ago, and people don't actually seem to fit more into their lives than they used to. I know many mothers didn't work outside the home, but plenty did. So what is it about life now that makes people stressed? I wonder if it's the pressures of keeping a job, worrying about the mortgage or how to pay the rent, rushing to get things done and not taking time out when it's needed. Does that add up to people being overwhelmed and feeling as if they don't have a spare minute?

Whatever it is, if you feel you are busy or rushed all the time, I encourage you to slow down, and *take more time* to do your work. It may surprise you when you get more done and feel better for it. When I closed down my business to return to my home, initially I rushed through my housework to make sure I got it all done. I never did, so I felt anxious and inadequate. Then I had one of my Eureka! moments, realising that

housework never ends, and I slowed down, took whatever time it took and concentrated on my work, and came out better for it. And I got more work done. Rushing doesn't facilitate work; it blurs it, making you feel you're constantly behind and you have to hurry. Remember that fable, 'The Hare and the Tortoise'? The tortoise, slow and steady, came first.

This minute is all you have. Yesterday has gone, tomorrow hasn't happened; you only have now. If you constantly rush through what you're doing, thinking of what you'll do next, you don't truly experience your minutes or your hours. Slow down, think about what you're doing, experience it fully, and get something out of it. Everything you do is part of your life. Make your minutes memorable.

When you're more relaxed you'll feel more capable, you'll be able to do what you have to do and you won't get into bed at night exhausted and wondering what you did all day. If you've made a commitment to yourself to live a more simple life and you know that it will be better for your family, start by slowing down and looking at your work as being productive and creative, not just as chores to be rushed.

Home management journals

There is no doubt about it, simple life is easier when everything is organised. Quite a bit of the information we use in our simple homes is freely available, but you need to actively gather it and keep it in one place.

A few years ago I started a home management journal that turned into a kind of all-purpose encyclopaedia of the practical things we do here. When I started making soap I collected recipes from the web, from people I know and from books – they all went in the journal. I experimented with those recipes and now that I have my favourite soap recipes, only they remain in the journal. Bread was the same – I collected a lot of recipes and info about technique and ingredients and placed it in my journal. I worked with them all and chose what suited us, then got rid of the rest. Launching the household into a more natural cleaning regime added yet more information to the journal. Then came vegetable garden plans and planting times, seed catalogues, harvests, egg numbers, the dates we bought new chooks, the chooks' names, how to knit mittens, weather and rain records, telephone numbers and email addresses. It's an ever-evolving thing – now I'm collecting knitting and sewing patterns for babies and finding information about working effectively with solar panels. As I collect what I want to keep as reference materials, it is all added to the journal.

I would like you to make your own home management journal. It can be like mine: a ring binder with some hole-punched hand-written pages, some printed pages, and some plastic sheet protectors to hold things like business cards, seed catalogues, your budget, to-do lists, school schedules, your calendar, water and electricity meter readings, menu plans and grocery lists. Or it can be something else. It can be as fancy or plain as you care to make it; it can be anything you want it to be. Whatever it looks like, it should hold all those loose pieces of household and garden information that need to be in one place. You will build it up over the years, and it's important to review it every six months or so to keep it as current as possible. I transfer everything I'm not currently using into a second folder. I guess that's my history folder – an archive that shows my journey as much as this book does. Look around the house for an old folder you can use, or buy one when you're out shopping, so that you can start adding those vital pieces of information to your own home management journal.

Decluttering

Opening up your home and your life

One of the most liberating and symbolic things you can do on your journey to simplified living is to declutter your home. It's liberating because you don't have to look after all that junk any more, and it's symbolic because it opens up your home and your mind while rejecting a more materialistic past life. It's amazing how energised you feel after getting rid of the items you no longer need or want. Clear your cupboards out so you can let more life in.

We all have 'stuff' in our lives: junk that we keep because we think it's important, or because we haven't thought to throw it out or because we believe we might need it someday. Get tough with yourself and your possessions; they are holding you down under the weight of a hundred Saturday shopping trips and all those unwanted birthday and Christmas gifts. How many times have you 'needed' something, tried looking for it in your home and given up before you found it? How many times have you bought a replacement for that item, then found the old one a week later? Those days are over.

When you've decluttered your home you'll be surprised at just how much expensive junk you've paid money for and kept over the years. Keep only those things that you really need or those that give you pleasure. If something is kept in a cupboard and you don't see it for months or years, get rid of it. When you finish your first decluttering session, look at what you have left and enjoy it.

Clear your cupboards out so you can let more life in.

Decluttering is a major investment in your future wellbeing. Don't try to declutter your entire house in one purging frenzy. Do it properly; it's not a race. This is a readjustment to your life and it needs to be done with care and consideration. Concentrate on one room or one area at a time. Do one room a week until you've finished, then revisit every room and make sure you got everything.

ACTION PLAN: *Decluttering*

There are hundreds of ways to declutter. This is how I do it

* Get four large boxes or garbage bags and mark them: 'Put away', 'Give away', 'Sell' and 'Rubbish'.

* Start at the door of the room and work in one direction around the room.

* When you pick something up, don't put it down anywhere except in one of the bags or boxes. If you're not sure about an item, ask yourself these questions:

  • Is this important to me or my family?
  • Would I be sad if I didn't have this?
  • Have I used this in the past year?

* Don't leave the room to put things away until you've finished, or you'll take too long. If the 'Put away' box is full before you've finished, put those things in their rightful places, then continue.

* Never skip an area, even if it seems overwhelming – just take more time with it. Just starting is the biggest step for some areas. Keep that in mind and if it looks like too big a job, tell yourself that you'll work on it for fifteen minutes. Set a timer and when fifteen minutes is up, stop. Often you'll find that this will be enough to make a big dent in a problem area. You can go back and finish it later, even if you do it fifteen minutes at a time.

* When the boxes/bags are full, everything in the 'Put away' box should be put away in the appropriate place in your home, and everything in the 'Give away' box can be given to charity, family, friends or neighbours. Take your 'Sell' box to the garage and keep it with other things you want to sell on eBay or at a big garage sale you could organise at the end of your decluttering. When you make money by selling those items, don't waste it. Put it towards the mortgage or in your emergency or savings account. It's not extra money; it's money you've earned. The 'Rubbish' items can be put into the rubbish bin or recycle bin.

* As you work through your rooms, resist the temptation to clean while you go. Leave things tidy but save your cleaning and organising for another day. When all your decluttering is finished and you have moved all the boxes to their appropriate places, go back to each room and assess what needs to be done next. Now that you've removed all the excess items you can really clean and organise your rooms into functional areas that support the way you want to live.

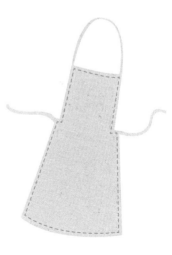

Routines

How a routine helped me

Establishing a housekeeping routine that suits you can be a daunting task. When I took up the broom and pegs as my tools of trade, I started with a little list of jobs I would do within a certain amount of time. For instance, I would shower, write my blog, feed the animals and chooks, make breakfast, make the bed and make bread all before my self-imposed time limit of 9 a.m. By twelve o'clock I had to have swept the floor, cleaned the kitchen benches and stove, and done any laundry that needed doing. Keeping a list of tasks within a flexible timeframe helped and I was surprised that, in the space of about a month, I had established a routine for myself that felt comfortable and easy to work with – and it got my housework done.

When I had that rhythm, I slowed down and started thinking about what I was doing. Sweeping the floor, making the bed, washing up, cooking from scratch, growing vegetables, collecting eggs and baking bread all connected me to my female ancestors. Hanno's grandparents had a very productive garden that he often talks about. I have no doubt he feels connected to them when he's planting and harvesting. When I made that ancestral connection, I started liking most of what I did, because I saw it all in a different light. I was taking control and making the house exactly how I wanted it to be, rather than cooking and cleaning up after everyone. I looked for new things to learn, I started making a lot of what we were using, I began to live more generously and I settled into my home. At last, I felt truly comfortable living and working there.

When I look back on it, I know that getting into the rhythm of doing chores each day, understanding what I was doing and not rushing through my work changed my habits and established positive new ones.

Establishing your own routine

I'd like to share with you five things you can do every day to help establish your own routine. As you can see, they are very common tasks that most of us need to do each day.

- Make the beds and tidy the bedrooms. When they are old enough, teach your children to make their own beds. This should be one of their chores so they contribute to the running of the home and learn how to look after themselves. Don't expect perfection from them but expect them to do it every day.
- Sweep the floor.
- Wash up or run the dishwasher.
- Organise and tidy one area a day. This might be the laundry, kids' rooms, the family room or your finances, snail mail or email.
- Make sure you know what you'll eat today and tomorrow.

If the list helps you, expand on it with a second list of five. This second list will be specific to you and your circumstances – whether you have children or not, whether you work outside the home or not, and it would possibly change according to where you live. For example, if you live in an apartment, your chores would be different from those you would need to do in a house with a garden and chooks.

If you can make a realistic list, with times on certain activities, it will probably help you get through your work. Earlier in the book I wrote about how housework never ends and I always keep that in mind, especially when I'm very busy.

As I've mentioned, the best way for me to work is to divide my work into time periods – this, for me, is usually morning and afternoon, but it could be any time that you're prepared to do the work, such as early morning and the evening.

ACTION PLAN: *Daily routine*

✳ Let's say I had the following chores to do on one day: bake bread, clean kitchen, make bed, tend garden, check worm farm, feed worms and chooks, pick and blanch vegetables, make tomato sauce and process it in water bath, do laundry, sweep floor, wash up, make dinner, write, answer emails, mend and knit.

✳ First I would decide which I would do in the morning and which in the afternoon.

Morning

- make bed
- feed chooks
- load washing machine
- make bread and set to rise
- make tomato sauce and process – leave jars to cool
- bake bread
- clean kitchen
- wash up
- hang out washing
- collect eggs
- sweep floor
- write until lunch (this last one is restricted by the amount of time I have)

✳ Then I would have lunch and relax for a while.

Afternoon

- feed worms
- tend garden and pick vegetables
- blanch vegetables, set to cool, then freeze
- two hours of writing
- knit for thirty minutes or so
- bring laundry in and fold
- make dinner, answer emails while it's cooking
- eat dinner, clean up kitchen and wash up

✱ If I felt like it, I could mend after dinner, but usually I'm tired by then, so it could wait till tomorrow. If I was falling behind, or feeling tired, I could leave the tomato sauce or blanching until tomorrow as well. I could spend more time writing and not knit.

As you can see, I do a fair bit of juggling and I think that gives me some leeway. The important thing is to do the work in blocks of time. Don't toil for hours on one thing. Do a bit, do something else, then come back to your longer job. It does make it easier.

And I always remember:

- I can move chores around.
- I can put things off till tomorrow.
- I don't have to finish everything.
- It doesn't have to be perfect, it just has to be the best I can do on that day.
- I'm not living in a showroom; this is my home.

Sometimes I don't do any work at all. If I've had a really busy time at work and at home, I give myself a day off to recover. That day off is a powerful thing. I want to look after myself and I want to enjoy my work. I'm in this for the long haul; I don't want my housework to become a burden. I'm sure many of you think it's an absolute luxury to have a day off but I am at the stage of life when it is possible and necessary. If you can't give yourself an entire day, make sure you take an hour. It's important; it will make a difference.

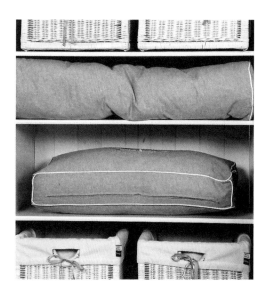

Remember, whether you're the bread-winner and doing housework, the mother of young children or a new baby, working at a small home business while being a full-time housekeeper, or struggling in any way to keep up with things, take time out. It might sound like the wrong thing to do because it takes more time, but if you get sick, it will be worse for everyone. Give yourself as much care as you give everyone else and take time out to regenerate when you need it. Doing that is a strength, not a weakness.

Some household tasks need to be done only once a week. These commonly include menu planning, grocery shopping, changing the sheets and towels, ironing, vacuuming, cleaning the bathroom and kitchen, dusting, mending, paying bills and gardening. Write your weekly list, then you can plan what you will do on which day. For example, in my daily routine on the previous page, I could replace the tomato-sauce making or doing the washing with any of these weekly chores. Add something from your weekly list as often as you can. This will help you get through your weekly tasks as well as the daily ones.

> *Give yourself as much care as you give everyone else and take time out to regenerate when you need it.*

One routine might not cover all you need to do at home, so you could break down your routines into smaller sets that relate to different tasks and times. The most important thing is that you have a routine that works for you. If you're working to a fairly loose time frame, tell yourself you have to have finished a certain set of chores before a certain time. If you're on a stricter schedule, put times next to each task. This is supposed to help you, not stress you. If the routine doesn't work, modify it to suit your needs.

I know there are many of you who struggle to get everything done. I know there are some who don't do much at all and feel guilty about it, but can't seem to find the motivation to do what you feel you should. I hope that sharing how I work, and how I feel about it, may help you with your work. Try to work with an open heart. You are your own boss in your home; be kind to yourself and take the pressure off – you don't need to be perfect. If you have trouble starting, set the timer for fifteen minutes and make yourself get up and work solidly for that quarter of an hour. Anyone can do that. When fifteen minutes is up, rest, then set your timer again. You'll be surprised how much you can achieve like this.

Quick organisation tips for the busy home

- **Get up early:** This is a difficult one to develop but if you can do it, it will make a big difference to your day. Getting up before anyone else gives you extra quality time. The phone won't ring, the children will be asleep; you will be able to do more between 6 a.m. and 7 a.m. than between 6 p.m. and 7 p.m. You can either do something you want to do for yourself but never get time for, or start on the laundry, do the ironing or make school and work lunches.

- **Write lists:** If you're a list person, or until you get into the rhythm of your home, writing a to-do list each day will probably make your day-to-day life run more smoothly. However, be prepared to be flexible with your list so that if important things crop up, you include them. Plan your trip to the shops according to your list and when you're out, try to get everything you need so you won't have to make several trips. If you work outside the home most days this sort of organisation is even more important.

- **Plan your menus:** Having your meals organised will help make you more relaxed for your other tasks. You'll know what you'll be preparing for dinner that night and have all the ingredients waiting for you. No last-minute panic, no rushing to the store to buy something that is missing.

- **Delegate:** Children benefit if they grow up knowing they contribute in a practical way to their home. Give them tasks, within the limits of their ages and abilities, that help with the overall running of the house and teach them how to look after themselves in the process. From an early age they can start by putting dirty clothes in the laundry hamper, picking up toys and feeding the cat, and progress to more involved tasks as they mature.

- **Do a bit of housework every day:** If you're working outside the home try to do some housework every day. You might clean the bathroom, wash a load of laundry or vacuum the family room. Whatever you can manage during the week will keep your home in order and give you more time on the weekend to spend with the family.

- **Say no to time wasters:** Turn off the TV, walk away from the computer, say no to the neighbour who always pops in for morning coffee. Say no to whatever it is that lures you away from what you have to do and want to do. This will free you up to build the kind of life you want. It will give you time with your family, for exercise, to spend on sewing, or a spare thirty minutes to sit alone with your thoughts and a cup of tea.

- **Stockpile:** Stockpiling groceries can turn your weekly trip to the supermarket into one that you do maybe once a month. Shopping once a month instead of weekly will free up quite a few hours for other things you need or want to do.

- **Say goodbye to morning stress:** Most families are in a rush in the morning, and doing a few extra things at night can help a great deal. Do a quick tidy up, make the next day's lunches, put on a load of laundry or pick out clothes to be worn the next day before you go to bed – you'll have more time the following morning.

Organising your belongings

The linen cupboard

It's an important part of my homemaker's responsibilities to properly care for everything that is used in our home. Our hard-earned money has been used to buy or make the sheets, quilts, towels, napkins and tablecloths we use, and I want them to last as long as possible and to look fresh and lovely when we use them. So when the seasons call me to take the quilts from the beds, and when they are returned to the beds later in the year when it's cool again, I organise the linen cupboard. If I organise the cupboards and have everything neatly folded and in its place, I know if items need to be repaired or recycled. I check everything as it's being put back in the cupboard after washing, so mending and repurposing happen in a timely manner and the linen cupboard doesn't often become untidy or out of control.

It's a good idea, although not always possible, to have a dedicated linen cupboard where you keep sheets, pillowcases, towels, face washers, tablecloths, napkins and any other household linens you may have. The shelves or drawers should be painted or lined, because untreated wood may stain whatever sits on it.

The shelves at eye height and within easy reach should be used to store your most frequently used linens, like towels and sheets. Use your top and bottom shelves for items like quilts and blankets that you don't use as often. Experiment with the folding of each item so that you use your shelves efficiently, and always put the folded side to the front. It will make the cupboard easier to look after, it will look tidy and functional each time you go to it and it will be a pleasure to use.

When you organise the linen cupboard, check your fabrics for wear and tear. If a towel or sheet is too damaged to repair and is pure cotton or linen, cut it up for cleaning cloths instead of throwing it away. If it's a poly/cotton blend, you may be able to patch it together to make fabric storage bags for your quilts or blankets. Try to re-use these things in some way instead of throwing them out.

Sheets and towels

I keep sheets of the same size and shape together, but you could also sort your sheets into sets. I have found that having two or three sets of sheets and pillowcases in the cupboard for each bed will give you a good rotation and you'll get quite a few years' wear out of them. Dust mites that cause allergies live in bedding, and washing the sheets and pillowcases weekly after use will keep this to a minimum. After washing, fold them to your requirements and store at the bottom of the sheet stack in the cupboard. Always take your clean sheets from the top of the stack. Rotating your sheet sets like this will keep them looking fresh for years.

Sort your towels into colours and sizes and stack them on the shelf with the folded side to the front. Take new towels from the top and put clean towels back into the stack at the bottom. Rotate them in the same way as your sheets.

I wash all our laundry, including towels and sheets, with homemade laundry powder or liquid (the recipes are in the previous chapter) and sometimes add a little white vinegar in the final rinse. This softens them and helps remove all traces of laundry powder or liquid. The towels will come out smelling slightly of vinegar but when they are dry the smell is completely gone.

Quilts and blankets

If your quilts and blankets are to be put away for a period of time, try to find a fabric or plastic bag to store them in to keep moths and insects away. The plastic zippered covers that doonas are often sold in are ideal for storing blankets, and this is a good second use for the packaging that would otherwise be thrown away. If you don't have one of these bags, you could make a large calico bag.

Make sure your blankets, quilts or doonas are clean before you store them. Storing anything with a spill on it will attract silverfish and cockroaches. Check the care instructions on the blanket or doona and, if possible, wash it gently and dry outside. Woollen blankets that are in use on the beds should be washed in cold water and dried in the shade every six weeks, and again at the end of the cold season just before storing them away. Adding a splash of eucalyptus oil to the wash will protect the wool from moths. Do not wash woollen blankets in hot water or hang them in hot sun – this will shrink them. Cotton and synthetic blankets can be washed in the washing machine every six weeks and dried in the sun. Quilts and doonas can be machine washed if your washing machine is big enough and has a gentle wash and spin cycle; otherwise, take them to the laundromat to wash in their large machines.

If you cannot wash your doonas and quilts, hang them in the sunlight, with the underside facing the sun, to air and sanitise every couple of months. Blankets, quilts and doonas will all be sanitised if they're hung in the sun to dry. Make sure everything is completely dry before storing, otherwise you may have a problem with mildew.

> **HERB BAGS**
>
> Small calico, cotton or linen bags containing herbs or aromatic leaves can be easily made and are very useful in a linen cupboard. Any herb with a strong aroma is suitable. I sometimes use crushed bay leaves, lavender, mint, rose petals or lemon myrtle leaves. You can either sew small bags for the herbs or just use an old handkerchief and tie the herbs in with a small piece of ribbon.

Clothes and shoes

If possible, most of your clothing should be on coathangers in a wardrobe. This will allow them to be stored crease-free and protected from sunlight and dust. If they are seasonal clothes and will not be used for a while, wash them before hanging or folding. Fold woollen jumpers and cardigans and store them in a drawer – keeping them on a hanger during the year will misshape the shoulders. If you have the time and spare fabric, make cotton storage bags or find large recycled plastic bags for your woollen jumpers and cardigans to keep moths and insects at bay. Adding cedar disks to the coat hangers or cedar balls to the drawers will also help guard against moths.

Store shoes, in pairs, in a cupboard. Make sure your shoes are clean if they're to sit there for a few months. If you have a long period of wet weather, check your leather shoes and handbags for mould and mildew. If you find it is growing, wipe it off with a rag dipped in white vinegar. When the area is dry again, wipe it over with one drop of oil of cloves on a clean rag. The oil of cloves will help prevent the mould growing back.

Mending

Sometimes I come across a small rip or missing button in the course of my day but I usually find mending jobs when I'm washing, ironing or putting things away. I look carefully at the fabrics and fasteners and put aside any that need repair. I have a mending box in my sewing room where torn clothes and broken household goods sit until I have enough for a mending session. If you're new to mending and repairing, get into the habit of collecting buttons, buckles and clips that you find in your home. Have a small, recycled jar handy to collect them so that when you find the shirt or dress with the button or clip missing, you'll know exactly where to go to find it. When you're ironing, check hems and collars so you can repair them before they get out of hand. Caring for household linens and clothes is a small part of caring for your family and your home. It is a simple and ordinary task that can be a silent and private expression of love for your family, the respect you have for your role of homemaker and the importance you place on caring for what you own.

The kitchen

If you've never given your kitchen much thought, now is the time to do it. If you love cooking, a well-organised kitchen will make it a pleasure to work in; if you don't like cooking, a well-organised kitchen will make it easier for you to feed yourself.

The best way to organise a kitchen is to look at the space you have to work with. If you have a modern kitchen with plenty of storage and bench space, have the things you use all the time close to your main workspace. If you have a small kitchen with only one work bench, you may like to use the kitchen table for extra work space or pack your appliances away to make more room. Use hooks on doors, on walls and under high cupboards to hang things. Think about how you work in the kitchen. You may be making things harder for yourself just because things happen to be in the wrong position. Be creative and don't be afraid to try different ways of working. If they don't work, just change back again.

Some kitchen organisation tips

- A tray holding tea, coffee, sugar, honey, teaspoons and tea balls near the cupboard you store your cups and mugs in would be handy if you make tea and coffee regularly.
- Your plates and bowls should either be close to the stove so you can reach for them when you're serving food, or close to the dishwasher so it's easier to unpack and put things back in their place. If they're close to both, that's a bonus.
- Keep your tea towels, cheesecloths, tea cosies, jug covers, cloth napkins and tablecloths either in the kitchen or close to it.
- Store your plastic wrap, baking paper, aluminium foil, freezer bags and greaseproof paper in a drawer close to your working bench.
- If you bake a lot, put all your baking equipment together.
- If you have young children, make sure they can reach the items they need – and can't reach the breakables.
- Store your kitchen cleaning kit under the sink so it's always at hand.

Reducing, recycling and re-using

A good way to deal with garbage is to reduce the amount of packaging you bring into your home. I don't buy little packets of anything that is packaged in a bigger pack; I try to buy large containers to decant into smaller ones at home. My general strategy on packaging is to buy in bulk when I can, and buy products stored in paper, cans or glass. If they're in plastic, I check what type of plastic it is and if it's recyclable in my area and I need it, I buy it.

> I don't buy anything that is over-packaged, and I try to find someone in the store to explain that I want the product but won't buy it because it's over-packaged. The more people who do this the better, otherwise manufacturers don't know.

Not every local area recycles every type of plastic. Check your own shire council or local authority to see what their facilities recycle. If you're in Australia, you can find your nearest recycle station online. Learn what types of paper, cardboard and plastic your local rubbish dump accepts, then monitor your shopping to buy only that type of packaging.

I keep glass jars and some glass and plastic bottles. They come in very handy when I'm making jam, relish, chutney, lemon butter, ginger beer and cordials.

Taking the time to organise your work and storage areas and looking after what you own will pay off in the long run. Being tidy, doing simple maintenance when it's needed, organising cupboards, keeping things clean and being aware of how you store your possessions will keep everything in good order. Being organised will help you create a productive home that, hopefully, will help you feel in control and calm. There is something about a clean and tidy cupboard that makes you go back again and admire it. Try it – I'm sure you'll agree with me.

HOME-GROWN SELF-RELIANCE

Being a gardener helps you become a provider
of fresh, local food in your own kitchen.
With careful planning you can provide food
you often cannot buy in the supermarket and,
even if it's the same, your garden produce will
be fresher than anything you can buy. You
have never really tasted a potato until you taste
a new potato, dug that afternoon and steamed
with butter and parsley. Almost all foods taste
better when they're grown in backyards
and eaten soon after picking.

Gardening grows the spirit

For many of us, being able to grow some of our own food is an important part of simple living. Being a gardener helps you become a provider of fresh, organic food in your own kitchen, at a thrifty price. With careful planning you can provide food you often cannot buy in the supermarket and, even if it's the same, your garden produce will be fresher than anything you can buy. You have never really tasted a potato until you taste a new potato, dug that afternoon and steamed with butter and parsley. Almost all foods taste better when they're grown in backyards and eaten soon after picking.

But gardening isn't just about freshness and taste; it's also a life skill. It's one our ancestors took seriously because it helped them survive. They learnt all they could about growing food and made sure they passed that skill on to their children. We don't do that now, and here we are with the luxurious option of choosing whether to produce food in our backyard or to buy it. Of course, for some of us that option has been taken away by illness or lack of time or outdoor space, but those who have the choice should grab it with both hands. Learn how to produce the foods that will grow in your area and show your children the satisfaction and pleasure of gardening.

Gardening also helps you slow down. Growing plants is about time: the slowness and never-ending nature of it. If you use that time in a meaningful and productive way it has the potential to make you healthier, in mind and body. Your garden will not allow you to rush – there is a time for planning and a natural requirement for preparation and attention to detail.

If you're lucky, not only will you harvest healthy vegetables and fruits, but you'll grow in confidence and blossom in spirit too.

When you decide you want to start growing your own vegetables, take your time and make sure you're planting the right things for your climate. When you know what to plant, make sure you have the right varieties. This is especially necessary if you have a short growing season because you only have one chance at a crop each year. If this is your first year in the garden, take it slow, don't overdo it, and be patient. Take the time to discover your soil and backyard. Listen to the birds, look at the insects and come to know them – they are not all bad and some can be your friend rather than your enemy. When you're in the garden, be there, both physically and mentally. Don't think of what you'll be doing later. There is a lot to learn in any garden. If you're lucky, not only will you harvest healthy vegetables and fruits, but you'll grow in confidence and blossom in spirit too.

Enriching your soil

There is one thing you can do that will improve your harvests and the quality of your produce more than any other: enrich your soil before you start planting. There is an old gardeners' saying that is as true today as when it was first said: 'Feed the soil, not the plant.' Garden soil is not just rock particles, organic matter, water and air; good soil also contains microbes, fungus, worms, nematodes and a range of other 'life' that hasn't yet been identified. Good soil is alive.

If you're starting off with mediocre soil that has struggled to produce food in previous years, or has never been productive, I urge you to work on your soil before you even think about planting. When we started vegetable and fruit gardening fourteen years ago, the soil here was undisturbed, heavy clay. We started by enriching the soil and making compost long before we planted anything. Then we planted various plants directly into bucket-size pockets in the soil that we filled with compost. We had small yields during those first years, but eventually, with continued additions of compost and other organic matter such as lawn clippings and manure, we eventually turned that heavy clay soil into fertile, free-draining, rich loam.

We like to dig our garden. We believe you get the best crops and the full measure of your soils – with all the nutrients and minerals they can provide – if you plant directly into the topsoil. If you keep your topsoil alive by adding worm castings, worm liquid, manures and compost, you'll be giving whatever you plant the best chance of producing maximum crops and keeping your soil healthy at the same time.

Even if you've been working on your soil for a while, you need to keep enriching it every year. Each season you plant, that crop of plants will use the nutrients you add to the soil. So adding organic matter and supplementing the soil are continuing tasks.

Garden soil is not just rock particles, organic matter, water and air. Good soil is alive.

If you've never planted anything in your garden before, you'll need to know the pH level – the level of acidity/alkalinity – of your soil. Dig your soil over and test it for pH. You can buy cheap pH testing kits at the nursery and in the garden sections of large department stores. Some plants like a higher acid soil, some like it more alkaline, but the vast majority of vegetables grow well in a pH range of 6–7. If your soil is too acid – under pH6 – add agricultural lime to help balance it out. If it is too alkaline – pH8 or above – add compost and organic matter. Then water the garden. You are trying to encourage microbes and worms to live there and it must be moist and nutritious for that to happen. As soon as you start adding compost and other organic matter like manure, and if you keep the garden moist, the garden worms will come from nowhere. They will further help you break up the soil because they'll burrow through it, making tunnels for water and nutrients to flow. They will eat and excrete and, over time, will help develop the life in your soil.

Soil types

To see what kind of soil you have, wet some soil, scoop it out into your hand and roll it into a sausage shape. If the sausage stays firm and doesn't fall apart, you've got clay. If the sausage won't hold its shape and keeps falling apart, you have sandy soil. If it holds its shape but as you roll it in the palm of your hand, it breaks apart slightly, it's good loam – the best of all soils.

Clay soil

Clay soil contains a lot of nutrients but it has poor drainage. You will have to enrich it to stop your plants drowning when it rains, but if you improve the structure of the soil and the drainage, and continue to improve it every season, you'll release the nutrients and have great soil. Add a couple of barrow loads of compost to each garden bed and on top of that sprinkle over a few handfuls of gypsum. Gypsum is an organic compound that will improve the soil structure and help with drainage. When you have added the compost and the gypsum, dig the bed over to mix it all together. Add a thick layer of straw mulch and enough water to moisten the soil, and wait for two weeks before you use the bed.

Sandy soil

The solution for fixing sandy soil is almost the same as the one above for clay soil, but instead of using gypsum, you'll need manure and compost. Dig the garden bed over and add as much compost as possible. Then spade over horse, cow, sheep or pig manure that you know is weed-free. You can often buy animal manure at roadside stalls on the outskirts of cities; if not, you'll find it at your local nursery or large department store's gardening section. Dig it all in and mix everything into the soil. Cover with a thick layer of straw mulch and water it. Allow the bed to settle for two weeks before you plant anything.

Loam

Loam is what we all aim for, but even loam should be enriched before you plant your season's seeds or seedlings. You'll increase your chance of success if you plant into fertile soil that is teeming with microbes and organic matter. No amount of fertiliser added later will equal the benefits of having the plant's roots in rich soil.

Other tips for soil

When you're starting to set up the garden, think also about your natural fertilisers. Some plants, like comfrey, send down deep tap roots that mine the soil for minerals. Those minerals are stored in the leaves of the plant, so when you use something like comfrey for fertilising or activating your compost, you'll get the benefit of the high-nitrogen leaves and the minerals they contain. Comfrey will grow in poor soil but it likes moisture while it gets established. It grows better from roots than from seeds. It is a good idea to plant comfrey at the edges of your garden but be sure of the place you plant it in. Even though it does not spread by growing outwards, like bamboo it will regrow from a tiny piece of root: once it's in, it's difficult to get rid of.

If you have chooks, let them into the garden while you're building up the soil. They'll scratch around, leave their droppings, eat bugs and insect eggs that you can't see and generally improve the fertility of the soil simply by being there. We let our chooks into the garden in the month before we do our main planting in March. They eat the comfrey down to the roots, pick all the leaves from the capsicums, turn over the compost heap several times and eat every caterpillar and grasshopper in the place. We don't worry about the damage; the leaves grow back and the chooks do much more good than harm. Because of their hard work, we start off our gardening year with a clean slate. Once you plant seedlings and have your garden in full production, you'll have to keep the chickens out of your garden.

QUICK SOIL TIPS

- Start a compost heap.
- Dig the soil over and remove the weeds.
- Test for pH and make any necessary adjustments.
- Add compost and organic matter like cow, horse, pig or sheep manures.
- Let the chickens in to scratch and feed while you're preparing the garden.
- Once you've planted your seeds and seedlings, fence the garden off from chickens and pets.
- Water the soil and apply mulch to keep the soil moist.

Choosing what to grow

When you take up your trowel and fork and start planting vegetable seeds for the first time, there is a very strong tendency to overdo it or to dive in with no thought of order, outcome or orthodoxy. When the gardening bug grabs you, you're in it for production; nothing else matters. Or does it?

It will help you considerably if you can think a little about what you're about to plant, because if you're in your early years of gardening and you overdo it, or go through a season with few vegetables making it to your kitchen table, you might give up. I don't want that to happen. Never give up because it's too difficult – in gardening or anything else. You just need to think about your planting in a different way, work out your strategy and start again. You learn the best lessons from your own mistakes or when times are tough.

The first thing to do if you're planning your first vegetable garden is to decide what you'll plant. Find a good organic vegetable gardening book suitable for the climate you live in, or do some research on the internet (check the resources at the back of the book for suggestions).

Write a list of your favourite vegetables, then work out, by reading your book or looking online, what can be easily grown in your climate at this particular time of year. Remember, no matter how dearly you want something to grow, it won't grow out of season or if you're in the wrong climate.

There are far too many variables in climate and soil type in Australia for me to give you one good list of vegetables that you should plant in your first garden. However, as an example garden, if you're in the vast area south of Brisbane, a good spring garden might contain tomatoes, lettuce, green beans, peas, radishes, carrots, silverbeet, beetroot, pumpkin, zucchini and onions. In the areas of north of Brisbane, you could plant these same seeds, but from March onwards, right through to the end of the year. Again, be guided by your reference material and learn as you go. It is a good idea to start a plant diary, listing what you plant and when, and the success you had with each plant and harvest.

Don't fret about what you can't grow in your area. Appreciate your successes and focus on growing as many of your favourites as you can. As your gardening skills develop or your living circumstances change, you will be able to grow a bigger variety of vegetables, and plants that gave you problems when you started may suddenly grow in abundance. When you're a gardener, you never stop learning, even when you've been at it for fifty years.

Think big

If you have the space and hope to make your backyard close to self-sufficient, you should plant fruit and nut trees and fruiting vines. The traditional backyard lemon tree is a good start. We have a Eureka lemon planted in our chicken run and it gives us lemons almost all year long. We have a big harvest in late winter that I squeeze and freeze. This results in about 12 litres of lemon juice for cordials, lemon butter and general cooking. Then, by January, the tree is full of lemons again, which we pick as we need them. We also have a couple of Washington Navel orange trees, a pink grapefruit, a mandarin and a few groups of bananas.

Fruit and nut trees generally don't give instant results; growing them is another slow process. We stripped the flowers from our lemon tree for the first two years, which gave it time to establish itself properly before producing fruit. After that we had about twenty lemons the first year, and now it yields well over a hundred per year. The year before we bought this place a pecan tree was planted. It took twelve years to produce nuts and even now it's only a few handfuls.

Fruit vines are much quicker. Passionfruit and grapes will produce fruit in the first year or two. Kiwifruit vines take a few years to start, but it's worth the wait. When you buy your kiwi vines, make sure you ask about pollination. Most vines need another vine for pollination.

Berry fruits also earn a place in the sustainable backyard, and they'll give you fruit in the first year. We've successfully grown strawberries, raspberries and blueberries here. All these will grow well in colder climates but if you're in Queensland, see if you can find a Queensland raspberry – it's a delicious native. Don't forget your recycled fruit either. If you're in a warm climate and buy a good, sweet pineapple with the top still attached, remove the top and strip its bottom leaves. Let the top dry for a week, then plant it in good, rich soil. It will take about eighteen to twenty-four months to produce a pineapple, but if you pick that, twelve months later, another pineapple will grow. After the second year you pull it out and start again.

If you're in a colder climate you can try apples, pears, apricots, peaches and cherries, as well as almonds, walnuts and hazelnuts.

Growing vegetables from seeds

Food seeds are valuable items. They have the potential to feed the people of the world and without seeds, we have no corn, rye, barley, wheat, rice or vegetables. So we should be concerned about who controls our seeds. For the past fifty years or so, companies have been 'hybridising' seeds so they grow to a specific type and size, and in doing so, they remove the ability of that plant to reproduce itself. These seeds are called hybrid or F1 seeds, and are the popular seeds you can buy at the nursery or in supermarkets. They cannot be saved at the end of the season to grow again the following year. When you plant hybrid or F1 seeds, you must go back to the store and buy new seeds every year.

Heirloom seeds

In the old days, before the commercial seed market was established, people collected seeds from their own harvested vegetables and saved them for the following year. This was seen as a very important part of the gardening season because if seeds were not collected and stored correctly, there would be no seeds on hand to grow vegetables the following year. These seeds are what we now know as open-pollinated or heirloom seeds. Seeds used to be swapped with neighbours and bartered for goods; they were a valuable commodity.

Price, availability of old varieties, and the taste of these old vegetables still attract people all round the world to heirloom seeds – myself included. But there is also another advantage: every year open-pollinated seeds grow in your garden, they acclimatise to the specific conditions there. Every year you grow them, they get to know your soils, climate and conditions better, and they will be easier to grow and get good results from.

Whoever controls the seeds controls the food. And that is why it's important for us backyarders to save seeds and keep this valuable seed pool of old vegetables going. Our great grandparents saved them all so we have the choice. We cannot turn our backs on this heritage because it's easier or more convenient to buy seedlings or new seeds each year. There is more information about saving seeds later in the chapter.

Sowing seeds

There are many seeds you can plant straight into the soil, but others benefit from being grown in a container in sheltered conditions, and then being planted as a seedling. If you want a very orderly garden, you might want to plant seedlings rather than seeds in the garden because with seeds you can either over- or under-plant, and some seeds don't germinate so you're left with empty spaces. Planting from a seedling tray will allow you to plant out the garden exactly to your liking and to fill in spaces as they happen.

Medium-sized seeds like tomato and lettuce are best planted in seed-raising trays and grown to seedling stage before being transferred to the garden. We also prefer to raise capsicum, cabbage, leek and celery seeds in trays and plant them out as seedlings. Seeds for root vegetables like carrots, radishes, parsnips, turnips and legumes (peas and beans), are best planted directly into the garden soil. For the rest of your seeds, be guided by the instructions on the seed packet.

TESTING SEEDS

If you're using new seeds, you should be fine as long as you check their use-by date. If you're using older seeds that you've had for a while, or seeds given to you by a friend or seed swapper, you can test them for viability before you plant.

Sprinkle some of the seeds you want to test over some moist paper towel or newspaper. Roll the paper up in a long cigar shape and fold in the ends. Keep the cigar moist for seven to ten days and then check to see if any of the seeds have germinated. If they have, the seeds are fine to use.

Sowing seeds in a tray

When planting seeds in trays, use a good-quality seed-raising mix, not potting mix or garden soil. You need a mix that is open and drains perfectly, with no lumps of bark or charcoal that will stop a tiny seedling from emerging.

Fill the trays, poke your finger into each cell to flatten the soil slightly, then top up the cell with the mix again. Plant according to the instructions on the seed packet. Generally, the larger the seed, the deeper it's planted. So, for tiny seeds, you only have to place them on the top of the soil and scatter seed-raising mix over the top to cover them, then pat down. For a larger seed, plant it at a depth twice its size – so a seed that is ½ mm would be planted 1 mm deep, and a 1 mm seed would be planted 2 mm deep.

Pat the soil down over the top so the seed stays where it is planted, then gently water it in. A hose is too forceful, so get a plastic spray bottle and spray gently. It will take a while to completely wet the soil, but that's what it takes – gardening helps you slow down. The seed and all the soil in the cell need to be saturated, and then the water should freely drain away, leaving a moist seed and cell. The water is what causes the seed to germinate.

Once the tray has been planted up, you must keep it moist. Seedlings don't cope well if you let them dry out, so give them a good spray of water every day. Seeds contain everything, except water, to make them grow – they don't need fertiliser. Once the first few leaves appear you can gently fertilise them, but not before. We deliberately plant more seeds than we need so we can choose the strongest-looking seedlings and discard the weak ones.

Light plays a part too. Seeds don't need any light before they germinate but when they do, they need strong light – not full sunlight, but enough light to cast a shadow. As soon as you see green growth, move them somewhere they'll get good light and will be protected from the wind and rain. As they grow taller, they need stronger light. If seedlings don't get enough light they grow tall and leggy and they'll be weaker plants because of that. Just before I plant my seedlings out, I move them out of the green-house into full sunlight in their tray. This gets them used to full sunlight before they're transplanted.

Sowing seeds in the garden

Large seeds like beans, peas, pumpkin, beetroot and cucumber can generally be sown straight into a garden bed that has been dug over and enriched. They don't need the special care some other seeds need. Plants grown for their roots like carrots, radishes, turnips, parsnips and swedes are also sown directly into the garden soil. If you sow these seeds in a tray, then transplant, you run the risk of the root being damaged or misshapen. Scatter them along a shallow trench then cover with soil mixed with sand. It's better to use this sandy mix because the lighter soil colour will remind you every time you're in the garden that you have tiny seeds in that spot.

You can sow very small seeds like radish and carrot together. Get an old spice or salt shaker, and put the seeds in it along with a spoonful of fine dry sand. Prepare a trench for sowing and shake the seeds in. Cover with soil, and water in very gently with a fine spray. In about a week, the radishes will germinate and grow; the carrots take longer. By the time the radishes are ready to pick, the carrot tops will be showing and they'll be putting on root growth. Harvesting the radishes will make way for all those carrots.

When you plant seeds in the garden bed, you usually plant in dry or almost dry soil. Give large seeds a good watering only once – they will absorb enough water to keep them going until they germinate. When you see green growth, water again. Small seeds can absorb much less water but will easily be dislodged if you blast them with the garden hose. A fine spray once a day is all they need to keep them moist until you see green growth. Then water as normal.

The seeds of legumes need to be treated a bit differently. When planting peas or beans, water the ground well before you plant the seeds. Then place the seeds into the moist soil, according to the spacing directions on the seed packet. Don't water again until you see the new shoots emerge. If legumes get too much moisture, they'll rot.

Fertilising your seedlings

When the seedlings emerge they'll need some food. We only ever use organic fertilisers – either bought or homemade. Generally, as soon as we see the seedlings emerge and put on leaves, either in the garden or in a seedling tray, we fertilise them with weak fish emulsion, weak liquid blood and bone or weak homemade comfrey or worm liquid. Not all of them – just choose one. Comfrey is an excellent homemade fertiliser for both leafy green vegies and for fruiting ones, like tomatoes, chillies, potatoes, cucumbers and capsicums, because it contains calcium, potassium and phosphorus. Use worm liquid, fish emulsion or liquid blood and bone for your non-fruiting leafy vegetables like lettuce, cabbages, spinach, silverbeet and kale. I never go by the recommendations given on the fertiliser container; I find I get better results making a weaker brew and doing it more frequently. I make up a 50 per cent solution and apply it twice as often.

For instance, if your fertiliser instructions recommend making up a 10-litre watering can with two caps of fertiliser concentrate and applying it fortnightly, I would make up a watering can with one capful of concentrate and apply it weekly.

Planting tomatoes

Tomatoes are Australia's most popular backyard crop, so I want to spend a bit more time talking about them. You can plant tomatoes according to the directions on the packet but I do it a little differently. I plant the seeds in punnets or a seed tray as normal and wait for germination. When the plant has grown to be about two inches above the top of the soil, I transplant it to a slightly bigger pot, fertilising with comfrey and a pinch of sulphate of potash (it's organic). Each time I transplant, I water the plants with seaweed tea – this helps to avoid transplant shock. Concentrated seaweed solution can be bought at any gardening store and made up according to the instructions on the bottle.

I wait again until it grows another inch or two, then I transplant it to a slightly larger pot. Each time, I remove the bottom leaves, plant it deep, and water with seaweed tea. This would kill most plants, but tomatoes have the ability to produce more roots along their main stem and the more roots you have on a tomato plant (if it's healthy), the more fruit it will produce. Make sure your tomato seedlings have good light during this period or they will grow long and lanky and that will weaken them.

Keep your tomato seedlings going like this until they're strong and healthy and when you see the first flower, plant them in the garden – again, deep, in soil that has been enriched with compost and to which a teaspoon of sulphate of potash has been added. You might even bury half the stem and have the top half of the tomatoes above the soil. Put the stakes in before you plant the seedlings so you don't damage the roots by doing it later. If the plant is big enough, tie it to the stake straight away; if not, as soon as the tomato grows enough, tie it up before the wind has a chance to snap or damage the stem.

You'll sometimes see new shoots growing at an angle between the main stem and a large side branch. Remove these because if you allow them to grow, they'll make a very bushy plant and you'll get fewer tomatoes. When you cut them off you can make new plants with them. Plant them in a pot to develop roots and grow a bit, then plant out in the garden.

Once you've planted the tomatoes and tied them to their stakes, mulch heavily with straw, packing it in around the stem and up about three inches. Again, most plants would hate this but tomatoes thrive with this treatment. Water the mulch well without watering the tomato leaves. Always water tomatoes from below the plant, never over the top, as splashing mud onto the leaves with the hose will encourage disease. If you mulch well, the tomatoes will send more roots out into the mulch. Do not over-fertilise tomatoes with nitrogen, as it will make the bush grow like mad but you'll get almost no tomatoes.

Make sure you keep staking, and keep the branches off the ground. When the tomatoes are big enough, pick them while they're still green and ripen them in the house, out of the sun. They will develop their full flavour that way and be out of harm's way.

> Tomatoes suffer from a disease called blossom-end rot. This lack of calcium in the plants is caused by inconsistent watering. You'll see a big circle that runs around the blossom-end of the fruit. To avoid this, set up a watering schedule so your plants get consistent watering and don't suffer dry periods.

That's one of many ways of growing tomatoes. I'm sure you won't be disappointed if you try it. Just think of all those delicious tomato sandwiches and jars of tomato relish standing like jewels in your cupboard. If you're growing heirlooms this year, don't forget to save seeds from your very best tomatoes in the middle of the season. Yes, I know it's a huge sacrifice to save *the best* tomatoes, but you want to pass on *the best* seeds.

Saving vegetable seeds

If you're going to save vegetable seeds, you'll need to know how they're pollinated and if the vegetable is annual, biennial or perennial. (Technically, some common things like tomatoes, squash and cucumbers are fruit, but for the purposes of this section, I'm referring to everything as 'vegetable'.) Annuals will produce viable seed in the first year, biennials take two years to mature and produce seed, and perennials produce viable seed in the second year and from then on until the plant dies. Most of the common vegetables we grow in our gardens are annuals.

Points to remember:

- **Seeds need to be dry before you store them**, both inside and out. Initially, you can dry seeds on a clean rag or newspaper, but when they look dry, transfer them to a china or glass plate for a number of days or weeks to dry out completely. Leaving them on the rag or paper will allow them to stick and you might damage the seeds when you move them.

- **Always pick the best examples** of your vegetables when you collect seeds. You provide a stronger gene pool if you have seeds from more than one plant, so look for two or three to collect seeds from.
- **The biggest threat to your seeds is mould.** Make sure they're completely dry and then stored in dry conditions. A fridge is ideal for most seeds. Pack them in a little packet labelled with the name and date of collection, and place that, along with all the other packets or little jars, into a larger sealed plastic box and keep it in the fridge until needed. If you live in very humid conditions and this way of storing doesn't work for you, add a little diatomaceous earth to the seeds, shake off most of it, and store them like that. If you want to be an organic grower, don't use seed fungicides.

Types of seed

For the purpose of seed saving, I categorise vegetables into three groups: wet seeds, dry seeds and legumes.

Wet seeds

Vegetables like tomatoes and cucumbers have wet seeds, with thick flesh around the seed that needs to be removed and, in the case of tomatoes, fermented. Fermentation will happen when you add the seeds to a jar of water and leave it for two to four days. The fermentation process kills viruses that might be present on the seed while separating the viable seed from the bad seed and the pulp. When fermentation is complete, the good seeds will sink to the bottom of the container and the rubbish will float. Scoop the rubbish from the top and pour the rest of the jar's contents into a sieve under running water. Whatever is left of the flesh will come off. Then tip all the clean seeds onto newspaper or a clean rag. When they're dry transfer them to a plate to dry out completely.

Melons and cucumbers don't have to be fermented but can be if you're having problems with plant viruses. If not, watermelon, honeydew melon and cucumber seeds just need to be dried. Scoop the seeds out and put them in a sieve under running water until all the flesh is removed. Then dry them in the same way as the tomato seeds.

Dry seeds

Vegetables like pumpkin, squash and corn have dry seeds. These are the easiest seeds to harvest. Let pumpkin and squash mature for a few days after you pick them. Then cut them open, scoop out the seeds and dry them. To harvest corn seeds, pick all the corn you will eat, leaving behind the best cobs. Let them sit on the plant for another month and when they look dry, pick them, peel back the husks and let them dry out more. Tie the cobs together by the husks, and hang them up to finish drying, then pick the kernels off or rub two corn cobs together and they will fall off. The kernels are the seeds.

Loofahs have wet seeds but can be dried on the vine and treated as dry seeds. They don't have to be fermented. Leave the loofah on the vine until it's brown, then crack it open and pour out the seeds. If you're in a cooler climate, you can pick the loofahs green and store them in a dry place until they turn brown and crackly.

Lettuce, carrots, celery and parsley all form dry seeds in flower heads. You have to wait for the flowers to turn to seed, but if you can't do that for reasons of weather, wait until the flower head is almost ready to seed, then cut the whole flower off and store it in a paper bag in the house. After a couple of weeks you will hear the seeds rattling around in the bag when you shake it. All you have to do then is clean the dried old bits of flower away from the seeds and store them.

Legumes

Beans and peas have pods that are just broken open and the seeds are there waiting. They need to be dried before storing.

Choosing the best plant

In the case of flower-forming vegetables like carrots and lettuce, you only need to put one plant aside to harvest seeds from, but it must be the best plant. Look for vegetables that are healthy and strong and display the qualities you want, such as size, colour and abundance of the harvest. If there is one perfect fruit on the vine, that is not the plant to select. Go instead for a vine or plant that has a good yield of many healthy, good-sized vegetables and pick the best from that plant.

Choose the plant that looks healthy, is true to type and has had a large number of good-quality fruit.

If you have a number of the same plants to collect seeds from, choose the plant that looks healthy, is true to type and has had a large number of good-quality fruit. If any of your plants look diseased, don't collect seeds from them because you'll probably pass on the disease.

Pollination

If you want to save seeds, you'll need to make sure your plants are being pollinated. While your vegetables are growing, look for bees early in the morning. If there are none around, you'll have to hand-pollinate. To do that, go into the garden early in the morning and identify the male and female flowers on the plant you want to pollinate. The male flowers usually have a long, straight stem and anthers inside the flower; female flowers have a small round stigma inside the flower. Pick a strong male flower and peel off the petals to expose the inside of the flower. Find a female flower and lightly apply the male flower to the reproductive parts of the female flower (the stigma). You can usually pollinate three female flowers in this way with one male flower.

CROSS-POLLINATION

Some vegetables can cross-pollinate. That means that insects or wind – whatever pollinates them – takes pollen from one vegetable, such as a particular variety of tomato, and pollinates a different variety of tomato. The seed of that tomato may not grow true to type and you won't grow the tomatoes you expect to grow.

If the vegetables you want seed from are easily cross-pollinated you'll need to plant those vegetables away from their cross-pollinators. For instance, chillies and capsicums may cross-pollinate, even though they're different varieties of the same vegetable, so you need to be mindful of the pollination factor and grow the plants you want to sow seeds from at least 15 metres apart.

If you are serious about your vegetable growing, it's a good idea to grow a small number of flowers in with your vegetables to attract the pollinators like bees and other insects. These flowers can be things like nasturtiums (which are edible), alyssum, cosmos, daisies, marigolds and sunflowers, or flowering herbs such as tansy, oregano, thyme and borage.

If you're going to get involved in saving seeds – and I encourage you to do so – I'd recommend you buy *The Seed Savers' Handbook*, available on the Seed Savers website (seedsavers.net), or join an online forum.

Fertilising

Most plants like to be planted into rich soil, then fertilised at regular periods to grow at their best. It is quite easy to make your own fertiliser if you grow comfrey, keep chickens or worms, or make compost. Homemade fertilisers are very effective and don't contain any harsh chemicals that might be present in the commercial products. If you can't make your own, look for a good commercial organic fertiliser to keep your vegetables and garden free of chemicals.

Homemade fertilisers

Comfrey liquid fertiliser

Cut the leaves from the comfrey plant before it flowers and throw the leaves into a bucket that has a lid. Half-fill the bucket with the leaves and put a brick on top of them to stop them floating. Fill the bucket with water and put the lid on. It will smell . . . a lot. Stir it every couple of days and in two or three weeks you'll have a nice brown nitrogen-rich liquid that is an excellent feed for your plants.

Strain the leaves out of the mixture and put them in the compost. Comfrey makes an excellent compost activator. To use comfrey fertiliser in the garden, simply add a cup of comfrey concentrate to a watering can full of water and pour on. If you want to use it as a foliar spray – it is easily taken up by plant leaves – add a cup of your comfrey mix to every bucket of water and add a small amount of grated or liquid soap to help it stick to the leaves when you spray it on.

Manure tea

Take two full shovels of manure (either horse, cow, sheep or pig) or one shovel of chook poo, and place it in a hessian bag. Secure the top with string so everything stays in the bag – like a tea bag. Place the bag in a large barrel and fill to the top with water. Put a lid on the barrel and let it sit for two weeks to mature. To use this mixture, first dilute it so it looks like weak tea. It might take one cup of manure concentrate to one bucket of water, or more or less. You can use this on the garden or, if it's very weak, on young seedlings. Don't waste what's left of the manure in the hessian bag – dig it into the compost heap.

Worm-casting tea

This is an excellent all-purpose fertiliser. To make some, fill a watering can or bucket with water almost to the top. Add half a cup of worm castings, one tablespoon of molasses, one tablespoon of fish fertiliser, and half a tablespoon of seaweed concentrate. Stir this well for at least five minutes. Pour this on and around your plants first thing in the morning.

Green manure

If your garden bed will be standing empty for a while, plant a green manure crop. This can be any legume-type plant like cow peas or broad beans, or you could try a grass like oats or barley. If you have leftover pea or bean seeds, use them, or buy green manure seeds from your heirloom seed supplier. When the crop is about a metre high, cut it off and leave it as mulch or dig it into the soil. When you're ready to plant again your soil will be alive and healthy and ready for the new crops.

Harvesting your crops

Whether you live in a colder area and have one harvest a year, or in a warmer place, like I do, and have continuous harvests, picking your fruit and vegetables is when all your hard work pays off. Learn all you can about harvesting and storing your produce because you won't want to waste one beautiful ripe tomato or one crisp lettuce leaf.

With vine crops that flower, like **peas, beans, cucumbers and zucchini**, you get many more vegetables if you pick them continuously. Green leaves also benefit from continuous picking. We pick **lettuce, kale, silverbeet and spinach** from the outside, just taking the leaves we need for that day. The plant will keep producing leaves and you can keep harvesting them. However, if you want to put some silverbeet, kale or spinach in the freezer, you can harvest the leaves from the entire plant, making sure you leave the centre intact. After harvesting, give the plants a drink of weak fertiliser tea such as comfrey, compost or worm tea and within a few weeks, you'll have full plants again.

Tomatoes may be harvested when deep red, pink or green. You can pick them at any size if you need to clear the land or if weather such as hailstorms or extreme heat threatens them, but it's best to let them develop to a reasonable size. We find that if we leave tomatoes to ripen on the bush, the grubs will get to them before we do. We wait until they're a decent size and showing just the first twinges of pink, then we pick them. They ripen inside on the kitchen bench, away from birds and insects. Tomatoes don't need sunlight to ripen, they just need a warm temperature, so don't store tomatoes in the fridge. Don't worry that they'll go off – the only ones you'll lose will be those that have a grub in them. The rest will last a few weeks in a bowl on the bench.

Learn all you can about harvesting and storing your produce because you won't want to waste one beautiful ripe tomato or one crisp lettuce leaf.

Some vegetables, like **pumpkins, beetroot, turnips, potatoes and onions,** can be left growing until they're ripe and you need them. Naturally, you have to use your common sense when using the garden as a storage area. For instance, if you have continuous rain you'd have to rescue these vegetables or they'd rot in all that water. But if you're hoping to leave them for a few more weeks or even a month in the garden before harvesting, most of the time with these vegetables, that's okay. You'll need to keep your pumpkins in check by waiting until you see the first pumpkins growing and then nipping off the growing stems around it, on the same vine. That will stop the vine rambling all over the garden. Pumpkins are ready to harvest when the vine starts dying and they feel heavy for their size. When you harvest your pumpkins, cut them from the vine, leaving about six inches of vine still attached to the pumpkin. If the vine comes away from the pumpkin, cover the circle at the top of the pumpkin with some melted beeswax to protect it while it's ripening and drying. Dry the pumpkins in the sun for a couple of weeks before bringing them inside to store in a cool dark place.

Radish, carrots, turnips and parsnips are sweeter and more tender when they're picked smaller rather than larger. **Leeks and Welsh spring onions** can be cut off at ground level and will usually regrow.

A good indication it's time to pick **potatoes** is when you see the green tops turn brown and die. Be guided by the growing times for the variety you're cultivating. If you're impatient for potatoes, you can put your hand into the side of the plant and pick off some small new potatoes underground. This is called bandicooting. If you're gentle, it will not damage the plant at all and these small potatoes are a gift when steamed or boiled and dressed simply with butter, parsley and a bit of seasoning.

What to do with the excess

Harvesting is one of the most important parts of the vegetable-growing process and getting it right will reduce wastage. We freshly pick **tomatoes** almost every day and eat them in salads or on sandwiches. When there are too many (a truly joyful occasion) I pick the excess – usually when they're still green – and ripen them in the shade. When they're ripe, I make relish, sauce or chutney, process it in a water bath and store it in the cupboard.

We eat **cucumbers and beetroot** fresh but when we have a lot of them, they're picked, pickled and stored in the fridge. We probably eat one **cabbage** every week or two during winter – raw in coleslaw and kimchi or cooked and served with meat. Like

the tomatoes, we grow more than we eat fresh and at some point in the season I make sauerkraut so that we can store the cabbage for longer.

Vegetables like **corn, beans, peas, silverbeet, spinach, cauliflower, broccoli, kale and carrots** are all good to freeze. To do that effectively, wait until you have enough for at least a serving for your family, pick, blanch, then bag them up for the freezer. Never skip the blanching step if you intend to freeze it for a long time – it makes a difference. Some days you'll only have enough excess for one or two bags for the freezer; other days you'll have a lot more than that. Just take it as it comes; it will only take you a few minutes to process a bag or two. Don't think it's too small an amount to worry about. You'll be happy to have it later when you can just take a family-size serving of home-grown vegetables from the freezer and have it on the table to eat that night.

Growing food in containers

Many vegetables can be grown successfully in pots or containers so if you're new to gardening, start off with a couple of potted herbs or vegetables. They're a great introduction to gardening.

There are a few factors you need to be mindful of when growing vegetables and herbs in pots:

- Generally the size and health of the root ball will determine the number of vegetables harvested, so if you want to grow large vegetables look for large containers that will allow the roots to spread a little.
- You'll need a good-quality potting mix, or an ordinary potting mix with compost and old manure added. Don't use garden soil – it doesn't drain well and the roots will suffocate.
- Do a bit of research and look for dwarf varieties of the large vegetables you wish to grow. You can get heirloom dwarf tomatoes, short carrots and golden nugget pumpkin as a bush rather than a vine.

- Growing vegetables up a trellis will maximise your space. One cucumber seedling in a pot with a trellis will give you more than enough cucumbers for two people.
- Consistent watering is essential. When a plant is in the ground, its roots will go looking for moisture. This can't happen in a pot so the plant will totally rely on you for water.
- Make sure all your containers have a lot of drainage holes. If you're planting in buckets or polystyrene boxes, drill drainage holes in the base. Long polystyrene boxes are good for planting a row of lettuce or short carrots.
- Don't sit your containers in drip trays – they must drain freely. If you have the containers indoors, stand them on bricks or pebbles so the pot is out of the collecting water.
- If you're in a hot climate, put your containers where they will get sun till about 2 p.m., then shade.
- When you plant, water in with seaweed tea.
- Apply a spoonful of sulphate of potash to the flowering vegetables like tomatoes, pumpkins and cucumbers when you plant.
- When the plants have grown a bit, add mulch to help keep the moisture in.
- If you have worm tea, add that every week but make sure it is a weak brew.
- Apply weak liquid fertiliser to the green leafy vegetables every week.
- Don't over-fertilise your fruiting vegetables (like tomatoes, capsicums and cucumbers). It will cause your plants to produce lush green leaves at the expense of fruit.

You'll be able to produce good vegetables in containers but you'll have to look after your plants well. They'll require more care than vegetables in the ground, as they're reliant on you for all their needs. But if you can give them some time and effort they will reward you with fresh food.

THE SUSTAINABLE BACKYARD

There is something about putting your hands into the soil that restores the human spirit. It brings you down to earth, it energises you and reminds you that we're all part of the natural world. Self-reliance and sustainability is more than vegetable gardening and keeping chickens. It's an attitude to life, which often gives the grower a sense of empowerment and independence. It teaches life lessons on seasonality, living locally, developing community, renewal, making do, productivity and abundance.

Garden maintenance

It seems like I've been gardening most of my life. My mother was a keen gardener and my sister, Tricia, has a magnificent garden in the Blue Mountains, so maybe the love of it is in my bones. There is something about putting your hands into the soil that restores the human spirit. It brings you down to earth, it energises you and reminds you that we're all part of the natural world. We are not separate.

Having a sustainable backyard means that if you chose to grow fruit and vegetables in your backyard for fifty years, and beyond, your soils would not be depleted, abundant nutrients would be in your produce and your food production would not have a negative impact on your backyard environment; in fact, it would improve it. It means you'd work with the natural elements and that when you left that piece of land it would be in better shape than you found it.

But self-reliance and sustainability is more than vegetable gardening and keeping chickens, a cow or goats. It's an attitude to life, which often gives the grower a sense of empowerment and independence. It teaches life lessons on seasonality, living locally, developing community, renewal, making do, productivity and abundance.

In defence of grass

The beginning of summer always means the start of that most mundane of garden chores – mowing the lawn, or as we think of it, harvesting the grass. We have quite a bit of open grass to harvest and it does take time, but despite what many others think of lawn or grass or turf or whatever you call it, we would not get rid of it. Here it's a vital resource that gives more than it takes.

Having a sustainable backyard means that your food production would not have a negative impact on your backyard environment.

Grass is not the enemy. If you have small children, pets or chickens, I'm sure you'll already be aware of the benefits of having grassed areas around the home. It doesn't have to be manicured perfection to be beneficial. Over-zealous care of grass and wanting grass to look like perfect lawn is not sustainable. Just let it grow with natural rainfall and I'm sure you'll be surprised how hardy it is. Then change your attitude towards grass. Even though it needs to be mown (or harvested) it is a productive crop that you can use for chook feed or as a soft place to fall.

We never water our grass. We have more than enough natural rainfall to keep it alive. In times of drought, our grass has stopped growing and turned brown and crunchy, but grass is such a hardy plant – even when it looks dead and it hasn't rained for months, it will usually come back to life when it receives water. We never fertilise it either, even with organic fertilisers. It gets enough nourishment from the pecked or cut remnants of grass that fall and decompose within the blades, and from the droppings when the chickens free range on the grass.

So what do we use our lawn for?

- It gives our chooks a wonderful place to graze and therefore gives the eggs we eat a much appreciated boost of omega-3 and -6 oils. If we were to eat our chooks, their meat would also be rich in these oils. Grass is rich in omega-3 and -6 and chickens will consume up to 30 percent of their daily food as grass if given a good area to range over.
- When harvested by the lawnmower, grass gives us most of the green component needed in our compost heap. If we didn't have grass, we'd struggle to find enough bulk to keep the compost going.
- It provides cooler air around the house than we would have with hard landscaping. All those pavers, bricks and cement that surround some houses make them hot in summer.
- It reduces noise and dust around the house.
- It absorbs carbon dioxide and produces oxygen (the same as trees do).
- It filters water run-off before it reaches waterways.

Mulching

Mulch is the material such as straw or spent sugarcane that you place on the soil around a plant. Mulching the vegetable garden has a number of benefits:

- It provides a cover for the bare soil that will help keep the moisture in, and therefore reduces the amount of water needed for the garden.
- It helps reduce weeds. Weeds need sunlight and bare soil to grow. Covering the soil with mulch cuts out both those ingredients.

- It insulates the soil surface against extreme heat or cold and helps maintain an even soil temperature.
- It eventually breaks down to add organic matter to the soil, increasing soil fertility.

When you apply mulch to your vegetable garden, make sure you don't let it sit too close to the plants, as you'll rot the stems of some vegetables. (This rule doesn't apply to tomatoes.) Always weed and water before you apply mulch. You'll find if you do that, you're giving the soil the best chance of producing bumper crops for you. The water you apply will stay in the soil longer, the temperature will remain fairly constant and you'll create the best conditions for growing healthy vegetables.

Day-to-day garden tasks

It sounds like a lot of work, but if you get into a routine with your gardening, it only requires observation and fixing problems as soon as you see them. During your active growing season, put aside thirty to sixty minutes a day for your garden if you can. There will always be something to fix, adjust, tie back, prune or move. The rest of it is pure enjoyment – both in the gardening and in the eating. And you will probably find that you're at your best in the garden – many of us are.

Here are some tasks to do during the growing season:

- All through the growing season, no matter what you're growing, keep the garden beds weed-free and pick off every dead or damaged leaf you see on your plants.
- Watch out for caterpillars, grasshoppers, slugs and snails and if you find a few, pick them off and give them to the chooks. Try to get into the habit of inspecting your plants early in the morning or late in the afternoon because that is when most insects will be feeding. There is more information about bugs and insects later in the chapter.
- Keep your green leaves growing well with some sort of fertiliser tea – it's easily made at home and costs very little. If you see any plant that is stressed or being

attacked by insects, apply a feeding of seaweed tea. It is a great plant tonic and can help plants survive harsh conditions. If your fruiting vegetables aren't producing flowers, apply sulphate of potash (according to the directions on the pack) around the base of the plant and water it in. All these applications are organic.

- Tie up your tomatoes before they become too unruly and keep all your climbing plants attached to their supports. It only takes a few minutes a week to do this and it makes all the difference. Vines that are allowed to fly around in the wind will get damaged or break.

- Keep applying mulch through the season as it breaks down.

- As you clear an area after harvesting, apply some compost, dig it in, and start another crop, even if it's just two or three plants. Gardening this way will give you the best return on the work you put in and it uses the soil productively and sustainably.

Looking after your tools

Your garden tools don't have to be the best or most expensive. Often you can buy very good-quality old tools at garage sales and markets – this is a better investment than buying cheap imports. Keep your tools in good working order by giving them a little time and effort after you've used them and they'll last a lifetime.

Lawnmower

- After using your lawnmower, check the oil level. If it is low and has not been changed for a while, now is the time to do it (while the engine is still warm).

- While checking the oil, look for wear and tear on the cutting blades. If they need replacing, do that straight away.

- A small amount of dirt and grass build-up helps protect the housing for the blades but clean it out if there's too much.

- Clean the air filter.

- Make sure the catcher is empty as it will smell if you store it with clippings still inside.
- Give the mower a quick wipe over with a clean cloth.
- Store it in a protected area.

Edge-trimmer

- When you finish your work, clean the unit with a rag. Remove any dirt or plant material.
- Check the oil level so the trimmer will be ready for work the next time.
- Store it in a protected area.

Garden tools

- Clean dirt off your tools after you finish using them.
- Don't leave your tools out in the rain or exposed to the sun for too long.
- If the metal is showing signs of deterioration, clean it well and apply a rust preventative.
- Every so often, check the wooden handles for splinters and roughness. If the handle starts to split, smooth it over with emery- or sandpaper and apply a mix of turpentine and linseed oil. Leave it overnight to sink in and dry, then smooth over again with emery paper and finish off with a light sanding with steel wool.
- Store your tools in a dry place.

Bugs and insects

If you're going to create a garden and be outside in the sunshine you have to expect to come across other living creatures. Don't be scared of them. Like us, they're a part of the beautiful, natural scheme of things and have a role to play in our world. If you're a new gardener, do some online research or visit your library to educate yourself about what to expect in your region. Work with the natural elements, not against them, and you'll be rewarded.

Not all bugs are bad, so don't go around killing every insect you see. Some bugs eat other bugs, or their eggs, and some of them lay their eggs in the bodies of other insects. It sounds pretty gruesome but it's how the natural world works and it can help you.

The troublemakers

In Australia, these insects are always pests:

- European wasps (aggressive and dangerous)
- ticks (the paralysis tick can kill dogs and cats)

- mosquitoes (carry disease)
- large earth bumblebees (accidentally released in Tasmania and have been an environmental disaster, competing with native bees for food)
- fire ants (a relatively new pest but a serious threat in areas they've colonised).

If you're going to create a garden and be outside in the sunshine you have to expect to come across other living creatures. Don't be scared of them.

Ants, other than fire ants, are sometimes good and sometimes not. They may carry scale insects that will attach themselves to your plants and suck the sap out of them. (Scale insects can't move themselves; ants move them around so they can eat the sticky honeydew the scale secrete.) If you see ants active on your plants and find scale insects, find the ant nest and pouring boiling water into it. Repeat if they rebuild the nest. You will also have to spray the scale with white oil.

Homemade white oil

White oil can be used on all types of scale, citrus leafminer and aphids.

Blend 2 cups of vegetable oil and 2 tablespoons of liquid soap in a blender, or shake vigorously in a sealed jar till thoroughly combined. The liquid soap helps the oil stick to the plant and the insect. Label the jar. It can be stored for about 12 months. To use, add a tablespoon of the oil to a litre of water and shake well. Spray all sides of the leaves and stems.

Organic remedies for chewing insects

When you're an organic gardener, it pays to work with the natural ecosystem in your backyard. Try to stay away from sprays, because even the organic options sometimes kill beneficial insects and have withholding periods (the time that must elapse between application and harvest). There will be times when you'll have to use a commercial

organic spray, bait or powder, but make sure it's the last option. I don't think that every recommended organic method works. For instance, over the thirty-plus years we've been growing vegetables, I've tried companion planting every so often, but it's never worked for us. However, there are other organic techniques that do work for us and we rely on them year after year.

We use Dipel on caterpillars. It's an organic remedy that uses bacteria instead of poison. Make it up according to the directions on the bottle and reapply if it rains. We usually catch grasshoppers and give them to the chooks but if there are a lot of them, we spray them with eco-neem, according to the directions on the bottle. We don't have a lot of snails here but we do have slugs. We use the old beer treatment for them – just pour ½ glass of beer into a low-sided container and leave it in the garden close to where you've seen snails and slugs. They will be attracted to it, slide in there to drink the beer and drown.

The good fellows

In Australia there are many species of native bees. We also have the honey bee, introduced into Australia in 1822 because the English thought there were no bees here. If you have any of these bees visiting your garden, particularly the native bees, you're very lucky.

Other insects that you want in your garden include:

- assassin bugs
- lacewings
- parasitic wasps and predator wasps like paper wasps and mud daubers
- many spiders
- dragonflies

- praying mantises
- hoverflies
- robber flies
- lady beetles, but not the 28-spot beetle that looks like a lady beetle – they eat plants.

If you have children, be careful if you have wasps visiting. Our rule of thumb here is that if wasps start building a nest close to where we are, we carefully remove the nest. Otherwise, they stay. If you see the occasional wasp in your garden, it is nothing to worry about; it's a healthy sign. Predatory and parasitic wasps are not aggressive (despite their name) and will only sting if you disturb their nest or attack them.

Now you know which bugs you want in your garden, how do you get them there? Flowers! The insects will come if you plant the flowers they love. Almost any flower will be suitable, but there are a group of flowers that attract beneficial insects. Those flowers include:

- cosmos
- daisies, including echinacea, feverfew, chrysanthemums, gerberas and chamomile
- red clover
- Queen Anne's lace
- carrot flowers
- dill flowers
- marigolds
- alyssum
- nasturtiums
- yarrow.

Most insects need water, so put out a small container, off the ground, full of pebbles or stones so the insects can land and leave the water safely. It would be best placed in a protected area, like under a tree, or close to some herbs. That would be an excellent project for the children. It would get them involved in the garden and it could be their job to refill the water container, keep it clean and make sure there is the right amount of water and pebbles.

Gardening, particularly organic gardening, is not just planting seeds and watering; it's more involved than that. It's all these little things that make the difference between a garden and a productive, healthy garden. And the thing about gardening is you learn something new every year. You never know it all, but even in those first few years, it gives rewards and pleasures that will bring you back year after year.

Keeping chickens

If you're living in a suburban or rural location you can probably keep chickens. You should give this a lot of thought first, because although chickens don't require a lot of time, you will be responsible for them for their entire lives. That means providing safe accommodation, feeding, fresh water, and maintenance in the form of checking for lice and cleaning out the coop. In return, the chickens will give you the freshest eggs and many a laugh as you watch them go about their daily business in your backyard.

Chicken housing

Chickens need a place where they feel safe and can lay their eggs. There are a lot of predators around: dogs, foxes, feral cats, snakes and other wildlife will wander in under the shadow of darkness. Their coop should have a door that you can close, and having separate areas for times when you want to quarantine a sick or new chicken is very good. You'll need nests, which should be in the quietest and darkest part of the hen house. One nest per five chooks is about right, but you often find that all the chickens want to lay in one or two nests. We have four nests here with twelve chickens, but we usually have at least one broody chicken taking up a nest all the time. If the nests are high off the ground, you'll need to provide a little ladder or steps for the chooks to reach them.

Your ladies will sleep on a roost, which is basically a horizontal bar. Using dried, stripped tree branches as roosts is better than buying dowelling or other material.

Cleaning the coop

If you have a dedicated henhouse, it will need to be cleaned out at least every week, depending on the number of chickens you have. If it is rainy and the henhouse is wet, it might smell. Laying straw on the floor will help with the smell, and this straw can be placed on the compost heap after a couple of weeks. Don't expect your coop to be sparkling clean every day – it is outside and in a natural setting where wind will blow dust in and spiders will spin webs. It does need to be fairly clean and not smelly, but it's not your kitchen.

Buying chickens

Local regulations

Most local authorities will have a by-law about keeping chickens. We can have up to twenty chooks where we live, and the chicken coop must not touch a neighbour's fence. We can't keep roosters. Phone your local shire or council to ask about their regulations before you buy your chickens, or look it up online.

How old should they be?

The vast majority of chickens are hatched in spring and summer. Day-old chicks are often available for sale but when I'm getting new chooks, I usually go for point-of-lay pullets that are eighteen to twenty-two weeks old. They will start laying a couple of weeks after you buy them. Point-of-lay pullets will have been checked by a chicken

sexer and grouped as either male or female, and you'll get only hens. Day-old chicks won't have been sex checked, and you'll get approximately half hens and half roosters.

Pure-breed chickens

Pure-breed chickens are similar to heirloom seeds: unless we buy them, they will die out and we'll lose more genetic diversity. Isa Browns, the small red chooks, are bred for the caged-egg industry. They've been bred to be good layers and often don't go broody. Chooks have a natural rest when they are broody because they stop laying eggs and try to reproduce, even when there are no roosters around. This is when they replenish their calcium levels and set themselves up for another year of egg production.

When you buy your chickens, please give some thought to pure breeds like Orpingtons, Rhode Island Reds and Sussex – all good dual-purpose birds for meat and eggs – or lighter breeds like Wyandottes, Faverolles or Pekin bantams for eggs alone. The pure breeds and the caged poultry cost about the same, but you'll help the gene pool survive if you choose any of the pure-breed chickens.

How many chickens should you buy?

The smallest number should be two. Solo chickens are sad birds, as they need to be part of a flock. There will be times when you have to isolate your chooks and keep them on their own, but generally chickens prefer to be with other chickens. Your chooks will know the other chooks by sight and when you introduce new chooks, the older ones will give them a hard time.

Get the number of chickens you have room for. Our twelve give us about eight eggs a day because we have a couple of older hens that lay infrequently. A little flock of three to five girls will give enough eggs for a family of four or six.

Bringing chickens home

When you bring your girls home, lock the gate on their coop and leave them to settle in. Don't let them out to free range for at least a week – during that time they will learn that the coop is their home. When chooks know their home, they will come home to roost when the daylight starts to fade, and usually you don't have to go looking for them.

Introducing new chooks

If you already have chickens, isolate any new birds you bring home, but put them where they can see and be seen by the other chooks. Keep them isolated for a few days. This will help them assimilate and when you let them out together, there will be less pecking. Isolating new chickens might also help you identify if the new girls are sick. If they are, take them back to the breeder.

Pecking order

Pecking each other to establish pecking order is natural behaviour for chickens. Don't intervene unless you can see an open wound or blood. Then you'll have to remove that chicken until she has healed. The higher up the chicken is when they go to sleep, the higher up in the pecking order they usually are. Generally your top chook will be up on the highest roost at night.

Lifespan

From my experience, a chicken's lifespan is about ten years. Cross-breed chooks generally live for eight years. They will continue to lay eggs up until they die, but when they're very old you will only get about one egg every few months.

We have found over the years that if you get a flock of about eight or ten girls, in five years you'll have maybe six or seven left. Some chickens get sick and die, and often you don't know why. If any of your chooks are obviously sick, isolate them – but make sure they still have good shelter and access to food and water.

Broody hens

Most pure-breed chooks and some hybrids will go broody at some point. They want to hatch eggs and become mothers, but unless you have a rooster, that will not happen. (Hens don't need a rooster to lay eggs but they need a rooster to fertilise the eggs.) When our chickens go broody, we let them, unless they sit there for too long – over a month – and start losing weight. Generally they'll sit for a couple of weeks in the darkest nest, hoping you don't see them. Just put your hand in and collect the eggs every day as you normally would. If you don't want the chook to sit on the nest, you'll have to lock her out of the nesting area, but even then, she might find another dark place in long grass or in the hay bales and keep sitting. They do no harm sitting, so we feel it's best to just let them sit.

Keeping chickens healthy

Food and water

Chooks must have clean water *all the time*. Get into the habit of giving them clean water every second day, or daily if they drink a lot. Chickens are omnivores; they eat meat, grains and vegetables. They love cheese, yoghurt, whey, sour milk and milk. If you have small chicks, they'll need chicken starter crumbles. If you have point-of-lays they'll need laying pellets or laying mash (a combination of grains).

Chickens rarely overeat so it's fine for you to fill up a feed hopper (available at the produce store) and let them feed themselves when they feel like it. This will save work for you because if you buy a large hopper and fill it up with pellets or mash, you'll only have to refill the hopper every few days.

It's a great idea to supplement their diet with greens from the garden or kitchen scraps. Start this early as they get picky later and will stay with what they know. They need a high-protein diet to produce eggs constantly, so if you have chickens that aren't laying, give them a boost with some day-old bread soaked in milk, or warm porridge made with milk. They will love this and the milk will boost their protein level.

If you have grain like wheat or barley, sprouting it for the chickens gives them a good nutritional boost. Simply soak the grains in water for a couple of hours in a large, flat container, or upturned bin lid, pour off the excess water and keep the container in the shade, covered with a cloth. Wet and rinse the grains every day and drain off the excess water. When the grains sprout, feed them to the chooks.

Free range

Your chickens will be healthier and will give you better eggs if you let them free range sometimes. When chooks eat grass, they will have omega-3 and -6 oils in their eggs, which is a great bonus for anyone eating the eggs.

Eggshells

Eggshells are a good natural supplement to help keep the hens' calcium levels at a healthy level. They need that to produce eggshells. Keep the shells of the eggs you use and wash them out so they don't smell. When you have quite a few, put them in the oven, on a medium setting, for 10 minutes to dry out. When they're cool, put them in a blender and blitz them, or crush them inside a tea towel with your rolling pin. Store them in a jar. The crushed shell powder can be added to a small dish left in the coop so the chickens can help themselves if they need extra calcium. Keep the dish off the ground so the chickens don't kick dirt into it.

Grit

Chickens need grit to help them digest the food they eat. As you know, chickens have no teeth, so food is passed into their system whole, partially digested by acids and enzymes in the oesophagus and then moves on to the gizzard. Grit accumulates in the gizzard and, by a grinding action, helps break down the food. If your chickens free range regularly, they will probably pick up enough grit by pecking in the backyard. If they're kept in a henhouse, they'll need a grit supplement. You can buy it at the produce store in the form of crushed oyster shells, which are high in calcium. Add them to the same dish you have the ground eggshells in.

Raspberry cordial

Another little thing that keeps your chooks healthy is adding some 'real' raspberry cordial, with at least 25 per cent real juice, or squashed frozen raspberries or jam to their water every so often. This is also a good treatment for diarrhoea in chickens and is commonly given as a tonic by bird keepers. Here are the ingredients for a homemade cordial:

- 2 cups crushed fresh or frozen raspberries
- juice of 1 lemon
- 1½ cups sugar syrup
- 8 cups water.

Bring to the boil and simmer for 5 minutes. Cool, then decant to clean plastic bottles. Store in the fridge for up to 2 months or freeze.

Add about 2 tablespoons to a bucket of water when you notice any sick-looking chooks, or when you want to boost them with a tonic.

Lice

If your chickens have lice – and it will happen from time to time – get some good-quality diatomaceous earth from the produce store or nursery and rub it all over the chooks. Make sure you rub under their wings and around their combs and wattles (the red bits on their faces). This will get rid of the lice. If you can't catch the chooks, sprinkle diatomaceous earth in the area where they have their dust baths. They'll roll in the dust and take on some of the diatomaceous earth as well.

Eggs

Hens start laying eggs when they're twenty to twenty-two weeks old. You will know your ladies are maturing and getting ready to lay when their combs and wattles get larger and redder. Depending on the weather, each hen will lay about five eggs a week in the first year. It will decrease slowly after that. They will stop laying when it is very hot or very cold and when they're moulting (replacing their feathers). When your girls first start laying, they might lay an egg with no shell or an egg with two yolks. The eggs usually start off small and get bigger as the hen matures. When the hen's hormones have settled down, you will get single-yolk eggs with the shell intact.

Your girls will usually lay in the morning. Collect the eggs once a day. If you let the eggs stay in the nests it might encourage the hens to start pecking at them. When a hen starts eating the eggs, you have a real problem. Don't wash the eggs, as that will remove a protective layer on the shell. If the egg is dirty, rub it with a cloth and remove as much dirt as you can. If you still need to wash it, do so – but use that egg next. Don't let it sit in the fridge.

Eggs should be stored in the fridge, in an egg holder so they don't roll around. There are regulations for selling eggs in most places, but eggs are excellent bartering produce. See if someone in the neighbourhood wants to barter eggs for honey or fruit.

Composting

What is compost?

Composting is an ideal activity for those of us who live simply. It reduces household waste and helps us use what we have to its fullest extent – from new, right through until it decomposes and returns to the earth. It helps us see waste in a more productive way, instead of giving it to someone else to take care of. It encourages us to look for natural products that will be compostable in a few years' time instead of buying plastic or polyester. But most of all, I love composting because it allows me to take full responsibility for what I buy. If it comes here, I want it to stay here and not be part of the growing problem of landfill.

Compost is the end result of organic matter that breaks down and decomposes. Organic matter, in this context, is anything that was once alive: vegetable scraps, lawn clippings, newspaper and cardboard, outer leaves of vegetables, leaves, hair, straw, and so on. You can also include tea bags, tea leaves and coffee grounds.

Just about any leafy product can go into compost, but never include diseased leaves, as that will just keep that disease in your garden and spread it around. Other things to avoid including are meat, fish, bones, dairy products, citrus and onions.

How to make compost

Compost can be made on bare earth in a sheltered area of your garden. It doesn't want too much sun or wind because it will dry out too quickly. If you have fussy neighbours, it might be a good idea to keep it away from their fence as well. Good compost shouldn't smell but it might look unsightly.

There are many different ways of making compost. The purists make sure their compost heap is a certain size to ensure it heats up – that encourages decomposition and kills some weed seeds. Other people use bins that are enclosed at the top and open at the bottom. This type of composting relies on anaerobic organisms. I have found that using one of these bins to make compost generally results in a very wet mix, so it needs more brown material (such as straw and newspapers) than green material.

There are three requirements for making compost: nitrogen, carbon and aeration. Your compost will need about three parts carbon to one part nitrogen. It sounds complicated, doesn't it? Well, it can be, but it is easy if you get your mix right.

- **Nitrogen** is wet green vegetable waste, scraps, fruit peels, lawn clippings and old vegetables. It's the stuff that's still juicy or slimy – all that waste that hasn't yet dried out. Nitrogen comes from the fresh kitchen scraps you'll have most days. All the ingredients should be as small as possible. If you have big pieces of cabbage or pumpkin, cut them into smaller pieces with your spade.
- **Carbon** is dry waste like straw, newspaper, cardboard and dried leaves. These items should also be as small as possible.
- **Aeration** is simply moving the nitrogen and carbon materials around to introduce air into the mix. You could do this by turning the compost over with a pitchfork, by using a tumbler that spins the compost around or by building your compost heap around a wide plumber's pipe that would allow air to go deep within the heap. Generally, it's best to turn the compost with a fork every week or two. The more air you get into the mix, the faster you'll make compost.

Of course, you could also enlist the help of your chickens. If you have an enclosed space for them – a yard that is fenced or surrounded with chicken wire – throw all your lawn clippings, straw, vegetable peelings and scraps, shredded paper, garden waste and old vegetables from the garden in there. The chickens will eat some of it but they'll also walk on it, scratch it around the yard, and leave their valuable manure on it. In about six weeks' time, you'll have a healthy compost.

Here are the steps to make good compost:

- You'll need 25 per cent wet/green nitrogen waste such as lawn clippings or vegetable scraps, and 75 per cent dry carbon waste like straw, dried leaves or shredded newspaper.

- Add the ingredients in layers – two layers of carbon then one layer of nitrogen – and mix it together.
- Add some manure or comfrey/yarrow leaves.
- Wet this with some water.
- Mix.
- Shape into a neat pile and leave it.
- Add to the pile as often as you can, making sure you always have more dry than wet waste.
- Keep the heap moist, not wet, and turn it as often as possible.

Compost troubleshooting

- **If the compost has a terrible smell**, you've got too much green wet waste (nitrogen) in there. Add a handful of lime and some shredded newspaper, straw or other dry carbon waste and mix it in.
- **If the compost looks dry and isn't decomposing**, add more wet/green waste, or a sprinkling of water from the hose, and mix. A half-bucket of comfrey tea or some animal manure will help a compost heap activate and start decomposing.
- **If you have a lot of wet weather**, cover your compost heap with a tarp or plastic to keep some of the rain out. It should always be moist, but not dripping wet.

Worm farming

Worm farming is another way to compost your kitchen scraps, cut down the amount of food waste you send to the local landfill dump, and increase the fertility of your garden soil. Compost worms produce castings (waste products), and from these worm castings you can make worm tea, which is a great fertiliser. You can also mix the castings into your topsoil, which will help to make your soil fertile and alive with beneficial microbes. A worm farm is a container with bedding made up of either straw, coconut coir, shredded paper, or a mixture of all of them. The worms live in the bedding, and feed on food scraps and various microbes that also live in the bedding, helping to decompose the scraps.

You can buy ready-made worm farms at a plant nursery or large hardware stores if you prefer not to make your own. They're a system of black plastic boxes and trays and come with complete instructions and, often, a bag of worms. We built our own worm farm in an old bathtub.

Where to put your worm farm

I live in a fairly dry and sometimes hot environment but when it rains, it can be torrential. If you live in a moderate climate, you'll be able to keep your covered worm farm under a tree. If you're in a cold place, it will have to go somewhere protected from the cold. If it's really hot where you live, your worm farm will need to be in the coolest place. The idea is to provide a fairly stable temperature, with moist conditions. If the temperature is too hot or too cold, the worms will either die or they'll escape to find a better home. When you start your worm farm, monitor it to make sure the worms are okay and like where you've put them.

Making your own worm farm

When I first got my compost worms, I kept them in a couple of polystyrene boxes. They were happy enough but then they started reproducing and I realised they needed more room. So we bought an old bathtub from the local recycle shop for $20.

If you can't find a bathtub, any large plastic tub would be fine. In addition to your bathtub or large container, you'll need:

- a plastic tap you can screw into the container to allow the liquid to pour out
- an adapter and elbow to attach the tap to the tub
- about two buckets of road gravel
- a sheet of microfilter, weed mat or tightly woven shade cloth
- lots of compost or good garden soil
- aged animal manure
- shredded computer paper, newspaper or cardboard, straw or hay
- coverings like hessian bags, thick wads of newspaper or cardboard
- covering for the tub to keep the rodents and rain out (such as a corrugated roofing sheet)
- kitchen scraps
- our old friend, the compost worm: about 2000–10000 reds, tigers or blues (not earthworms).

ACTION PLAN: *Making a worm farm*

* Fill a wheelbarrow with water, add two tablespoons of molasses and mix well. This will help feed the beneficial bacteria that will live in the bedding with the worms. Place the dry materials like the shredded paper and straw in it to soak while you prepare the container.

* If you're using a bathtub, locate the old tub outlet and screw in the plastic tap attachment and elbow. Then screw the tap onto the attachment and make sure the tap opens easily. If you're not using a bathtub, make a hole in the side of the container and screw the tap in.

* Using an angle grinder, cut slits in the bathtub about 5 cm from the base, to allow air in. If you're using a plastic container, cut holes with a sharp knife on the lower sides, 5 cm from the base. Although the worms will be living in the bedding, it needs to have air in it or they will die. When you've added the slits, place the container where it will sit permanently. Make sure the tap is in a convenient place and that you can put a bucket or watering can underneath to collect the worm liquid.

* When the tap is in place, add the gravel. The gravel provides good drainage so that the bottom of the bathtub doesn't fill with water and drown some of the worms. When the gravel is in, cover it with the filter sheet or weed mat to prevent the worm castings mixing into the gravel.

* Now you're ready to start placing the bedding. You need to make a nice organic bed for your worms, one they'll happily eat, reproduce and live in. The better the conditions you give them, the faster they'll reproduce and the more castings you'll have for your garden. Wring out the paper/straw/hay bedding and put it into the container. Empty what is left of the molasses water onto your compost heap. Top the bedding with lots of compost and manure and mix it all together. Place a container under the open tap to catch the liquid as it drains out.

* The bedding should be about 40 per cent water. A good test is to wring out a handful of bedding material. If you can only get a couple of drops of water, that's great. If water drips out, that's too much and you'll need to drain the bedding to remove some of the water before placing the worms in there.

* When you've got the bedding in place and it's mixed well with just enough water, place some finely chopped food, such as stale bread or kitchen scraps, on the bedding and mix it in. Now put the worms on top of the bedding, and they'll burrow in themselves. Worms need a dark environment, so cover the bed with moist hessian or cardboard/paper, and place a rain-proof cover over the worm farm.

BE CAREFUL

If you're going to add animal manure, like cow or horse manure, to your worm farm, ask if the animals have recently been wormed when you're buying it. If the manure is contaminated with worm medication, it will kill your worms.

Feeding the worms

Feed the worms about once a week. Whatever you give your worms to eat needs to be finely cut or processed in the food processor. The faster they feed, the bigger they grow, and the more they reproduce – and the more worms and castings you'll have. Check how much food is in the bedding and feed accordingly – you don't want the feed sitting in the worm farm too long. Remember, worms eat the food you give them, the microbes you can't see that live in the bedding, and the bedding itself. Worms and the microbes will eat anything that was once alive, so give them your kitchen scraps, old dishcloths, hair, worn-out cotton or wool, tea leaves or tea bags, coffee grounds, old bread, eggs, finely crushed eggshells, shredded wet paper or wet cardboard. Do not give them too many citrus peels or onions, although they can take a small amount. As with the compost, avoid meat, fish and dairy products. Feed a variety of food to get the best possible worm castings. When you feed the worms, dig the food into the bedding so it's not available to wandering rats, mice or cockroaches.

WORM REPRODUCTION

When they're mating, worms will produce about twelve babies per adult per week. You'll know that they're mating when you see little worm capsules in the bedding. Each capsule contains around four babies. The babies hatch after about thirty days and are ready to breed about two months later.

Worm farm maintenance

The worms must remain moist, because if they dry out they'll escape or die. Check the moisture level by poking your finger into the worm farm every few days. If it feels dry, add some water. Make sure the drainage holes at the bottom of the container remain open so that water can freely drain out.

If the worm farm starts to smell a little, you're feeding them too much. Cut back the food and sprinkle a little lime over the worm farm. That should sweeten it up again. With a fork or a little claw rake, fluff up the bedding once a month to make sure there's enough air. Worms hate to be disturbed and they don't like light. Apart from this maintenance and feeding, leave them alone to do their thing.

Harvesting the castings

Worm castings are worm manure. They contains microbes, bacteria and nutrients in a water-soluble form that is easily taken up by plants. It is a very gentle and beneficial fertiliser. As you feed the worms they'll excrete the castings into the bedding. After a few months the bedding and everything else you added in the beginning will be eaten and you'll be left with a bed of dark-brown castings. They don't smell and they look like little balls of fine soil.

About two weeks before harvesting, start feeding the worms on one side of the farm only. They will all move to that side to feed. After a couple of weeks, look through the castings on the non-feeding side with the aid of your trowel to make sure there are no worms in there, then fill a container with the castings. When you have all the castings out, refill that side of the worm farm with bedding. When the worms have settled down again, start feeding on the new bedding side and harvest the remaining castings on the other side.

Worm liquid and worm tea

Liquid is released from the food you add to the worm farm and when you water down the bedding to keep the worms moist, that water filters down through the castings and animal manure and drains out into the bucket you put under the container. Dilute that worm liquid in water to the colour of weak black tea and apply to your seedlings, or undiluted to your garden plants.

To make worm tea from castings, scrape about a quarter of a bucket of castings from the top of the farm, or from the container you harvested, and soak them in water for a few hours. Dilute this with water to the colour of weak black tea. The microbes in the tea will stay active for about fifteen hours, so apply it within that time.

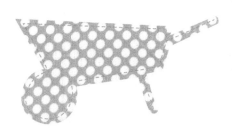

Harvesting your rainwater

I love rain. I love knowing it's watering our vegetables, being harvested from the roof and stored in our water tanks. Setting up a rain-harvesting system can be as simple or sophisticated as you like, but if you're growing your own vegetables and fruit and you want it to be a sustainable system, you should think about storing a substantial amount of water. Water is precious and your efforts at harvesting it will allow you to keep your plants going for a while longer if there is no rain, before you have to rely on town water or the plants die.

If you have stockpile cupboards inside that will see your family through a crisis, water barrels containing harvested water will fit right in with that way of thinking. Just like your stockpile, your rainwater can be used throughout the year, but that water will also be there to use more sparingly in a crisis.

We installed our first water tank – a 5000-litre steel tank – as soon as we moved into our house fourteen years ago. A few years ago, when our government decided to encourage all of us to save water, rebates came in and we bought a 10000-litre poly tank. Those two tanks have not been empty at the same time since we installed the second one. We only use the water in our tanks for the garden, the animals and outside cleaning.

It will cost some money to buy the materials, but over time you'll recoup that cost because you won't use as much tap water. It's also an environmentally sound practice. Instead of wasting the water that would go down the storm-water drainage system, or into a creek or river, you'll capture that water and use it when there is no rain.

Water tanks come in all shapes and sizes. There are poly tanks and steel tanks, all with food-grade lining, that can fit into just about any space. They're usually round but some are oval, and some are like a wine-cask bladder that will sit, out of sight, under decks. You'd be well advised to buy the largest tank you can afford, depending on the rainfall in your area.

I can't give general guidelines about water tanks or barrels because climate differences really do affect how and where you install your system. For instance, where we live, there are torrential downpours in summer, which means we must have our overflow going to an area running directly into our creek. We don't have to empty our barrels in winter to avoid the water freezing and cracking the barrels. Climate plays a big part not only in the size of the tanks but also in how you hook up your system. The store you buy your tank from will have instructions for that particular type of tank and you should be guided by that. No matter what you choose, you must make sure your tank or barrel cannot be accessed by children or animals.

You don't have to spend a lot of money to harvest rainwater. Suitable second-hand containers will do very nicely as your tanks/barrels, and all you'll have to do is connect them to the downpipe with some plumbing pipes – you might already have these on hand. Don't think that it's not worth doing unless you can have a brand-new, state-of-the-art system. Water harvesting is a big part of any self-reliance strategy and, as such, made from scratch with second-hand materials will do just fine.

NOURISHMENT

The kitchen will be a place where you make your memories, offer hospitality to family and friends, sit and talk, or sit and think with a cup in your hand. It's where you'll prepare and cook food and come together as a family for daily meals, as well as for special celebrations. Your kitchen is the heart of your home and it will beat to your rhythm. A good kitchen table will not just hold plates, glasses, flowers and candles; it is your meeting place and it has the potential to be as profound or as simple as you need it to be. 🌱

The heart of the home

We know that food keeps us alive and healthy, but real food is more than just nutrition; it's an important part of our culture and who we are as people. Food brings us together. Many of us have memories of Christmas or celebration dinners around the kitchen table with everyone laughing and catching up with the family news. Out in the kitchen the important work of the day was being taken care of with Mum, Grandma and a couple of aunties cooking a feast that would be talked about for days. This one room, the kitchen, will be a place where you make your memories, offer hospitality to family and friends, sit and talk, or sit and think with a cup in your hand. It's where you'll prepare and cook food and come together as a family for daily meals, as well as for special celebrations.

Your kitchen is the heart of your home and it will beat to your rhythm. A good kitchen table will not just hold plates, glasses, flowers and candles; it is your meeting place and it has the potential to be as profound or as simple as you need it to be.

Of course, food is something we all deal with every day of our lives. Many of the most practical of life skills centre around food – not only cooking and sharing it but also growing, selecting and storing it. Some of us produce a portion of our own food, or store food in stockpiles, jars and freezers, and almost all of us buy food at supermarkets, farmers' markets, butchers, greengrocers and small specialist stores. All of us eat.

Real food versus convenience

There are few products that take advantage of our love of convenience more than food. Whether it's takeaway chicken or hamburgers, precooked food in tins, cooked frozen meals on an aluminium tray, pizzas delivered to your door, soup in cans and plastic bowls, pre-washed salad greens, or pre-prepared vegetable and fruit salads, it's all made by someone else (or even by machines), all provided in polystyrene, plastic or paper packaging, and much of it contains preservatives, artificial colourings and flavours.

How do you find a balance between convenience and healthy food? And how do you know if you're providing your family with good nutrition or a ticking time bomb when so many claims are made about the health benefits of food and then proven totally false a few years later? Nourishment is a big part of a simple life, and without being obsessive about it, it requires that you think carefully about your choices and make a commitment to fresh, organic if possible, local food. If you can't hit your targets every time, aim to be as close as possible. Food is an excellent entry point to your simple-living journey. It's something you have every day so you see the changes straight away.

Organising
your food

Food waste

According to a recent Australia Institute survey, Australian households throw out $1.1 billion worth of fruit and vegetables every year. A similar figure is wasted on restaurant and takeaway meals – the leftovers of ordered meals not eaten and thrown in the bin. We shame ourselves with statistics like that. There should be no, or very little, food waste in your bin at the end of the week. This is something we can all work on – I know I am guilty of leaving food too long in the fridge.

Of course, the best way is to plan well. Often food doesn't even get to the cooking or leftover stage – it sits neglected in the fridge for weeks and is then thrown in the bin. Planning needs to be done before the buying stage, assisted by meal plans, freezer and stockpile lists.

Menu planning

One smart way to cut down on food waste and save time and anxiety is to plan your daily menus a week in advance. Menu planning is not for everyone. When we're fully stocked up in the stockpile cupboard and garden, I don't plan my menus. I take each day as it comes and decide after lunch what we'll eat, according to what the day has been like, how tired I am and which ingredients are available. Some people living close to shops prefer to shop for fresh food daily and others go in and out of menu planning at various stages of life. Generally, though, menu planning will save you time, effort and money. If you haven't tried it yet, give it a go.

A menu plan is a list of predetermined meals you'll cook fresh, cook and freeze, or have the ingredients for at home. They're a bit like budgets: they help you look at your resources in a way that cuts down or eliminates waste, and use what you have to get the best value for your dollar.

When you do your plan, it's wise to include all main meals, lunches and snacks, but main meals and work/school lunches are a good start. If you alternate between eating cereal, porridge, eggs, toast and tea or coffee for breakfast, all you need do is make sure you have those ingredients covered in your shopping and you'll have breakfasts taken care of. If you serve larger breakfasts with varied ingredients, each breakfast should be included in your menu plan.

Menu planning will save you time, effort and money. If you haven't tried it yet, give it a go.

Menu plans will be different for singles and couples and for families. Singles and couples will have a more spontaneous way of planning – perhaps by not tying down a meal to a specific day, and by leaving room for last-minute invitations. A family plan will need to be more structured, probably with more cook-once, eat-twice meals, variations of meals if there are special diets in the family and creative ways of dealing with leftovers. I encourage you to think about how you buy, cook and store your food and to plan your menus in a way that suits you and your circumstances.

Like most things we do in this simple life, organisation is the key. When you start menu planning, start with your favourite easy meals, then go through recipe books or search online to create a list of recipes that you can cook easily and will satisfy you and your family. Don't forget to include seasonal meals in your weekly plans to take advantage of the fresh food you'll find as the year progresses, as it will be cheaper, fresher and at its prime. If you can invest thirty minutes of your time to make up a menu plan for a week, you'll be on the road to simplifying your food and cutting down the time it takes to shop and prepare it.

Keep your weekly meal plans in a folder when you finish with them because they will be the foundation of a monthly meal plan you can work towards. When you have several months' worth of different plans that work with seasonal foods available in your area or your backyard, you'll have a wonderful resource to help you plan your cooking and shopping throughout the year.

How to plan your menus

Start by checking your calendar to see what special days are coming up. You might also have days when you eat at your parents' or a friend's home and have them at yours. Mark those days on your menu plan. Then ask your family what they'd like, check what you have in the garden, freezer and stockpile that needs to be eaten, and look at the weekly flyers when they're delivered to see what food is on special. Know what fruits and vegetables are in season and make a place for them in your plan. Finally, when you go to the markets or shops, be flexible enough to include anything you find that is a real bargain, just coming into season or something new you want to try. The aim here is not only to provide an organising framework to your meals, but also to eat fresh, nutritious food that is not too expensive.

If you don't stockpile, and instead shop for groceries on a weekly basis, start off your menu planning by using what you already have in the kitchen. Check your fridge and pantry for what food is available to work with. Don't forget to include whatever you're growing in the backyard. Many meals have been made here just from our backyard: herb omelettes, eggs with curried vegetables, and tomato and vegetable soups.

You might want to do your shopping first and buy only what looks fresh and delicious, then work out your menu plan from that. Or you might decide to do a mix of both by deciding on certain recipes that you're sure you'll cook, then supplementing them with whatever is appealing at the market and looking for recipes for those ingredients when you return. Whatever way works best for you is what you should stick with.

Make sure you understand the principles of good nutrition and be guided by your common sense. If you need to read about nutrition and the food groups, do that before you start and build your menu plan on that knowledge. The Dieticians Association of Australia's website (daa.asn.au) has some good information, recipes and tips. Be mindful of the different requirements for adults, children, adolescents, pregnant and breastfeeding women and the elderly. The differences are not great, but they're important, and you should know about them if you're the main provider of food in your family. Don't be afraid to try new foods and give yourself a lot of variety.

If you plan before you buy, it's just a matter of marking up a sheet of paper with each day's meals on it. Make room on the sheet for a shopping list and if there's an ingredient you need but don't have, mark it on the shopping list. You'll save time and money if you cook double the quantity – cook once, eat twice. For instance, when I cook tuna and pasta bake, it serves four. We eat it two nights in a row, the second night being the best as the flavours have had time to develop. Or you can freeze leftovers that have a high liquid component, like soup, pasta sauces, casseroles, roast with gravy, curries and many other dishes. The meal takes the same amount of time to prepare but the second night you save on preparation time and energy bills by just using enough energy to reheat the food.

Sample meal plan

	Breakfast	Lunch	Snack	Dinner
Monday	Tea and toast with vegemite or jam, or porridge and milk and fresh juice	Sandwiches or leftovers with tea	Apples	Spinach pie and salad
				Leftover morning tea cake
Tuesday			Grapes	Corned beef, mashed potatoes, cabbage, carrots
				Fruit
Wednesday			Oranges	Corned beef fritters, potatoes, baby peas, carrots
				Date-stuffed baked apples
Thursday			Pineapple	Beef casserole, herb dumplings, green beans
				Fruit
Friday			Apples	Fresh fish and salad
				Yoghurt with stewed apricots
Saturday			Fruit salad	Roast chicken, potatoes, pumpkin, golden beets
				Fruit salad with yoghurt
Sunday	Bacon, eggs, toast	Lunch with Susan	Dried apricots	Leftover roast chicken as curried chicken and vegetables
				Leftover fruit salad
To buy	Bacon, milk	Bread flour	Dried apricots, pineapple, oranges, lemons	Frozen spinach, filo pastry, salad greens, tomatoes, carrots, yoghurt, golden beets

Storing your food

Food is usually a never-ending expense in the household budget. If you can save money on food, you'll generally save big money over the course of your life. It makes sense that you look for bargains, buy local and get the freshest food available, and you should also store your food so it doesn't deteriorate before you eat it. This is an important subject because food needs to be healthy and safe every time you eat it. One of your jobs as a homemaker or provider of food is to learn about how to safely store food in the way that's most suited to your climate and way of living.

Stockpiling

If you're driving to the shops a few times a week to buy a few items, now is a good time to rethink your strategy. You're using more fuel than you need to, and adding to the emissions already attached to the items you buy. If you would love to have a little shop close by, where you could find all those things you forgot to buy and where items are always on sale, create that store for yourself in your own home. That is what a stockpile is: your own open-all-hours convenience store offering the best prices.

The main idea behind stockpiling is that you work out what you usually eat and use in your home and, over time, buy those things that can be stored safely in a cupboard or freezer when they're on sale, storing them in a separate area.

> *A stockpile is your own open-all-hours convenience store offering the best prices.*

To start a stockpile from scratch, your first step is to work out what you need to store. The easy, non-food things to think of are soap, toilet paper, tissues, toothpaste, toothbrushes and cleaning products. If you make your own cleaners, you'll need baking soda, white vinegar, borax, washing soda and laundry soap.

Then work out your food list. The key to a successful stockpile is to include only what you know you'll eat and will use. There is absolutely no use in buying and stockpiling a great bargain if you don't eat it or use it in some way.

If you bake bread, include bread flour, seeds and yeast; if you bake cakes and biscuits, include things like sultanas, dates, brown sugar, cocoa, choc chips and nuts. Also make room for baked beans, dried beans, tinned salmon and tuna, honey, tea, coffee, milk powder, Vegemite, peanut butter, olive oil, vinegar, seasonings, dried pasta, sugar, salt, pepper and spices. We buy olive oil and rice bran oil for cooking and soap making in 4-litre tins when it's on sale. We always have powdered milk in the cupboard as well and I usually cook with it instead of using fresh milk. Powered milk is bought in a 1-kilogram foil bag and stored in a glass jar when opened.

When you know what you need to buy, work out where you will store your food. If you're like me, you'll have a few different spaces. I have a pantry and two stockpile cupboards. The pantry is where I keep everything I am currently using – the things that are open and being used regularly. My pantry is in the kitchen. The stockpile cupboard contains unopened items that are being stored for future use. I have one food stockpile cupboard near the kitchen and another, containing toiletries and laundry products, in the second bathroom. As you can see, stockpiling is an organic thing that tends to fit in wherever you have space. Don't be afraid to store your stockpiled goods in the bedroom or garage if you have no room near your kitchen. Your pantry needs to be in the kitchen because you're using those foods every day, but the stockpile can be anywhere in the house or garage.

STOCKPILING BENEFITS

- You'll shop monthly instead of weekly, saving all that time you now spend on grocery shopping. When your stockpile is fully operational, you'll only need to top it up and buy the fresh foods like milk, meat, fruit and vegetables.
- You'll save money because much of what is in your stockpile cupboard will be bought in bulk and on sale.
- If there's an unusual family situation – you are sick, your partner is out of work, your children need much more of your time for school projects or sports, you'll know you can still feed everyone with what's already in your home, sitting in the stockpile cupboard.
- If there is an emergency (floods, cyclones, bushfires) you won't need to go out as you'll have all your provisions safely stored at home.

When you buy dried goods like bread flour, self-raising flour, nuts, seeds, pasta, corn flour, lentils and rice, it's a good idea to put them in your freezer for a few days to kill off any bug larvae that happen to be in there. It's horrible to think they are there, but they usually are. If you've ever wondered how weevils or pantry moths can hatch out in a sealed container, it's because the larvae were in the product when you bought it. Freezing will kill them.

When you have your stockpile working well, make sure you look after it. Check there are no rodents, bugs or water that could ruin your food. Add new food at the back and always take from the front, as that will rotate your stock. Every so often, go through your stockpile to make sure everything is okay, that there are no moths, bugs or leaks and your home-processed food is not mouldy. If you find anything like that, empty your stockpile cupboard, wipe up any moisture, vacuum the shelves to pick up insect eggs, then wipe your shelves over with a terry cloth dipped in hot water and eucalyptus or tea-tree oil. Don't make your solution too strong because you don't want the smell to get into your food. You just want to deter the bugs.

If possible, keep all your dry goods in airtight containers to protect them from bugs. Beans, chickpeas, lentils, dried fruit, salt, rice, sugar, coconut, polenta and so on are stored in the original packages in the stockpile cupboard and, when in use, transferred to a glass jar and stored in the pantry. If you don't have storage jars, it's a good idea to buy one every time you do your shopping.

STORAGE CONTAINERS

There are various concerns about plastic having contact with food and it is a good general rule to use glass for storage if you can, or food-quality plastic. I try to use glass containers for the dried goods but for the bulk amounts I use food-grade plastic. I got some food-grade, round plastic buckets for storing flour from my local baker. These are really handy, but recently I also found some Decor square buckets capable of holding 10 kilograms. Square buckets will fit in the cupboard and use the space you have more efficiently than round buckets.

As with most things in life, you should do the best you can do and don't stress if you can't do what you would like to. If you can't afford to use purpose-built glass storage jars, use food-quality plastic. If you have few containers, keep food in its package until you need to use it, and if you have no container to store it in, seal it in a plastic bag or cover it with a clean tea towel and store it in the fridge or a sealed cupboard.

Don't forget to add home-produced food to your stockpile as well. We often use home-grown fruit and vegetables, or cheap seasonal boxes of fruit and vegetables, to make relish, chutneys, sauces, jams, pickles and preserved fruit. All these are made to the recipes I've been using for years, processed in a water bath and stored for up to a year in the stockpile cupboard. When you have all this beautiful home-preserved fruit and jam, don't be tempted to display it on your dresser or kitchen shelves. It should be kept in a dark, cool cupboard and lined up so you use the oldest first.

Stockpiling groceries is the best way I know of to lower your food bills and it can also help you survive an emergency – both a national emergency and a personal emergency. But remember, it's an investment and worth a lot of money; it must be looked after. If you do an audit every three months, as well as when you add new stock to your cupboard, you'll reap all the benefits of your stockpile.

Storing fresh fruit and vegetables

Fresh fruit and vegetables should be stored in a few different ways.

- **Potatoes and sweet potatoes** should not be refrigerated. Remove them from the plastic bag, as plastic will make them sweat and they'll rot. Check for damage – throw away any damaged or green ones, and place the good potatoes in a basket or container that allows air circulation. Store in a cool, dry, dark place.
- **Onions** need the same storage conditions as potatoes, but keep them in their own container in a cool, dry, dark place. Onions and potatoes each emit a gas that can cause the other to rot.
- **Tomatoes** tend to lose flavour in the fridge, so it's best to place them in a bowl and keep them on the bench. They will continue to ripen and are best eaten when they're fully ripe.
- **Garlic** can be stored with tomatoes on the kitchen bench.
- **Citrus** can be left on the bench in a bowl if they're fresh and you'll eat them within a week. They'll develop their true flavour if not in the fridge. If you're not sure how old they are, store in the fridge in the crisper.

- **Bananas** should be bought fresh and eaten as soon as possible. Don't store them in the fridge as they'll go brown. If you don't think you'll eat the bananas soon, put them in a plastic bag in the freezer. Do not peel – store them in the freezer as they are. Defrosted, they can be used in cakes and muffins.

- **Pears** should be left on the bench to ripen properly and eaten as soon as they're ripe.

- **Leafy greens** are stored in the fridge. Wash, shake off the excess water and store in a plastic bag or plastic container. Clean, recycled plastic bags are perfect for this. The bags can be washed and reused many times.

- **Spinach** is kept unwashed in the fridge. It has a very short shelf life, so if you want to store it, it's best to freeze it.

- **Herbs** should be washed and placed on a clean, moist cloth in a recycled plastic bag.

- **Celery** should be washed, then shake off excess water and wrap tightly in two sheets of aluminium foil. Seal it up so there's no celery sticking out, and store in the fridge. It will stay crisp for at least two months.

- **Root vegetables** such as carrots, parsnips and turnips always need their green tops cut off as they will take moisture from the root. Wash, dry completely and store in a plastic container in the fridge, or wrap in foil in a similar way to celery.

- **Mushrooms** should not be washed, as they will absorb the water, making them difficult to cook. Place in a brown paper bag, or put them in a bowl and cover with another bowl or cotton cloth. Use within a week.

- **Apples, capsicums, eggplant, beans and cucumbers** all go in the crisper of the fridge.

- **Rockmelon, pawpaw, pumpkin** and other similar fruit will store better in the fridge if you remove all the seeds after cutting them open.
- **Peaches and nectarines** can be ripened on the bench. If they're ripe, store them in the fridge.
- **Avocados** can ripen on the bench. When they're ripe, store in the fridge and eat as soon as you can.
- **Nuts** are placed in small jars and kept in the fridge.

> Food such as tomatoes, bananas and passionfruit do not benefit from refrigeration, and give off gasses that accelerate ripening in other fruit and vegetables, so I store them on the kitchen bench. None of them last long and they're fine for their short life in a bowl on the bench.

Freezing

Freezing is an easy way of preserving food. It does not sterilise food, like a water bath or pressure canner does, but it slows down changes in food and retards the growth of microorganisms due to the extreme cold. It doesn't require special equipment, except the freezer itself, and it doesn't take much time. It's much faster than using a water bath and if treated properly, the food usually retains its nutrition, texture and colour. I believe freezing is the best method of preserving food but it does cost money to keep the freezer going and you run the risk of losing the food to spoilage if your power is cut for a length of time.

> If your freezer is under a window, make sure the sun doesn't shine on it. If sun comes through that window, put up a curtain.

Freezing will not preserve your food indefinitely. It stops the fast growth of bacteria, but the sooner you can eat the food, the better. Long-term freezing is not good for any food. Be guided by your freezer manual, but generally three months is a good rule to work by.

That is the length of a season, so if you're freezing to see you through winter, the three-month rule should work well.

For the best results, keep your freezer below –18°C. While freezing will not kill the bacteria that cause botulism, if the bacteria are present, they cannot multiply and produce harmful toxins in a freezer kept at this temperature. The freezer that is inside your fridge usually isn't cold enough for long-term storage. When we know we will be adding new foods to our freezer, I set the temperature lower twenty-four hours before adding the food. That allows the food to freeze faster. The faster food freezes, the less damage done to the cell wall structure of the food.

We freeze meat that we buy in bulk, as well as small amounts of fish from the local fishing co-op. I have also been using my large chest freezer as a cool room for storing grains and dry goods. In our humid climate, especially in summer, it's been a very good way of making sure bugs and mildew don't spoil our food. I also freeze excess vegetables from our garden. Some plastic containers will crack when subjected to very low temperatures so make sure you have the right kind of container. Don't freeze glass, as most of it will break.

Blanching vegetables

If you grow your own vegetables or buy cheap seasonal vegetables by the box you will get their full value by eating some fresh and freezing the rest. If you decide to freeze them you'll need to do it when they're still in their prime. If you know you'll only store something for a couple of weeks, it doesn't need to be blanched. But I tend to blanch all vegetables I freeze because I generally don't know when they'll be used. Blanching vegetables before freezing them inactivates enzymes that can spoil the food and it helps kills some microorganisms on the surface of the vegetables. Blanching will also collapse the vegetables a little and that helps pack more food into a small space. Garlic, onion and capsicum don't need blanching. Peel the garlic and onions before freezing, and slice the capsicum and place in a plastic bag.

ACTION PLAN: *Blanching vegetables*

* Wash all the vegetables thoroughly, then peel and chop to a suitable size for cooking.

* Prepare a deep pot of boiling water and have a colander and tongs ready.

* Fill your kitchen sinks or large bowls with cold water and ice. It's fine to use the same water for all the different vegetables.

* Put small amounts of the vegetables into the boiling water and time them, from the moment the water returns to the boil. There is a blanching time list below but generally, greens are ready when they turn bright green. Dense vegetables like pumpkin and sweet potato should be cooked before freezing.

* When blanching is complete, remove the vegetables from the boiling water and plunge them into the iced water to prevent overheating.

* When the vegetables are cool, drain in a colander.

BLANCHING TIMES FOR COMMON VEGETABLES

Asparagus (whole): 2 minutes	Fennel (whole): 3 minutes
Beans (whole): 2–3 minutes	Parsnips (chunks): 2–3 minutes
Beetroot (whole): 5–10 minutes	Peas (shelled): 1 minute
Broccoli (florets): 3–4 minutes	Snow peas (whole): 30 seconds
Brussels sprouts (whole): 4–5 minutes	Spinach, silverbeet and other green
Cabbage (slices): 2–3 minutes	leaves (not lettuce): 2 minutes
Carrots (slices): 3 minutes	Sweet corn (whole, small): 4 minutes
Carrots (whole, small): 5 minutes	Turnips (chunks): 2–3 minutes
Cauliflower (florets): 4–5 minutes	Zucchini (chunks): 2 minutes

Wrapping food

I always use freezer bags to store food in the freezer (you can buy these from the supermarket) but two layers of greaseproof paper is suitable for short-term storage.

Place the food into the freezer bag and press gently to expel as much air as possible. If you can, move the contents of the bag around a little to make a flat, square package, so it will stack better in the freezer and will defrost faster. Small packs are better than big ones.

If you can twist the bag around and double it back over the food, do it. A double layer will help prevent freezer burn. Otherwise you could use two freezer bags, or wrap the food in greaseproof paper first, then place it in the freezer bag. Freezer bags can be washed and re-used if they're not ripped.

Freezing liquids

Freezing is also a good way to store liquids like meat and vegetable stock, milk, or pasta and curry sauces. Food expands when it freezes so make sure you leave a small amount of headspace, but don't leave too much as you don't want a lot of air in the container. The larger the container, the more headspace you'll need. For example, about 500 ml of liquid will require a headspace of about 12 mm. A litre of the same liquid in a 1-litre pack needs about 25 mm. If you're freezing commercial milk straight from the shop, you will have to take a little bit out of the bottle to allow for expansion.

If you have time, it's best to defrost liquids in the fridge. Milk must be defrosted in the fridge, but juice can be left out to defrost if you don't have time to let it defrost in the fridge. Stock, curry and pasta sauces can also be defrosted on the stove if you'll be using them straight away.

Freezer records

It's a very good idea to keep a record of what you have in your freezer. This will allow you to manage your frozen food effectively. A freezer, particularly a chest freezer, is a difficult space to manage and a record of what goes in, with the date, and what comes out, will give you an accurate freezer inventory at any time without you having to unpack it to see what's at the bottom.

Make sure you mark all bags or containers you put in the freezer with the type of food and the date it was frozen.

IF THE POWER GOES OFF

If you know the power will be off on a particular day, turn up the freezer the day before. Then, when the power goes off, unplug the freezer and cover it with blankets or quilts to insulate it. Don't open the freezer until the power comes on again. When the power comes back on, plug the freezer in again and switch it on. A freezer will usually be able to keep food safe this way for two days.

If power outages are frequent and long where you live, freezing large amounts of food might not turn out to be so frugal after all.

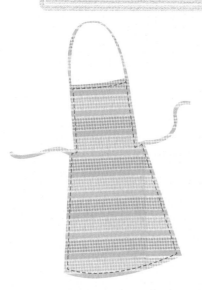

Preserving food

In Australia, there is a long, fine tradition of homesteaders 'putting up' food – to see them through tougher times, and also because they were so far away from the shops. They would do it when the season was high and crops were plentiful. If you want to cook from scratch and consume fewer preservatives, preserving food is still a good skill to have. Used in conjunction with other methods of long-term storage, preserving will give you good food out of season, or allow you to have your favourite jam or tomato sauce ready in the cupboard.

Most of the preserving I do is not to keep us going through the leaner seasons – our garden does that – it's to make a delicious sauce from a glut of tomatoes, to make the most of a cheap or free box of peaches, or to make jams and relishes. All those things I make are family favourites now and all much tastier and cheaper than anything I can buy at the supermarket.

People have been preserving food in jars for a long time, so many different methods have been developed. There is a small risk

of botulism poisoning from incorrectly processed food, but serious problems are very rare. Most of the guidelines have been updated in the past twenty years, so don't use an old preserving book or recipes. Please be guided by your thermometer, the newer information available and your common sense. If you intend to do a lot of preserving I encourage you to buy an up-to-date Australian preserving book or borrow one from the library. I recommend the *Australian Women's Weekly Preserves*, which will probably be available at your local newsagent, bookshop or online.

The simple kind of preserving I do is called water bath processing. The principle behind it is to make a jam, sauce or relish, or prepare fresh fruit such as peaches, then place the food in clean jars that will seal and be sterilised after being boiled in a pot for the required time. When food is processed in this way, the prolonged heat kills most bacteria and yeasts. It is suitable only for high-acid foods like tomatoes and rhubarb, and some foods to which acid, in the form of vinegar or lemon juice, has been added (such as jams and relish). You cannot process foods like meat, soup or low-acid vegetables such as corn, peas, beans or cucumber in a water bath. You can pickle cucumbers in vinegar, however – the vinegar adds the required acidity. Pickled cucumbers can be stored in the fridge for up to six months.

A frugal set-up

While there are plenty of jars and preserving units you can buy to help you preserve food in jars, you may be able to do it with what you already have in your home.

You will need:

- **A stockpot** large enough for you to have at least an inch of water over the top of your tallest jar.
- **A tea towel** folded up to prevent the jars touching the hot bottom of the pot. Alternatively you could use newspaper or a round cake rack.
- **A thermometer** to clip to the side of the pot and monitor the temperature while the jars are in there. I use a milk thermometer that I bought for $15 at a kitchen store.
- **Recycled jars** to store the food in. Pop-top lids that have a thin ring of rubber on the inside are best – they will help you seal the jar. Some people advise against using recycled jars with metal lids but I have been using them for many years and have never had a problem. You must make your own decision on what equipment you use, but make sure you carefully check your jars and lids for damage. Don't use jars larger than a litre, as there is no guarantee that the heat necessary to kill bacteria will penetrate into the middle of a firmly packed large jar. Also avoid jars with plastic lids, like Vegemite or peanut butter jars.
- **Tongs** to lift the jars out of the pot.

The water bath method

This method of processing is suitable for the frugal set-up with recycled jars or for a commercial processor and jars bought specifically for processing.

ACTION PLAN: *The water bath method*

Check and sterilise the jars

✳ Before you start your preserving session, wash all your jars and lids and run your fingers around the rims to check for chips or cracks. Check the lids for dents, rust or holes. Never use damaged jars or lids.

✳ Wash the jars, lids and tongs in warm soapy water and rinse in warm water, then place them in your oven set on 160°C for twenty minutes. Keep the jars warm until you fill them. Hot food may crack the glass if you allow it to cool.

Fill the jars

✳ Now you are ready to deal with the contents of the jars. This can be either a recipe like jam or chutney that you cook and pour, hot, into the warm jar, or fruit that you add syrup to, or vegetables (pickles) that you add spiced vinegar to.

✳ If you're cooking jam, make it according to the recipe and, using a wide-mouth funnel, pack the jars to within about 7 mm of the jar top. This allows the contents to expand when boiling, without bursting out of the jar.

✳ If you're packing fruit or pickles, pack your jars firmly and neatly, using a packing stick or wooden spoon handle to remove any air bubbles. Air in the jar might cause mould to form when the jar is being stored.

✳ When the jar is packed, pour syrup, fruit juice or water over the fruit (according to the recipe), or the spiced vinegar over the pickles, to within about 8 mm of the jar top. It is important not to change any preserving recipes because they'll have correct levels of sugar, lemon juice or vinegar that assist with the preservation of the food.

✳ If you're using screw-on lids, screw them on fairly tightly, but not too tight, and wipe the jars to make sure no jam or syrup is on the outside.

Heat, cool and store

✳ Place the jars into your processor/pot that is half-filled with warm water, then add enough water to cover the jars by one or two inches of water.

✻ Bring the processor/pot slowly up to the boil on a low heat – this will take 45–60 minutes. When it's boiling gently, hold it at a slow boil for another 45 minutes for small jars, or 1 hour for larger jars.

✻ When the time is up, use your tongs to remove the jars from the saucepan. Place them on a tea towel on the bench to cool slowly for 24 hours. The prolonged heat will form a vacuum in the jars.

✻ When the jars are cool, check that all the lids (or the pop-tops, if your jars have them) are inverted. If you're unsure, if the lid is not inverted, or if there has been a spillage, put that jar in the fridge and use it as soon as you can. All the jars must have a perfect seal to be stored in a cupboard.

✻ For long-term storage, the jars should be stored in a cool dark cupboard. They will keep well for about a year without losing their nutrition. Don't be tempted to display your jars on an open shelf. They will lose their colour.

Simple syrup and spiced vinegar recipes

SYRUP FOR FRUIT

Light, medium and heavy refer to the amount of sugar in the syrup. Use whichever suits your taste.

Ingredients

- light – 1 cup sugar to 3 cups water makes 3½ cups of syrup
- medium – 1 cup sugar to 2 cups water makes 2½ cups of syrup
- heavy – 1 cup sugar to 1 cup water makes 1¾ cups of syrup

Method

Add the sugar and water to a saucepan and bring to the boil. Stir to dissolve the sugar. Remove from heat and allow to cool.

You could use fruit juice, honey, molasses or golden syrup instead of sugar, but it will add another flavour to your fruit. Fruit may also be preserved in plain water but it won't keep as well as that preserved in a sweet liquid. Artificial sweeteners are not recommended for preserving as they develop a bitter taste over time.

SPICED VINEGAR FOR PICKLES

Good-quality vinegar needs to be used for preserving, with an acid content of at least 5 per cent. Brown malt, white, balsamic, white wine, red wine or apple cider vinegar are all good to use.

Ingredients

- 1½ cups vinegar
- ¾ cup water
- ¾ cup sugar
- ½ teaspoon peppercorns
- ½ teaspoon mustard seeds
- ¼ teaspoon pure salt
- 2 bay leaves

Method

Place all ingredients in a saucepan and bring to the boil. Simmer for 5 minutes.

Remove from heat and allow to cool. Strain off the chunky bits with a sieve before using.

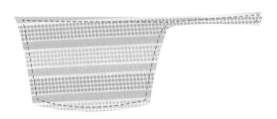

Shopping for food

Fruit and vegetables

If you're not growing your own food, the best way to buy fruit and vegetables is seasonally. Eating what is in season will give you the freshest and possibly the cheapest food. It is really difficult to know what is in season when you're shopping at a mainstream supermarket because most of the fruit and vegetables will look fresh, even when they're not. Sometimes apples will be months old and just out of storage; tomatoes might be weeks old and if you're not a gardener yourself it's difficult to know the signs to look for. If you can, shop at local markets and ask the seller when the produce was picked. If you can't do that, and supermarkets are your only option, do some research on what is in season in your area, and also be guided by price. Tomatoes and bananas are warm-weather crops so in summer, when they're in season, they're cheaper. In winter, when berries, spinach, broccoli, cabbages and kale thrive, they're cheaper.

It's easy to find out online what is in season in your area – check the resources at the back of the book for suggestions. Print out the information you find and keep it in your household management journal.

Supermarkets

Before you rush off to fill up your stockpile cupboard, do a bit of research and find out which is your closest and cheapest supermarket. That will be your base supermarket. For me it's Aldi, as their prices seem to be consistently lower than those at Woolworths and Coles. We buy as much as we can there. I always read the labels to see where the produce is from. If there is a choice, we buy produce from our own state; if not, and we're shopping at Aldi – a German supermarket – we buy Australian or German (Hanno is German and I used to live there, so I feel very comfortable buying their products). I never buy food imported from China, as there are lots of questions about the growing practices used there. My next favoured supermarket is my local IGA. It's close to where I do my voluntary work, and that is where I top up on fresh foods like milk, dairy and fruit and vegetables if we aren't growing them at home.

If you can, shop at local markets and ask the seller when the produce was picked.

You will find that most supermarkets have a large stable of groceries and food that they put on special regularly over a period of about three months. All those foods will be on special at various times during those three months and you should try to work out when your supermarket cycles their specials. When something you need comes on special, if it can be stored safely, buy as much as you need to carry you through until it comes on special again, or as much as you can afford.

Be aware that not everything you buy will go on special. Things like vanilla extract, baking supplies and unprocessed products rarely do. You should buy those items at your cheapest supermarket or bulk food store. In some towns and cities, bulk food stores offer a great service. You can buy bulk bread flour, as well as all the other flours, a wide variety of dried fruits and nuts, tea and coffee, spices, grains like rice and wheat, and pulses such as beans and dried peas. These places are generally cheaper because you don't pay for extravagant packaging. If you can find such a shop close by, it will probably be cheaper to buy as many products as you can from there. You can also take your own containers or bags to these stores to save on taking plastic bags home.

Choosing your products

Make sure you buy food with perfect packaging. You don't want dents in your cans, rips in paper or plastic bags or squashed boxes. Check 'use by' and 'best before' dates while still in the shop. If you intend storing your purchase for a few months, make sure the use-by date doesn't expire before that time. Look through the products on the shelf to see if any have later dates, and if they do, choose those. If you do a big stockpile shop, pack everything well for the trip home and go home as soon as you can so you can get frozen or fresh goods into their appropriate places before they start to warm up. When you bring home new food from the supermarket, pack your cold items away first, then go on to everything else.

GUIDES TO FRESHNESS

Best before: This means the food, if still in the intact package, is at its premium on or before the date marked. If the date has passed, the food may still be edible, but may not be at its best. Sometimes you will see 'best before' food that has passed its date reduced for sale in the shops.

Use by: This date indicates the end of the acceptable storage life of the food. All food that should be eaten within a certain period of time for health and safety reasons will be marked with a use-by date. It is illegal to sell food after the use-by date.

Baked on: This is used on bread that has a shelf life of less than seven days.

Organic food

Organic food is food that has been grown in natural conditions without chemical fertilisers, pesticides or artificial additives. The fruit and vegetables we grow and our chooks' eggs are all organic. We try to grow our garden so we have a continuation of supply but that doesn't always happen so sometimes we have to buy what we need.

We can't afford to buy certified organic fruit and vegetables, but I don't worry about it. I prefer to buy what is in season and what is freshest. I have no doubt some of the produce at the local Sunday farmers' market is organic but isn't sold with that label because it's not certified. The only organic product I continue to buy is bakers' flour. It's more expensive than the ordinary flour but we eat bread every day and I prefer it to be organic. We usually buy local, fresh Guernsey milk from Maleny Dairies. I see these cows grazing on pastures around our area every time I drive up the mountain. They live in a healthy and natural environment. The dairy industry is a small but important part of the area I live in. We want to support them, so we buy local dairy foods, and that includes local cheese and, sometimes, yoghurt. I make my own yoghurt when I can, but when I buy it, it's locally made, but not organic.

When you do your shopping, and if you can't afford to buy organic food, try to buy local. You might find that your local butcher or greengrocer has sourced local food and will know a lot about the produce they sell. They usually know their primary producers. If you live in an area where people are growing food, try to barter with them. If you're growing some of your own food, you might be able to barter eggs for honey, tomatoes for local milk or a box of your produce for some meat from your local butcher. Anything is possible; you just have to ask around.

As homemakers we are responsible for the food brought into our homes and for buying the healthiest food for the dollars we have available. I believe that if you are living on a limited income you will do more for your health if you cook from scratch, with as much fresh produce as possible, than trying to buy all organic food. Get rid of the food that contains preservatives and added flavourings and colours. Buy oatmeal instead of processed cereal, make macaroni and cheese from scratch, not from a box, encourage your family to eat fresh fruit by having a bowl of it on the kitchen table. Start your own vegetable garden if you have the space and time. These will be big steps towards a healthier life, and will cost you less rather than more.

As homemakers we are responsible for the food brought into our homes and for buying the healthiest food for the dollars we have available.

Don't be pressured into buying organic food if you can't afford it. Of course it's great to eat organic if you can because you'll be eating food that has been grown naturally without artificial additives, but when you have to stretch your dollars as far as possible, all organic usually isn't an option. Like everything else in this simple life, it takes a bit of organising to discover where you'll get value for money, but always be guided by your own values, not by what someone tells you or what you read – and I include myself in that. If what I write here doesn't fit well with your value system and how you've decided to live, don't do it. Simple living is about being authentic and living an examined life and if you've thought about the values you want to live by, be confident and stick with them no matter what others around you are doing.

Cooking
from scratch

If you're a new mother staying at home with your baby, if you've recently moved away from your parents' home, or you're just looking for a way to start simplifying your life, learning to cook from scratch is a significant step on your road to simple independence. A home-cooked meal is real food – just like those meals your mum or grandma made that used wholesome, fresh ingredients and staples from the cupboard. There were few cookbooks for those meals; they came from a long history of understanding food and how to mix it together with good results, and sometimes from recipes written on a piece of paper or in an old exercise book and passed down through the family.

Food producers know the appeal of home cooking and try to use that longing for real food to sell their products. They name their food items 'Mama's Choice', 'Grandma's Favourite' or 'Granny's Pie'. Don't be fooled: many of them contain preservatives, artificial colourings, stabilisers, firming agents, colour fixatives and flavour enhancers.

Even some organic foods come with preservatives, so if you're trying to eat healthy food, the best way is to cook it yourself.

What you cook will be healthier, cheaper and fresher than any convenience food you buy, and it will contain only what you put in it. I'm not telling you that you should never buy another take-away meal or eat convenience food, but I encourage you to move towards home cooking and to try to make most of your meals from scratch.

THE TIME FACTOR

Home cooking does take longer – that is why you pay so much for convenience food. You are paying for someone else's time and experience to make your food, along with all the ingredients they use. But over time, as you develop your skills, and your desire to cook increases, you'll realise you can cut back on the time it takes for many things. You can cook double the amount and freeze another meal for later, you can do all the preparation at a convenient time and just do the cooking part when it's needed, you can use a slow cooker that will cook while you're at work. There are ways around the time issue.

Developing flavour

There is more to good home cooking than following a recipe. To consistently cook well, you need to understand how flavours develop. There are ways of developing flavour in your home cooking that don't involve adding anything from a packet or opening a can of soup. For instance, certain foods like onions, garlic, ginger and bacon hold strong flavours that transfer readily to the foods they're cooked with. All these techniques involve good wholesome food, with no artificial flavours. And don't be afraid to experiment. Start off with a good basic dish that you find appealing and modify it by adding the flavours that your family likes. Once you've mastered that skill, you're on your way to being a good home cook.

Caramelisation

One of the best ways to add flavour to some food – meat, fish, fruit and vegetables – is to caramelise it. Many foods have natural sugars in them but they don't make the food sweet. Caramelising changes the colour of the food to brown and intensifies the flavour by removing water from the food's sugars.

If you are making a casserole or stew, caramelising the meat first, before you do anything else, will make it taste better. Add a small amount of oil – I always use extra virgin olive oil – to your pan, heat the oil so it's hot and add the chopped meat. Don't add too much meat: if you have a large amount to cook, add it in batches and brown the meat a small amount at a time. If you add too much meat at once, the juices from the meat will release and it will stew instead of dry fry. You're trying to remove the water from the sugars in the meat, so if you stew the meat at this point it won't caramelise and therefore won't develop that delicious flavour you're after.

The process is the same for other foods. Your aim is to cook the food until it is golden brown, not dark brown or black. When you have reached that stage you will have developed the flavour and you can go on to the next step in your cooking.

Spices

Spices are the flowers, bark, roots, berries or seeds of various plants used to develop flavour in cooking. Common spices include pepper, chilli powder, cardamom, coriander seeds and paprika. Spices are usually dried to a powdered form and added in small amounts. You will release more flavour from spices if you dry fry them in a pan before using them in your cooking. Spices are often used in long, slow cooking, such as curries, which use a combination of various spices. Other spices such as pepper can be added raw, sprinkled on the top of food to add a quick burst of flavour.

When you buy spices, only buy small amounts as they lose flavour when stored for a long time. Store your spices in a cool dark place in a sealed jar.

Herbs

A herb is any plant that is useful in cooking and adds flavour, such as parsley, chives, sage, oregano and thyme. They can be used fresh or dried. Adding herbs at the beginning of a recipe will develop flavour while cooking, but you can also add them at the end of cooking to give freshness to the dish. For instance, you might add parsley, oregano and thyme when you begin cooking a spaghetti sauce, then add more parsley at the end, giving the meal a fresh taste.

Sugar

Sugar or honey can be added in very small amounts to bring out the flavour in certain foods. For instance, half a teaspoon of sugar in a tomato dish such as pasta sauce or tomato sauce will make the tomato flavour more intense. The same amount of sugar added to onions will help them caramelise. Cook them slowly, over a low heat, stirring occasionally until golden.

Evaporation

You can also add flavour by evaporating the water out of food. To do this, simply bring it to the boil, then simmer with the lid off the pot. As the steam evaporates it intensifies the flavour in the dish. A good example of evaporation is when you make a meat sauce for pasta. You add stock, wine and tomatoes at the beginning, and the major portion of the time for cooking this type of food is taken up with the sauce reducing and thickening; that is evaporation.

Stock

Cooking bones with vegetables and herbs in water will make stock. Stock can be used to make a variety of delicious soups or can be added to casseroles, sauces or curries for a real depth of flavour. Make good stock whenever you have the bones of chicken or beef or if you have spare vegetables. If you roast the bones in the oven for an hour beforehand, you'll caramelise the flavours and make better stock.

The hierarchy of food waste

When you buy anything you are responsible for it – and if you're living frugally, you want to get the full value of it. If you have a dog you must make sure it stays healthy and doesn't bark day and night, upsetting the neighbours; your car needs to be kept in good mechanical condition and only those licensed to drive can operate it. Everything comes with its own set of responsibilities – and food is no exception. When you bring it home you must store it so that it doesn't deteriorate before you have a chance to eat it, and if there is food that will not be eaten by the family, it should be disposed of in an environmentally friendly way. For me, throwing food in the bin to be taken to the rubbish tip or putting it in the garbage disposal system isn't a solution, as I'm just passing my responsibility on to someone else. If you believe that living more simply involves personal responsibility and independence, this is an area that you'll need to focus on.

We deal with food scraps and waste according to the value they return to us. At the top of that hierarchy are the chickens – they turn scraps into food again. The chooks get plate leftovers including meat and fish, day-old bread, leftover salad, tops of tomatoes, fruit and vegetable peels. Along with the fresh greens they're fed from the garden and the grain we buy for them, they use that food to lay eggs for us.

Everything you buy comes with its own set of responsibilities – and food is no exception.

We love our dog, so even though there is no returned value except for the look on her face, Alice gets leftover cake, soft biscuits, leftover meat and fish that's not going to the chickens, and all the pieces of meaty fat or gristle I trim off meat before cooking.

The worms are the next level in the hierarchy. They get whatever food no one else wants. I put it through the food processor so it's in tiny pieces. They don't need much feeding so their leftover feasts are an occasional thing – definitely not daily.

Potato and onion peels are put in a closed compost bin to slowly decompose. If left in the open compost, they would take too long. Eggshells are left to dry, then pulverised and added to the chook food as a calcium supplement. Tea leaves or tea bags go into the general compost; coffee grounds go around acid-loving plants like blueberries. Pineapple tops can be planted – in a semi-tropical or tropical climate they'll fruit in their second year. Everything else goes into the general compost.

Of course, all this is dependent on having those systems and animals in your backyard, but it's a good idea to think about your food waste no matter where you're living. The Bokashi compost system can be easily set up in the kitchen if you don't have a garden. This is a composting system in a container that reduces kitchen waste to soil conditioner through a process of fermentation.

If you cook at home there will be waste in some form – either eggshells, vegetable peels or food left on a plate. Take the time to work out a system to deal with this kind of waste. It's not a huge problem but you need to take responsibility for it and dispose of it as naturally and easily as you can.

Kitchen checklist

If you haven't done much cooking in the past, here are a few things to think about. Remember, you don't have to know everything straight away. Learn slowly and build up your skills as you go.

- Do you plan your menus in advance? (This works for some families and not others.)
- Do you have enough cooked-from-scratch main meal recipes to cover a six- or seven-day meal rotation?
- Are you able to fill school and work lunch boxes with healthy snacks?
- If you're growing food, how do you intend to use or store your excess?
- Do you minimise food waste?
- Do you use leftovers wisely?
- Are there skills you need to learn, such as how to preserve, blanch, freeze, bake or ferment?
- Can you safely store your food?

- Do you have a place to store recycled bottles and jars?
- Do you have enough large glass or plastic storage containers?
- Is the fridge cooling as efficiently as it should? Are the seals working?
- Do you use your oven efficiently? (Baking two things at once, making twice the amount of food and freezing half.)
- Is your kitchen set up properly for the tasks you carry out frequently?
- If you're composting, do you have a covered container for your kitchen scraps?
- Do you need to make cloth food covers for when you're making bread, ginger beer, sourdough, yoghurt?
- Do you have enough dishcloths and tea towels?

RECIPES

Is there anything more heartwarming, comforting and nourishing than a homemade meal shared with loved ones? Meals can be as simple as a fresh salad with boiled eggs from the backyard, or as special as a five-course feast. Cooking is the only common household task that uses all the senses: sight, sound, smell, taste and touch. No wonder so many of us love serving and eating home-cooked food.

Baking

Bread

Baking bread makes sense economically. Even if you buy a breadmaker, it will still be much cheaper in the long run than buying premade bread. It will also be healthier, as your homemade bread will contain only those ingredients you include, not flavour enhancers, preservatives or colourings.

You can use this recipe to make bread-machine bread, but these instructions are written for a beginner who is making hand-kneaded bread. There are photo tutorials on my blog if you need further information.

When you make your first loaves of bread, you may have trouble getting a good rise from the dough. Adding gluten flour to the recipe will help you get a good loaf of bread even if you have not yet got the kneading under control. When you're more proficient, or if you're using a bread machine, you can leave the gluten flour out. You can also add gluten flour to plain flour to make it high in protein – and therefore suitable to make bread dough – instead of using baker's flour. The ratio is 1 teaspoon of gluten flour to 1 cup of plain flour. Gluten flour is available at supermarkets and health food stores.

As you know, flour and water have virtually no taste. Adding salt and sugar to your flour mix will add flavour, so don't be tempted to leave it out. Another thing you need to know about flour is that it's different all over the country because of the type of wheat used and the level of humidity in the air, so it takes different amounts of water. And even if you use the same bag of flour at different times of the year, you'll probably use slightly more or less water, according to the weather conditions. This just means you have to know what your dough should look and feel like before going to the next step.

Breadmaking is very tactile, even when making the dough in a bread machine. You need to learn what the dough should feel like and that involves putting your fingers into it, feeling it and remembering that for the next time. What you're aiming for is moist dough that is not sticky, so even though the recipe advises 350 ml, use your common sense, feel the dough and adjust it to suit your conditions.

BEGINNER'S WHITE EVERYDAY LOAF

- 100 ml warm water
- 2 teaspoons dried yeast
- 1 tablespoon sugar
- 4 cups baker's flour – also called strong flour or high-protein flour
- 3 teaspoons gluten flour (optional)
- 2 teaspoons salt
- 250 ml warm water + more if necessary

Step 1: Activating the yeast

Here you're making sure the yeast is fresh and alive. If you use old yeast, your bread won't rise. Pour the warm water into a teacup. Don't use hot water because it will kill the yeast. It should be comfortable to hold your finger in the water. Tip in the yeast and sugar and stir for 15 seconds, then leave it on the bench and prepare your other ingredients. The yeast is activated when it starts to bubble and become frothy. This indicates the yeast is alive.

Step 2: Mixing the dough

Add your dry ingredients to a large mixing bowl. Add the activated yeast and the 250 ml of warm water. Mix all the ingredients with a spoon until it gets to the point where your hands will mix it better, then start bringing the mixture together with your hands. This is the first point when you check the moisture content.

You're aiming for a ball of dough that has combined all the ingredients, with a slightly moist feel. You don't want it wet but it shouldn't be dry either. If your dough looks too dry, get half a cup of warm water and a dessert spoon, and add the water to the dough one spoonful at a time. You have to be careful not to add too much, so do it slowly. Knead the dough, and if it needs more water, add another spoonful. If it looks too wet, add a small amount of extra flour. If it looks and feels okay, go on to the next step.

Step 3: Kneading the dough

Gluten is one of the proteins found in wheat, barley and rye flour. When gluten is mixed with water and kneaded, it develops long strings that help bread rise. It is very difficult to make a light loaf of bread without gluten.

If you've had problems with handmade bread before, you're probably not kneading the dough long enough. This is a very important step if you want light bread with a good crumb. If you're good at kneading, this step will take you *at least* 8 minutes. If you're light-handed, you'll take *at least* 10 minutes. You need a firm and stable surface on which to knead your dough. It's best done on a clean benchtop. Wipe your benchtop with a clean cloth and warm soapy water – don't use antiseptic wipes, as you could kill the yeasts. When you're satisfied the bench is clean, wipe it with a clean tea towel. This surface is ideal for kneading.

If your benchtop is not suitable, use a large bread board with a slightly wet tea towel folded in half underneath. The moistened tea towel will stop the board moving while you're kneading. Sprinkle a small amount of the same flour you used in the recipe onto your benchtop and place the dough on it. Before you start kneading, poke your finger into the dough – the indent should stay there. Poking the dough is a good way to test it as you go through the kneading process.

Start kneading the dough. What you're trying to do is work the dough to get the gluten strands to develop. Push the top of the dough away from you with the heel of your hand while holding the dough steady with your other hand.

The dough stays right in front of you all the time, but you push a portion of it away with every action. After you've pushed out, fold that portion of the dough back on itself like the top of an envelope. Turn the dough a quarter-turn and push it out again with the heel of your hand. Fold it back on itself. Another quarter-turn.

As you knead the dough it will look drier and smoother. Keep kneading until your dough is smooth and elastic, and springs out nicely when you poke your finger in it. If you've been kneading for *at least* 8 minutes (longer if you have a light hand) and your dough is smooth and elastic, then you're ready to move on. Don't rush things just for the sake of a few minutes, because the work you do here will make or break your bread.

Step 4: First rise

The ball of dough will have a smooth side; place it smooth side up, in a clean bowl that's been very lightly greased with cooking oil. Cover the dough with a clean, moist tea towel or a lightly greased piece of plastic wrap. You want the dough to rise in a warm, draft-free area. If the dough stays cold, it will take hours to rise. You could place it in an oven that you've heated to about 150°C for 3 minutes then turned off. Or you could put it outside in the sun (I do this), but make sure it's covered properly as you don't want flies or ants in your mix. You could place a heated wheat bag near the bowl. If you have a hot-water system that is warm during the day, that might be a good place for you. You're looking for a temperature of around 20–24°C. If the area is too hot or too cold it will affect the taste and texture of the finished loaf. Leave the covered dough in the warm spot untouched for about 30 minutes and check. It needs to double in size.

Step 5: Punching down and forming the dough

When the dough has doubled in size, punch the dough to deflate it. Sprinkle flour on your benchtop again, scoop the dough up out of the bowl, and place it on the floured bench. Knead the dough for 2 minutes, using the same technique as before with the heel of your hand.

After 2 minutes of kneading, flatten the dough and roll it into a cigar shape, or whatever shape you want your loaf to be. You will have one smooth side and the underside will be tucked and folded.

At this stage you have the opportunity to add more nutrition to the loaf with oats, wheatgerm, sesame or poppy seeds, polenta, oats, soaked linseed, caraway or any other topping you want to use. I often use a mixture of sesame and poppy seeds with oats on my bread.

If you'd like to add seeds, pick the loaf up with the smooth side on top and, with your other hand, moisten the loaf all over with water. Roll the loaf in the seeds/oats so that it's completely covered. The water will make the coating stick to the loaf.

Water also makes a crisp crust. If you don't want seeds on the loaf but would still like it crusty, just moisten the dough with the water. If you want a softer loaf, skip this step entirely.

Preheat your oven to 230°C and grease a loaf tin lightly. Put the loaf into the tin and sprinkle with a small amount of flour. Making 5 mm deep slashes in the top of the loaf will allow steam to escape and gives you a better rise.

Step 6: Second rise

Let the loaf sit in the loaf tin for the second rise until it has lifted 5 cm or so but is not bulging over the sides. Handle the dough gently at this point.

Step 7: Baking

You need a hot oven to get a good lift, so when it's reached 230°C, gently place the loaf in to bake. After 10 minutes, turn the oven down to 200°C and cook for another 15–20 minutes, or until you can smell baked bread and the loaf is golden brown. Take the bread from the tin and place it on a cake rack to cool. Get the butter ready because you are about to enjoy your bread.

Scones

Scones are easy to make and you can have a batch made and baked in under 30 minutes. The key to good scones is to use buttermilk or whey instead of plain milk, to have fairly moist dough and to treat them gently. If you overwork scones, they'll be tough. You'll need more or less buttermilk or whey depending on your flour.

If you don't have buttermilk, use plain milk with a teaspoon of vinegar or lemon juice added.

2 cups self-raising flour *or*
  2 cups plain flour with 2 teaspoons
  baking powder
pinch of salt

1 tablespoon sugar
30 g cold butter, chopped
1 cup buttermilk *or* whey

1. Preheat oven to 220 °C. Get your tray ready by greasing it or adding baking paper.

2. Sift flour into a large bowl, along with salt and sugar. Add cold butter and rub in lightly with your fingertips until it looks like breadcrumbs.

3. Pour in buttermilk and mix in, using a butter knife, until you have a soft, moist and sticky dough. Over-mixing will result in tough scones.

4. Turn onto a lightly floured surface. Knead lightly for 15 seconds. Press out the dough into a rough circle, about 4 cm thick. Cut into smaller rounds using a cutter or floured wine glass. A cut edge will give you a better rise than a formed edge.

5. Place the cut scones on the baking tray and then into the hot oven, then turn the temperature down to 200 °C and bake for about 20 minutes or until golden brown.

Whole orange cake

Wash the orange thoroughly, particularly if it's not organic or from your backyard.

This is one of the easiest cakes you'll ever make and it's full of flavour and orangey goodness. It's all mixed in the food processor too, so there is very little washing up. Simple!

1 orange, washed and quartered
3 eggs
180 g butter, melted
1 cup white sugar

1½ cups self-raising flour *or*
   1½ cups plain flour and 1½ teaspoons
   baking powder

1. Preheat your oven to 180°C and grease cake tin – I use a large loaf tin.

2. Put the orange quarters into the food processor and process until they're completely broken down and no large pieces remain.

3. Add the rest of the ingredients and process again for about 30 seconds, or until everything is mixed together.

4. Scrape the batter into the tin and bake for around 40 minutes or until the cake is golden brown, and a skewer inserted in the centre comes out clean. Cool on a cake rack.

Cinnamon tea cake

This is a good cake for the lunch box. It has no icing or filling so it carries well.

1 cup self-raising flour
½ teaspoon ground cinnamon
1 egg, separated
½ cup sugar
½ cup milk
20 g butter, melted
¼ teaspoon vanilla extract

Topping
15 g butter, melted
1 teaspoon ground cinnamon
1 tablespoon sugar

1. Preheat the oven to 180°C and grease an 18 cm round cake tin.

2. Sift the flour and cinnamon into a large bowl and set to the side.

3. In a second bowl, beat the egg white until it's stiff, then stir the egg yolk in gently.

4. Gradually add the sugar to the egg, mixing as you add it, then stir in the milk, melted butter and vanilla.

5. Add the dry ingredients to the egg and sugar mix and stir until combined.

6. Pour the mixture into the greased tin and bake for about 30 minutes, or until a skewer inserted in the centre comes out clean.

7. Take the cake from the tin while it's still hot, turn it out and place it on a wire rack. Spoon over the butter and sprinkle the cinnamon and sugar over the cake while it is still warm.

Basic muffins *Makes 12*

This recipe can be the basis of many different flavoured muffins. You could add ½ cup cheese, or 1 cup apple pie filling, or 1 cup mashed banana and walnuts, or 1 cup drained tinned cherries, frozen blueberries or raspberries, or choc chips, for deliciously flavoured muffins.

¼ cup olive oil
1 egg
1 cup milk
½ cup sugar
2 cups self-raising flour

1. Preheat oven to 180°C and butter a standard 12-hole muffin tin.

2. Combine the oil, egg, milk and sugar in a mixing bowl. Mix thoroughly with a fork or wooden spoon.

3. Pour in the flour and mix. Make sure there is no dry flour, but do not over-mix it. It's best for it to look under-mixed than be over-mixed.

4. Spoon the batter into the muffin tin and bake for about 20 minutes or until a skewer inserted comes out clean. Remove from the oven and allow to sit in the tin to cool slightly before turning out on a wire rack.

Cheap and easy biscuits *Makes 70–80 biscuits*

This recipe uses only 4 ingredients, but you can make the basic dough into jam drops, lemon biscuits, choc-chip biscuits or whatever you want to – add what's in your pantry. The dough freezes well for about 6 weeks so you can divide it up into batches, freeze the dough in a long tube and defrost to make 20 or 30 biscuits as you need them.

500 g butter

1 cup sugar

1 × 395 g can condensed milk *or* use the
recipe for homemade condensed milk
in this chapter

5 cups self-raising flour

1. Preheat oven to 180°C and grease a biscuit tray or line with baking paper.

2. Cream the butter and sugar together, add the condensed milk and mix well. Add the choc chips, nuts or other flavouring if using.

3. Stir in the flour with a spoon.

4. Roll the dough into balls the size of a walnut and flatten. Make a thumbprint in the dough and add lemon butter or jam if using.

5. Place on the prepared tray and bake for about 10 minutes or until golden brown, then allow to cool on a wire rack.

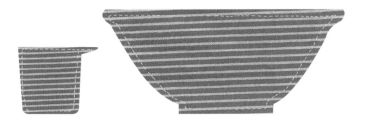

Dairy food

Yoghurt *Makes 1 litre*

I make this in the early morning so I can monitor it during the day. If you overheat the yoghurt, you'll kill the beneficial bacteria. If you let the temperature fall too far, the bacteria won't grow.

You can buy the yoghurt you start with from the shop. It should contain live cultures and will state that on the label. Check the use-by date, making sure it is as fresh as possible and you've got plenty of time before the expiry date. Use natural yoghurt, not vanilla or any other flavour, nor anything with gelatine in it. You can also use yoghurt starter, which I buy online.

You can sterilise your jar by placing it in the oven for 20 minutes at 120°C. Sterilise the lid by boiling it in a saucepan for 10 minutes.

1 litre milk (can be UHT or pasteurised –
   homogenised or non-homogenised)
½ cup good natural yoghurt *or* the
   quantity of yoghurt starter specified
   on the packet.
½ cup milk powder (optional)

You will also need
milk or candy thermometer
1-litre preserving jar, sterilised
esky

1. Clip the thermometer to the side of the saucepan and warm the milk on the stovetop to 80°C, then remove from the heat. This process pasteurises the milk again, killing any harmful bacteria.

2. Allow the milk to cool to 45°C.

3. When the milk has cooled, add the yoghurt. If you want a thick yoghurt, add the milk powder as well.

4. Stir until the yoghurt has dissolved in the milk.

5. Pour the mixture into the warm, sterilised jar and wrap it tightly with a towel straight away, so no heat escapes.

6. Place the wrapped jar in your esky. Check it after 6 hours; if it's cooling down, heat up a rice bag in the microwave or fill a water bottle with hot water and place it in the esky. This added heat should keep it going for a few hours. You might need to repeat the process.

7. The yoghurt is set when its texture is more like custard than milk. If you've used a good-quality, fresh, natural yoghurt it will usually set in 12 hours. The longer the yoghurt takes to set, the stronger the taste will be. It lasts for weeks in the fridge.

If you don't have an esky, you could use an oven or slow cooker instead – either set very low, or turned on and off during the day. You could also use a wide-mouthed thermos flask that can retain the heat for 12 hours. If you live in a warm climate, the yoghurt will be fine in the jar, wrapped in a towel on the bench to set.

Condensed milk

Condensed milk can be used in many recipes for biscuits, cheesecakes, ice-cream and other sweets. This homemade version is much cheaper than a tin of condensed milk and it tastes the same. It can be stored in a glass jar for up to a month in the fridge.

⅓ cup hot water
⅔ cup white sugar
3 tablespoons soft butter
1 cup powdered milk

1. Put the hot water, sugar and butter in a small food processor or mixer and whiz until the sugar dissolves.

2. Add the milk powder and whiz until it's combined and creamy.

Vanilla ice-cream

The ice-cream will be smoother if you have an ice-cream machine but it's mighty fine made with muscle power.
You can use any milk you have in the house: skim, no fat, soy, powdered or full cream.

Please don't use vanilla essence, which is fake vanilla and will not do the ice-cream justice.

2 cups milk

1 cup cream

1 vanilla bean *or* 2 teaspoons vanilla extract

400 ml condensed milk (recipe on previous page)

1. Add the milk and cream to a saucepan and warm over a medium heat.

2. Split the vanilla bean in two, scrape out the seeds, and add bean and seeds to the milk mixture; or add the vanilla extract. Bring to the boil and allow to simmer slowly for a few minutes.

3. Remove the vanilla bean, if using, then add the condensed milk and stir.

4. Remove from heat and allow to cool. When the mixture is cold, place it in a container and put it in the freezer.

5. *If you have an ice-cream machine*, wait until the mix is forming ice crystals, then add it to the machine and start processing.
   If you don't have an ice-cream machine, when the mix has formed ice crystals, remove it from the freezer every 45 minutes and give it a good stir. Then smooth it out in the container and put it back in the freezer.

6. When the ice-cream is almost frozen solid, put it in a freezer container with a lid for storage.

Fermenting

Fermenting is a natural chemical process that occurs when beneficial bacteria and wild yeasts create lactic acid and convert sugar into carbon dioxide. In home fermenting, natural wild yeasts and bacteria in the air are captured and multiply in the food or drink you are making. We've all been taught that bacteria and food don't mix but these beneficial bacteria and yeasts are similar to those in yoghurt, kimchee, sauerkraut, kefir, vinegar and sourdough.

Ginger beer

This is a delicious fizzy drink that even the kids will love.

Most tap water in Australia contains chlorine, which kills bacteria and yeasts. We don't want anything in our ginger beer that will kill the yeasts, but if you let tap water sit for 24 hours, the chlorine will kill what it's meant to kill, and won't harm our beneficial yeasts.

3 cups white or raw sugar
juice of 2 lemons
5 litres rainwater *or* spring water *or* tap water that
   has been allowed to stand for 24 hours

Culture
8 dessertspoons ground ginger
8 dessertspoons white or raw sugar
1½ cups rainwater *or* spring water *or* tap water that
   has been allowed to stand for 24 hours

You will also need

wide-mouthed jar

open-weave cotton cloth

piece of muslin or cheesecloth (to use as a strainer)

large mixing bowl capable of holding 4½ litres

funnel

large jug

several large plastic bottles or glass bottles with corks

Step 1: Making the culture

1. Add 1 dessertspoon ground ginger and 1 dessertspoon sugar to the jar.

2. Add 1½ cups water and mix. During the day let this mixture sit on the kitchen bench with the cover off. Cover it at night with the open-weave cotton cloth.

3. Every day for 7 days, add 1 dessertspoon of ginger and 1 dessertspoon of sugar to the jar, and mix it in. After a couple of days, depending on the temperature in your home (it happens faster when it's warm), you'll notice little bubbles start to form. That is good; the fermentation has begun. The mix should smell of ginger and, towards the end of the process, it might smell slightly of alcohol. That's fine too – the amount of alcohol that might form is tiny and it will be diluted.

Step 2: Making the ginger beer

1. On day 7, after you've added the ginger and sugar to the culture, mix it, and strain it through the muslin or cheesecloth into your large bowl.

2. Add the water, sugar and lemon juice. Mix well, then bottle the mixture, using the funnel and jug. Leave about 2 or 3 inches of space at the top of each bottle for the gasses that will develop. Put the lids on the bottles.

3. After the ginger beer has been bottled it needs to ferment further. Let the bottles sit on your kitchen bench or in the pantry for 2 days before putting them in the fridge. If you've used plastic bottles and you notice some of them puffing up, put them in the fridge straight away. When they're cool, they're ready to drink.

You never know how fizzy the drink will become because the yeasts in your home are invisible. If you capture a lot of yeast, you'll have an excellent brew and a lot of bubbles. This is live food! It's dynamic; it changes all the time. Plastic bottles can puff up and glass bottles can shoot their corks out if the pressure is too great. It sounds a bit scary but if you're careful to watch the bottles, you'll be fine. Ginger beer will last in the fridge for 4 weeks.

CULTURE TIP

Don't throw the dregs of the ginger beer culture out after you strain the mixture. Like other live cultures it can be used again to start up your next batch. Just add it back to the clean jar and start feeding it again.

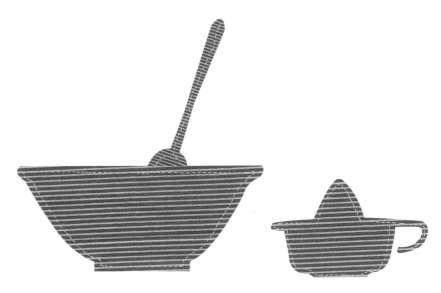

Simple everyday recipes

Tomato pasta sauce *Serves 4*

This basic tomato sauce is perfect for homemade pasta and, if made in large quantities, can be preserved in a jar or frozen.

1 tablespoon extra virgin olive oil
1 clove garlic, crushed
1 large onion, chopped
2 tablespoons tomato paste
1 kg tomatoes, chopped and peeled, *or*
   2 × 400 g cans chopped tomatoes

1 teaspoon sugar
¼ cup fresh oregano leaves, chopped, *or*
   1 tablespoon dried oregano
¼ cup parsley, chopped
¼ cup basil, torn
salt and pepper

1. Heat the oil in a wide saucepan or large frying pan over medium heat. Add the garlic and onion and cook for 4 minutes until softened and translucent.

2. Add the tomato paste and stir it around for 1 minute to get rid of the raw taste.

3. Add the tomato, sugar, herbs and salt and pepper to taste, bring to a slow boil then reduce the heat.

4. Simmer slowly for 30 minutes, tasting and adjusting the seasoning if necessary.

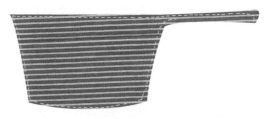

Fresh pasta *Serves 4*

If you know how to make fresh pasta, you'll have
the basis of many wonderful dishes. This is a
simple recipe that will make a variety of meals,
depending on the sauce you make to go with it.
Fresh pasta will last in the fridge for 2–3 days.

> *This pasta can be dried out for 2 days on a tray, or hung over a clean dowel stick covered with netting and away from insects. This dried pasta will keep in a glass jar for 6–8 weeks.*

500 g plain flour
½ teaspoon salt
4 eggs

1. Tip the flour and salt onto a clean benchtop and make a well in the middle. Crack the eggs into the well.

2. With your clean fingers, break the yolks and start combining the flour and eggs, taking the flour from the inner rim of the well and mixing it into the centre until all the flour is combined. If the dough is too firm and is hard to shape, add a tablespoon of water.

3. Knead the dough for 5 minutes then cover with a clean tea towel. Let it rest for 30 minutes.

4. *If you have a pasta machine*, pass the dough through the machine on the wide setting about 10 times. If it is still sticky after this, leave it to rest another 15 minutes. Then pass it through the pasta machine on a narrower setting. Keep using a narrower and narrower setting until it is smooth and thin.
   If you don't have a pasta machine, lightly flour your bench and roll out the dough with a rolling pin, turning the dough to achieve a long rectangle shape. Roll the dough as thin as you can get it without it breaking up.

5. Using a sharp, floured knife, cut the pasta dough into thin strips for linguine, wider strips for fettuccine, rectangles for lasagne or cannelloni, or fancy shapes for ravioli.

6. Cook the pasta fresh.

Slow beef stew in the slow cooker *Serves 4 or 5*

In the cooler months I love using my slow cooker. It tenderises cheaper cuts of meat over the long, slow cooking process and it makes many kinds of excellent soup. The trick is to keep using your cooking-from-scratch principles when using the slow cooker; using tins of soup or stock from a carton is not an option if you're trying to avoid flavour enhancers and preservatives. You can get excellent flavour without adding any packets of processed sauce mix or prepackaged soups.

The trick to adding flavour to a slow-cooker meal is to take some time at the beginning of the process to caramelise the meat in a frying pan. I have written about this process in the Nourishment chapter. It's an important step in building flavour, so don't skip it or try to hurry it up.

This is a basic recipe that can be changed. Adding curry powder instead of paprika will give you a tasty and spicy beef curry. Add tomatoes, some tomato paste and capsicum and you'll have an Italian beef casserole you could serve with pasta. Using chicken instead of beef would also make a fine meal.

olive oil

1 kg chuck, blade, skirt, round or
   topside beef, diced

salt and pepper

2 tablespoons paprika

2 onions, quartered (or diced if you're
   serving children)

2 tablespoons plain flour

1 cup water

2 carrots, sliced

2 sticks celery, sliced, including the tops

1 bay leaf

2 sprigs thyme

3 potatoes *or* 1 sweet potato, thinly sliced

1. Add enough olive oil to a frying pan to barely cover the bottom.

2. Divide the meat equally into 3 portions and add 1 portion to the pan. Adding more meat to the pan will make it produce liquid, which you don't want. Stir occasionally. You're aiming for nicely browned meat. Add salt and pepper to taste. I like to add about ½ teaspoon of salt and about ¼ teaspoon of pepper.

3. When the first portion of meat has browned properly, move it to the slow cooker and add the next portion of meat to the frying pan. You might have

to add a bit more oil if the pan is dry. You need oil for the meat to brown but you do not want oil swimming in the bottom of the pan. To this second portion, add the paprika and stir it in. When the meat is browned, add it to the slow cooker and put the final portion of beef into the pan. When that has browned, add the onions to the frying pan and brown them.

4. Add the flour to the pan and stir in. When the flour is coating the onions and meat, add the water and stir until the sauce thickens. You'll notice the nicely brown sauce. This is all natural flavour produced by taking the time to brown the meat and onions. The meat and vegetables will release moisture during the slow-cooking process, so don't be tempted to add more liquid.

5. Add the carrot, celery, bay leaf and thyme to the slow cooker, as well as all the remaining meat and sauce, and stir everything together. Turn the cooker to the 'auto' setting – this will heat on high for a couple of hours, then automatically turn itself to the low setting to finish cooking. Cook for about 4 or 5 hours, or all day on low if you're going out and you want a hot dinner waiting when you come home.

6. One hour before the end of cooking, add the potato or sweet potato. If you're going out all day you can add the potato with the rest of the vegetables, but chop them into large chunks rather than slices. I like adding them at the end so that they retain their shape.

And there you have it – beef stew cooked from scratch in a slow cooker. No need for commercial soup or stock. It's a delicious and healthy family meal.

SLOW COOKER TIP
If you have the time this is one of those dishes ideally suited for freezing, so make a double batch and freeze half for next week.

Spinach or silverbeet pie

This is the kind of recipe that should be in everyone's meal rotation. It's cheap, healthy, easy to make, delicious, and can be eaten hot or cold.

20 leaves spinach or silverbeet *or*
  2 × 250 g boxes frozen spinach
1 onion, chopped
1 clove garlic, crushed
2 tablespoons olive oil
5 eggs

250 g ricotta
salt and pepper
1 cup grated cheese (parmesan, cheddar,
  mozzarella or any cheese you have)
4 sheets filo pastry

1. Preheat oven to 180°C.

2. Add spinach/silverbeet, onion and garlic to a frying pan with 1 tablespoon of the oil. Cook over medium heat until the leaves wilt.

3. While the leaves are cooking, mix the eggs and ricotta together. Add salt and pepper to taste, then mix in the grated cheese.

4. Add the cooked spinach/silverbeet mixture to the egg mixture and combine well.

5. Using a pastry brush, take each sheet of filo pastry and brush some of the remaining olive oil over it. Fold each sheet in half and place it in a pie dish. Cover the base of your pie plate with all the sheets and fold the edges under as they reach the sides. You need to work quickly with filo as it dries out fast. If you need to leave for any reason, cover the pastry with a clean, moist tea towel.

6. Pour the egg and spinach mixture into the pie dish and bake until the top is golden and the pie looks set. Don't overcook as it will make the eggs rubbery.

7. Serve hot or cold with a salad or vegetables.

Split pea soup *Makes 9 litres*

I am always on the lookout for delicious thrifty
meals that are fairly easy to make, and in winter
I keep coming back to this old standby, which ticks
all those boxes. I think it's a favourite in many
families but this is how to cook it entirely from
scratch. No pre-made stock is needed, as it makes its own
stock as it cooks. This is one of those soups that tastes better
each day when you reheat it, and it also freezes very well.

I sometimes add croutons, which I make just before serving. Brush 2 slices of bread with extra virgin olive oil, cut the slices into small cubes and put them in the oven for about 15 minutes on 180°C.

500 g dried split peas
1 ham hock or ham bone *or*
   1 kg bacon bones
1 cup onion, chopped
1 cup celery, chopped

1 cup carrot, chopped
2 bay leaves
½ cup parsley, chopped
salt and pepper

1. Place the peas in a large bowl and wash them in cold water. Pour boiling water over them and leave to soak for a couple of hours. The longer you soak the peas, the less time it will take to cook the soup.

2. Add the bones to a large stockpot (about 9 litres in capacity) half full of water and bring to the boil.

3. Place the peas, chopped vegetables and herbs in the pot with the bones. Bring back to the boil, then reduce the heat and simmer for about 2 hours, or until the meat is tender and the vegetables are cooked to your liking. (Personally, I like the vegetables to be mushy.)

4. Remove the bones from the pot. Chop the meat into pieces and return it to the soup, then turn off the heat and add your seasoning. Pork tends to need a fair bit of salt and pepper, but taste before you add it.

Dressings and stocks

Simple vinaigrette

The classic recipe is 3 parts extra virgin olive oil to 1 part good vinegar or lemon juice. You can add a small amount of salt and pepper, a teaspoon of mustard powder or a little sugar. A dash of cream will make a richer dressing; some water will make a lighter one.

Try variations of this until you find what suits your taste. Just add all the ingredients to a small jar and shake it. Dress the salad just before serving.

Simple mayonnaise

Eggs must be fresh and at room temperature. This can be made by hand or in a small food processor.

2 egg yolks	2 cups olive oil
½ teaspoon salt	2 teaspoons lemon juice, or to taste
1 teaspoon Dijon mustard	salt and pepper
2 teaspoons good vinegar	

1. Whisk together the egg yolks, salt, mustard and vinegar in a bowl.
2. Add the olive oil very slowly – start whisking the yolk mixture and let the oil fall from the spout in a thin stream. When the mixture thickens up, you can add the rest of the oil more quickly. You must whisk all the time until you have achieved a thick, velvety mayonnaise.
3. Add lemon juice, salt and pepper to taste.

Meat stock

1 kg beef bones *or* 2 chicken carcasses

olive oil

6 litres of water

1 onion, chopped

2 sticks celery, chopped

1 carrot, chopped

2 bay leaves

1 teaspoon salt and ½ teaspoon pepper, to taste

½ cup parsley, chopped

1. Set the oven to 200°C and roast the bones in a baking tray for 1 hour with a small amount of olive oil drizzled over the top.

2. When the bones are golden, put them in a stockpot and cover with the water. Add the vegetables, herbs, and salt and pepper, then bring to the boil. Simmer for 1 hour with the lid on.

3. Pour the stock through a sieve to remove the bones, vegetables and bay leaves.

4. Allow to cool. If the stock has a layer of fat on it when it's cooled, skim this off with a spoon. (If you have chickens, give it to them on some stale bread.) When cold, stock can be frozen, or stored in the fridge for up to 3 days.

STOCK TIP

If you're cooking a roast chicken, reserve the bones and a cup of chicken meat and you'll be able to make a delicious soup the following day.

Let's begin

People tell us that alone, we can't make a difference. I don't believe that and I hope that after reading this book you might doubt it too. I think that we can all help to change our world by changing ourselves first.

I can't think of a better time to change. Prices are rising, many of us don't know our neighbours, and the world doesn't seem to be as simple or safe as it used to be. I am not nostalgic about the past; I do not yearn for everything to return to how it was, but I believe now is the right time to explore the possibilities of a simpler life that takes the very best from those earlier and gentler years.

And I think the change has begun. More and more I see it: families who want to work enough to pay the bills but not so much that they can't enjoy their lives during those working years. I see retired folk happily planting a vegie patch and buying their first chickens. I see younger men and women opting out of a life of consumerism, instead working sustainably towards the future. I see many more home-makers baking bread and preserving their own jams and relishes. There are more hens in backyards; there are many more vegetable gardens and people buying fresh vegetables and fruit from growers' markets. DIY, home cooking, knitting, mending, sewing and budgeting are returning to popularity. I hope there will be no going back.

When I first started on this path towards a more simple life it was difficult to stay as motivated as I wanted, and needed, to be.

There came a point, though, when my own life provided the motivation because I could see many changes and I was proud of what I was doing. Somehow it all fell into place, and instead of just undertaking new simple-living projects, one thing led to another and a genuine lifestyle was born. I'm not troubled by lack of motivation now but I do know that motivation is one of the most difficult things to maintain – not just in living this way, but in many things.

I think the key to motivation is to find someone (a neighbour or a friend) or something (perhaps a book or a blog) that inspires you. Seeing someone doing what you want to do, or reading about it, generally ignites a spark that keeps a flame burning for a while. If you keep that inspiration going, your flame will burn longer. The list of resources in this book may direct you to a book or blog where you find ongoing inspiration. But keep at it; don't give up if things get tough or you feel like it's taking too long to achieve your dreams. Never, ever give up. It's also a good strategy to keep in mind the reasons you want to change. What will you get out of it? How will it make your life better? Imagine how you want to be in your simple life and keep that image in your mind, and answer those two questions for yourself. Having end results squarely in view will help keep you on track.

I want every person who reads this book to be motivated and inspired to make the changes necessary to live to their true potential. I want you to feel energised enough to believe you can do whatever you need to do. I want the information here to seep into your brain so that it informs what you do and what you dream for yourself. Simple living is a series of small personal changes and adjustments to our lives; it's also about living generously and helping our family, friends and neighbours.

For me there is nothing better than waking to a new day that I know will be full of productive and interesting work around the home and garden. Pottering with this and that, putting things right, sitting and thinking – all the things that make a simple life also make a perfect day. I do not need many of those perfect days to keep me going; just the promise of one tomorrow or next week is enough. And enough is all I'm after.

I hope that this book has encouraged you to think about what is enough for you. You are not alone. Many people are making simple changes and there has never been a better time to work towards home production and self-reliance. Making that break away from consumption and debt can lead to a more sustainable future with time spent working in our backyards, making our homes warm and comfortable, cooking real food and being fulfilled by that simple work. Let's roll our sleeves up and begin.

Rhonda

Resources

LIVING SIMPLY

Walden and Civil Disobedience **by Henry David Thoreau, Penguin, USA**
An account of the simplest of lives. It documents the time Thoreau lived alone in the woods, when he formulated many of his ideas.

The Simple Living Guide **by Janet Luhrs, Random House, USA**
The first book about simple living that I read. It was a very good first step and helped me to clarify my thoughts and goals.

The Encyclopedia of Country Living **by Carla Emery, Sasquatch Books, USA**
A back-to-basics bible with information about hundreds of tasks like breadmaking, preserving and planting a garden.

down---to---earth.blogspot.com
Visit my blog for further information, photos and advice about the topics in this book. You will also find a longer list of resources with live links, for both *Down to Earth* and *The Simple Home*, on my blog under 'Resource lists'.

simple-green-frugal-co-op.blogspot.com
A cooperative of green-living writers from around the world (I'm the founder and a contributor).

AGES AND STAGES

asimplelivingjourney.blogspot.com

This blog features an Australian family, recently relocated to the mid-central coast of New South Wales, who are establishing a farm from scratch.

SAVING AND SPENDING

Your Money or Your Life **by Joe Dominguez and Vicki Robin, Penguin, USA**

This book gave me a good understanding of the links between lifestyle, consumption and overspending.

The Complete Tightwad Gazette **by Amy Dacyczyn, Random House, USA**

Dotted throughout this book are hundreds of ways to save money, some of which I didn't agree with when I read it, and others I still use.

mytotalmoneymakeover.com

American financial expert Dave Ramsey's money advice website. There is a sign-up fee but you get budgeting tools and access to an ad-free radio show for extra motivation and advice.

moneysmart.gov.au/budgeting/budget-planner

The Australian government's guide to budgeting, credit cards and saving, for all ages.

freemoneyfinance.com

A very good blog about managing money.

gettingout.info/moneymatters.htm

A young person's guide to spending and saving.

ingdirect.com.au/home_loans/calculators.htm

Some good online mortgage calculators.

sites.google.com/site/dsbudgethome

A free, simple open-source budgeting program.

HOME

knittingpatterncentral.com/directory/dishcloths.php

You'll find a knitted cotton dishcloth pattern here to suit you.

crochetpatterncentral.com/directory/dishcloths.php

Lovely crocheted dishcloth patterns.

Knitting Without Tears **by Elizabeth Zimmerman, Simon and Schuster, USA**

A book that enables you to knit items such as jumpers, cardigans, mittens and hats with basic patterns to suit all skill sets.

freeneedle.com

A sewing directory featuring free projects and tutorials.

sewing.about.com/od/techniques/tp/mendclothing.htm

Information and tutorials about basic sewing and mending.

babyvine.com.au/best-cloth-nappies

Your guide to the best modern cloth nappies in 2020.

modernclothnappies.org

A national organisation encouraging the use of cloth nappies.

ecoyarns.com.au

Vivian has a wide range of organic and ethically produced yarns.

clothingexchange.com.au

Swap clothes instead of buying new ones.

freecycle.org/group/AU

A network of people offering items for recycling. Find something you need or list something you think may be of use to others.

recyclingnearyou.com.au

Information about recycling and waste services offered by your local council.

soulemama.com

A beautiful blog about parenting, children and play.

HOUSEWORK

www.rd.com/list/how-to-remove-stains

How to remove every type of stain.

snowdriftfarm.com/soapcalculator.htm

A good soap calculator – just fill in the weight of the oil you'll use and it will calculate the amounts of lye and water you need.

oilsandsoap.com.au

A description of some soap-making oils.

soapnuts.com/indexcp.html

Some useful soap recipes.

candleandsoap.about.com/od/soaprecipes/a/cpshavingrecipe.htm

A recipe for shaving soap.

greenlivingaustralia.com.au

Suppliers of ingredients and kits for cheese, yoghurt and soap making as well as lids and jars for preserving.

ORGANISING YOUR LIFE

moneysmart.gov.au/tools-and-resources/calculators-and-tools/budget-planner

A free Australian government budget planner that allows you to enter your details, calculate your budget and print it out. You can also download a planner to your computer and work on it in Excel.

brendaarnall.typepad.com

Download some beautiful planners and calendars for free.

unclutterer.com/2008/02/20/creating-a-weekly-meal-plan

Download a free menu plan, either as a PDF to print or an Excel template to fill in on your computer.

HOME-GROWN SELF-RELIANCE

The Permaculture Home Garden by Linda Woodrow, Penguin, Australia

This was my bible when I set up my garden. It gave me ideas, but most of all it made me want to produce food in an ethical and thoughtful way.

Easy Organic Gardening and Moon Planting by Lyn Bagnall, Scribe Publications, Australia

The best Australian organic gardening book I've read.

edenseeds.com.au

A good Australian vegetable and herb planting guide.

greenharvest.com.au

diggers.com.au

selectorganic.com.au

edenseeds.com.au

seedsavers.net

Sources for open-pollinated, heirloom vegetable seeds, and herb and flower seeds that are usually not treated or modified in any way.

daleysfruit.com.au

Buy mail-order fruit trees.

foodwise.com.au/the-community-gardening-movement

Information about Australia's community gardens.

THE SUSTAINABLE BACKYARD

sagehenfarmlodi.com/chooks/chooks

A comprehensive chart of chicken breeds and characteristics.

rarepoultry.net

Information about rare-breed poultry.

sgaonline.org.au

The Sustainable Gardening Australia website has a free gardening newsletter and fact sheets.

online.retrosuburbia.com

Permaculture expert David Holmgren's ideas on sustainable suburbs.

NOURISHMENT

The Real Food Companion by Matthew Evans, Murdoch Books, Australia

If you're looking for books about nutritious and tasty Australian food, this is one of the best.

The Thrifty Kitchen by Suzanne Gibbs and Kate Gibbs, Penguin, Australia

A thoughtful and beautiful Australian cookbook for the thrifty home.

Stephanie Alexander's Kitchen Garden Companion by Stephanie Alexander, Penguin, Australia

If you cook from your backyard, you need this book.

Preserves, The Australian Women's Weekly, Octopus Publishing Group, UK

A no-fuss guide to preserving food in jars.

The River Cottage Cookbook by Hugh Fernly-Whittingstall, HarperCollins, Australia

Read not just the recipes but also the philosophy that inspired them.

Nourishing Traditions by Sally Fallon with Mary G. Enig, Newtrends Publishing Inc., USA

The book that brought me back from eight years as a vegetarian.

foodcentsprogram.com.au

A program that helps families make the most of the money they spend on food.

craftybaking.com

An excellent troubleshooting resource for bakers.

farmersmarkets.org.au/find-a-market

A list of Australian farmers' markets.

snk.com.au (Victoria)
simplygood.com.au (Queensland)
kiallafoods.com.au (Queensland)
allaboutbread.com.au (Western Australia)
santostrading.com.au/bulkfood/index.html (New South Wales)
biodistributors.com.au/prodinf.php (Tasmania)

Baking and breadmaking supplies around the country.

daa.asn.au

The Dieticians Association of Australia's website has some good information, recipes and tips under the title 'Smart eating for you'.

seasonalfoodguide.com

Download local information about which fruit and vegetables are in season throughout the year.

'Unhappy Meals' by Michael Pollan, *The New York Times Magazine*, 28 January 2007

A thought-provoking essay about modern food consumption, by a world expert.

'What a waste: An analysis of household expenditure on food' by David Baker, Josh Fear and Richard Denniss, The Australia Institute, November 2009, available at tai.org.au

A report about food wastage in Australia.

RECIPES

sbs.com.au/food/cuisine/australian

Australian recipes.

womensweeklyfood.com.au/traditional-australian-recipes-30070

Traditional Australian recipes.

Wild Fermentation by Sandor Ellix Katz, Chelsea Green Publishing, USA

An excellent reference book for fermenting, with many recipes.

Acknowledgements

Although my name appears on the cover, writing any book is rarely the result of only one person's endeavours. The way we have chosen to live requires a strong commitment to work in our home and the philosophy of handmade and from scratch. I would not have been able to continue living this way while writing the book without the ongoing help of my husband, Hanno. He kept the necessary wheels turning while I tapped away on the keyboard. For that, and for so many other things, I'm truly thankful.

More than anyone else, my sons, Shane and Kerry, have helped make me the person I am. Without them I doubt this book would have been written. While I was writing, both of them, with their partners Sarndra and Sunny, gave Hanno and me our first grandchildren. I hope that this book will help guide their future. Thanks also to my sister, Tricia de Chelard, for her interest and help, and to Susan Collings and Kathleen Tolman for reading bits and pieces of my text and telling me the truth.

I was encouraged by the daily contact I had with readers of my blog, who are far too many to name, but their ongoing interest and questions have kept me going over the years. I do want to single out one person, Sharon Fouillade, who has been a helper and friend right from the start. I have never met Sharon in person but our friendship reminds me every day of the power of the internet.

Jo Rosenberg has been my editor during this process and I've come to think of her as a friend. It was Jo's email asking if I was interested in discussing the possibility of publication that has resulted in this book being in your hands today. Thank you, Jo.

Thanks also to designer Nikki Townsend. All through the process of writing I had a vision of what this book would look like. I am thankful that Jo developed a deep understanding of my message and that Nikki realised that message so perfectly on the pages. Thanks also go to publisher Andrea McNamara, cover designer Allison Colpoys and photographer Greg Elms. I couldn't have asked for more.

And finally, I thank Penguin Australia for publishing and having faith in yet another unknown Australian author. If I could have chosen any publisher, it would have been Penguin. There is nothing like starting at the top.

VIKING

UK | USA | Canada | Ireland | Australia
India | New Zealand | South Africa | China

Viking is part of the Penguin Random House group of companies
whose addresses can be found at global.penguinrandomhouse.com.

First published by Penguin Group (Australia), 2012
This paperback edition published by Viking, 2020

Cover photography by Greg Elms, with special thanks to Est (estaustralia.com) for products
Cover design by Alison Colpoys © Penguin Random House Australia Pty Ltd
Text design and illustrations by Nikki Townsend © Penguin Random House Australia Pty Ltd
Typeset in Caecilia Light by Post Pre-press Group, Brisbane, Australia

Printed and bound in China by RR Donnelley

A catalogue record for this
book is available from the
NATIONAL
LIBRARY   National Library of Australia
OF AUSTRALIA

ISBN 978 1 76104 180 8

penguin.com.au